The cameras on Freedom Ridge followed my movements as I climbed up the low hill on the other side of the road, up dirt tracks fit only for a four-wheel-drive.

In response, the Jeep Cherokee finally began to move, turning and driving up a well-maintained road to a lookout post on the opposite hill. They were perhaps sixty feet away. Down in the wash between us were smaller versions of the warning signs, disappearing into the rugged land between the buttes.

My view into Area 51 was blocked by the mountain ridges to the west. I trained my binoculars on the Cherokee as one of the Cammo Dudes got out and uncovered a permanent binocular mounted on a tripod. I watched him watching me.

He was wearing gray pants and shirt that blended well with the desert, and his black gun holster was tied down to his thigh, the way SWAT teams and Special Forces do . . .

Whatever they're hiding in Area 51, they certainly protect it well.

UFO

HEADQUARTERS

Investigations
on Current
Extraterrestrial
Activity

SUSAN WRIGHT

St. Martin's Paperbacks

UFO HEADQUARTERS: INVESTIGATIONS ON CURRENT EXTRATERRESTRIAL ACTIVITY

Copyright © 1998 by Susan Wright.

Library of Congress Catalog Card Number: 98-21133

ISBN: 0-312-97181-8

Printed in the United States of America

St. Martin's Paperbacks edition/ September 1998
St. Martin's Paperbacks edition/ December 1999

10 9 8 7 6 5 4 3 2 1

**Dedicated to my loving supportive parents,
Bob and Ann Wright**

ACKNOWLEDGMENTS

As a survey of the UFO phenomenon, this book rests on the dedicated work of hundreds of scientists, ufologists, and journalists. I thank each and every one, with special thanks to: Glenn Campbell, Mark Farmer, Tom Mahood, Steve Douglass, Bill Hamilton, Jan Aldrich, Francis Ridge, and Barry Greenwood for answering my endless questions and giving generously of their time.

And many thanks to my agent, Peter Miller, and to my editor, Jim Fitzgerald, for his valuable guidance in developing this project.

SUSAN WRIGHT
JULY 6, 1997

CONTENTS

CHAPTER 1

At the Border of Area 51

As we pulled up to the border of Area 51, marked with large white signs, a brand-new Jeep Cherokee slowed to a stop on the other side, neatly blocking the dirt road. The windows of the Jeep were nearly black, so with the sun setting in the hills behind them, I could barely see silhouettes of the two men inside.

USE OF DEADLY FORCE AUTHORIZED, one of the two border signs stated in bold red letters. Both cited Federal Regulation #795 as forbidding entrance to the government installation.

Though the signs didn't say it, we were at the eastern border of Area 51, the secret government facility approximately ninety miles due north of Las Vegas, Nevada. From almost any vantage point, the six-by-ten-mile block of land that encompasses Area 51 is hidden behind low mountains.

But the mountains can't hide the aircraft that take off and land on the runways across Groom dry lake bed—said to be the longest in the world at nearly thirty thousand feet. The new stealthy aircraft, such as the mythical hypersonic Aurora, are rumored to be capable of reaching speeds of

Mach 8, which means it would take a racetrack half the size of America for it to turn in a circle at top speed.

People are drawn to Area 51 not only to see superso-phisticated aircraft, but because of the numerous sightings of flying saucers and UFOs. There is actually video footage of a UFO over Nellis Range that is remarkably like a video of a Brazilian UFO. And there have been strange cattle mutilations as well as reports of abductions by aliens while visitors were in the area.

In a 1989 interview with George Knapp on KLAS-TV, a former government employee named Bob Lazar said that he worked at S-4, just south of Area 51, in a project to back-engineer alien flying saucers. Lazar says our govern-ment has obtained nine discs and is trying to decipher the alien technology. He went public, he claims, in order to protect his own life after breaking his security oath.

No one knows for sure which government agency con-trols Area 51, so I tried to get in by contacting Nellis Air Force Base, which operates the Nellis Range Complex, a bombing and gunnery range that surrounds the Groom Lake area. During one of my phone conversations I was told, "It's dangerous out there—there's bombs dropping all over the place." One of the uses of the Nellis Range is "Red Flag," established in 1975 as a realistic combat training exercise involving the Air Force and its allies. These forces "attack" Nellis Range targets—mock airfields, vehicle con-voys, missile sites, tanks, parked aircraft, and bunkered and defensive positions. The Gulf War owed a measure of its success to Red Flag exercises.

The Air Force denied me access to Nellis Range, and Technical Sergeant James Brook sent me a fax of the of-ficial Groom Lake Statement (dated 26 October 1994):

There are a variety of activities, some of which are clas-sified, throughout what is often called the Air Force's Nellis Range Complex. The range is used for the testing of technologies and systems and training for operations critical to the effectiveness of U.S. military forces and the security of the United States. There is an operating location near Groom dry lake. Some specific activities and operations conducted on the Nellis Range, both past and present, remain classified and cannot be discussed.

Brook explained that he couldn't talk about anything regarding the Nellis Range, even about his personal feelings, because of security reasons. And he never let the words "Area 51" cross his lips—the secret base is officially known as "the Groom Lake facility." Brook then referred me to a next higher level: to Air Combat Command and the Secretary of the Air Force, Department of Defense.

I sent letters to the Pentagon requesting a tour of the Nellis Range, including but not limited to Papoose Lake and Area 51, but I wasn't surprised when one after another request simply disappeared into the black hole of "black project" secrecy. That's when I asked my congresswoman for help, and the Honorable Carolyn B. Maloney, member of the House of Representatives for the 14th District, New York, wrote several letters to Lieutenant Napoleon Byars, National Affairs Division, urging that my "request for a media tour receive prompt review and every possible consideration."

While the Pentagon never did answer *me*, Congresswoman Maloney kindly sent me a copy of her reply from Lieutenant Colonel Patricia M. Fornes, Congressional Inquiry Division. Fornes refused to grant my request on grounds of "policies and regulations relative to national security."

For further inquiries, a phone number was offered. So I called Major Guy Thompson, Public Affairs, and asked, Now that you've acknowledged the existence of the Groom Lake facilities, what would be the harm in allowing in a few select media? You've done it before at supersensitive government facilities, why not here?

Major Thompson was extremely pleasant and interested in my project, but he only replied, "We've had quite a few journalists ask for a tour, but we can't because of issues of national security."

The Department of Energy (DoE) was infinitely more accommodating, as per the dictates of former Energy Secretary Hazel O'Leary, who took President Clinton's request for openness literally. The DoE gave me an extensive tour of the Nevada Test Site (NTS), a 1,350-square-mile restricted area just west of the Nellis Range. On BLM maps, Area 51 is a small box of land barely connected to the northeastern part of NTS—and technically considered to be under the same land management.

NTS, otherwise known as "America's Nuclear Proving Ground," is a vast complex of underground test tunnels, assembly plants, bomb craters, and nuclear waste storage facilities. On my tour, I viewed the shafts where a warhead and a small amount of plutonium were going to be detonated 980 feet underground in June 1997. While eating lunch on Rainier Mesa, I had a fantastic view of the runways and the northernmost half of Groom Lake.

A few days later, at the eastern border of Area 51, I couldn't see the base, although I was physically much closer than I had been at NTS. With the narrow road blocked by the security Jeep, we were boxed into a narrow ravine where two mountain buttes overlapped. The two men didn't budge.

There were two cameras on the butte to the left, tracking our Dodge Diesel (equipped with two scanners and a CB radio). The sophisticated camera setups had video uplinks, parabolic dish reflectors, and yagi antennae. Near the white warning signs, another surveillance camera was tied to a yucca tree, an unsettling cyborg of ancient flora and silicon chips.

Ironically, this electronic Berlin wall was erected across what used to be known as Freedom Ridge, appropriated by the Air Force in a much-publicized "land grab." In April 1995, the border of Area 51 was pushed outward, eliminating the last two easily accessible vantage points to view the Groom Lake facility.

The name "Area 51" wasn't even acknowledged by the government until legal suits were filed against the Department of Defense, the Secretary of Defense, and the Environmental Protection Agency. These suits were filed by a group of Area 51 employees and their families because of alleged exposure to toxic wastes burned in open pits at the Groom Lake facility. This lawsuit finally forced the Department of Defense to release their 1994 "Groom Lake Statement," which tersely admits, "There is an operating location near Groom dry lake."

The waste lawsuit, meanwhile, trundled on in the court of appeals in San Francisco, after being dismissed by a federal district court judge in Las Vegas. On January 8, 1998, the 9th U.S. Circuit Court of Appeals held that state secrets privilege invoked by the Secretary of the Air Force makes discovery and trial on the claims of enviromental crimes "impossible."

Area 51 on the Internet

The government apparently intends to keep everything about Area 51 a secret. Jonathan Turley, attorney for the workers in the hazardous waste lawsuits, realized how serious the Department of Defense was when he tried to introduce as evidence an alleged Groom Lake/Area 51 security manual. The government retroactively classified the document and the judge sealed Professor Turley's offices at George Washington University.

Turley was simply using the document to illustrate the types of buildings at Groom Lake—such as a vehicle maintenance shop, which presumably dealt in everyday materials such as battery acid, antifreeze, and fuel oil that can be hazardous when burned. Yet the defense attorney for the government said that public exposure of the security manual could "endanger the national security."

Anyone is free to go on the Internet and download their very own "secret" copy of the *Area 51 Security Manual*. Glenn Campbell and Mark Farmer each received the manual from anonymous sources, and Campbell posted the text on his extensive website, Ufomind.

In the security manual, the section on "Field Sensor Guide" describes the "electronical sensors" planted throughout the ranges. These sensors look like little pots, and are marked "Government Property"—though they don't say which part of the government! These sensors are able to monitor vehicles or individuals entering or exiting the BLM land next to Nellis, which is in itself an illegal use of public land.

The precision arrival at the border by the "Cammo Dudes" (as Campbell nicknamed the security guards) made it clear they knew we were coming—and it wasn't just from the trail of dust we left in our wake driving down the long dirt road. The sensors had caused our scanners to squelch regularly, every half mile.

Glenn Campbell's website, Ufomind, turned out to be a goldmine of information on Area 51. The maps in his *"Area 51" Viewer's Guide* got us to the border, and the frequencies he listed allowed us to eavesdrop on the encrypted squelches as the two Cammo Dudes lifted their radios and reported back to their main base.

Glenn Campbell has run the Area 51 Research Center since 1993, releasing information on the secret base and actively raising awareness on civil issues such as the Air Force land grab and the designation of the Extraterrestrial Highway running along the northeastern edge of the Nellis Complex. Campbell also produces *The Groom Lake Desert Rat*, a World Wide Web newsletter that "walks a careful line about what may be out there at Papoose and Groom Lakes, trying to avoid speculation, but arguing that the secrecy here is excessive given the end of the Cold War."

Before coming out to the border of Area 51, we went to Rachel, Nevada, to visit the Area 51 Research Center, a single-wide trailer with all kinds of junk piled in front that has fallen out of the sky—pieces of aircraft and radar targets. Rachel is literally a handful of trailers in a vast empty desert valley, with several establishments devoted to selling alien-related merchandise.

As reports of UFO sightings in the area continued to increase, so did Campbell's reputation as the man to contact if you wanted a "native" guide to Area 51. By the end of 1994, Campbell had been interviewed by virtually every major media outlet in the country, from CNN, NBC, and ABC News to *The New York Times Magazine*—everyone wanted to see the secret base that had no name.

What's in a Name?

To this day no one knows where the term "Area 51" came from, but it could have originated in the Department of Energy, which currently operates the Nevada Test Site. Many of the sections of NTS are referred to by number—Area 15, Area 10, and Area 9 are near Area 51.

When I checked with the DoE database of declassified documents housed at the Coordination and Information Center (CIC), there were a number of documents recording radiation levels and structural examinations dating back to 1969 that referred to the Groom Lake area as "Area 51."

Despite the government's attempts at secrecy, the term "Area 51" has been in the popular vernacular for decades. George Knapp located official maps that show Area 51 in the region of Groom Lake. And the most damning evidence came from the defense contractor Lockheed, which flight-tested the U-2 spy plane and the F-117 stealth fighter. Lockheed black-and-white film footage shows aviation pioneer Kelly Johnson pointing to a blackboard that clearly states: "move out to Area 51."

On the drive up to Area 51, there were other more obvious indicators of a secret base hidden somewhere in the Nellis Range. Running along the narrow two-lane U.S. 93 were large power lines—three wires with six insulators each, in excess of 200,000 volts. Going where? Not to the tiny roadside towns of Aztec and Rachel, the largest population centers in Lincoln County, which totals 3,800 people.

Just south of Alamo, the power lines cross U.S. 93, sending a surge of static over both scanners and opening all forty channels of the CB. Then the power lines veer from the highway and head due west, directly toward Groom Lake.

Between the power lines and the sophisticated equipment scattered through the desert—underground transformer stations and fenced generator substations with propane tanks, not to mention double dump trucks with U.S. Government license plates and signs on the cab saying SANDIA NATIONAL LABORATORIES, LOS ALAMOS—I wondered how the government thought they had been hiding Area 51.

The Nellis Range was established as the Las Vegas Bombing and Gunnery Range in 1940, but the Groom Lake area wasn't utilized as an airstrip for at least another decade. It's not likely that any structures existed on Groom Lake before 1952, when Kermit H. Larson, chief of the Alamogordo section of the Atomic Energy Commission, wrote to Dan Sheehan asking if he and his colleagues could "stay in the Cabin" at Groom Mine again: "Four of our survey group have another assignment to do over in your territory, west of Groom Lake to the Water Tank and to the northwest of the Tank. . . ."

The DoE database holds a series of memos and letters between the Sheehan family, who worked Groom Mine overlooking Groom Lake, and the AEC, which was shaking things up in the area beginning with its 1951 series of nuclear bomb tests. Friendly relations soon turned sour, and Sheehan was reduced to writing to the director of the Test Division in August 1955 to request compensation for the damage done to the family's road and for the time lost when they had to evacuate their claim.

The facility on Groom dry lake was known as "Watertown" during the years of the U-2 program, until at least 1960. An unclassified press release from July 29, 1957, was unearthed first by Paul McGinnis, describing how a pilot landed his "small private aircraft" on the "Watertown air strip within the restricted air space over the Nevada Test Site." The release pinpoints the location as "in the Groom Lake area at the northeast corner of the Nevada Test Site."

The first mention of Watertown comes from an unclassified memo in October 1955 from Colonel Calfred Starbird, USAEC (U.S. Atomic Energy Commission), Washington, D.C. Starbird writes in response to a *Las Vegas Review Journal* request for a "progress report on Watertown Project." The approved release said,

Construction at the Nevada Test Site installation a few miles north of Yucca Flat which was announced last spring is continuing. Data secured to date has indicated need for limited additional facilities and modifications of the existing installation. The additional work which will not be completed until sometime in 1956 is being done by the Reynolds Electrical and Engineering Company, incorporated under the direction of the Atomic Energy Commission's Las Vegas Branch Office.

Tom Mahood, one of the Interceptors and webmaster of the Blue Fire website, believes REEC was working on the infrastructure, like the roads and power lines, while Lockheed Skunk Works was actually building the facilities on the sly to test their U-2. In Ben Rich's book *Skunk Works* (1994), the search for a testing facility is described—how Kelly Johnson and a representative of the CIA visited Groom Lake and decided that it was sufficiently remote and secure enough.

As a cover story for the CIA, the official government press release on Watertown in 1957 stated that NACA, the precursor agency to NASA, along with support from "the Air weather Service of the U.S. Air Force," was developing an aircraft that could "make weather observations" at unusually high altitudes. The U2 at Watertown was even painted in NACA markings.

It seems likely that there was no authorization for the covert facility between 1955 and the land withdrawal in 1958. Glenn Campbell found Public Land Order 1662, which went into effect in June 1958, withdrawing about sixty square miles of Groom Lake from public use and allocating it to the Atomic Energy Commission for use by the Test Site. As Campbell explains:

> I have yet to find any evidence that the land was part of the LVBGR [Las Vegas Bombing and Gunnery Range] prior to this—at least from the Federal Register. Such authority must have existed, I assume, I just can't find it. (In other words, I have found the withdrawal for most of the LVBGR, but it does not cover Groom Lake.)

To find out what the Watertown facility was like, I consulted another 1957 DoE document addressed to William Fairhall, manager of the Engineering Department at REEC. The 1957 nuclear test series, Operation Plumbob, included twenty-four nuclear detonations, so a lot of structural safety checking was done. The NTS headquarters at Mercury, Nevada, requested "information on the following structures at Watertown." Along with a battery shop, "Trailer 98," and the control tower, there was also a "Base Theater" and "Building 104 (Base headquarters)."

In the official press releases, Watertown remained under the jurisdiction of the Nevada Test Site. Most people believe that through some sort of subsequent agreement, the AEC then passed control of Groom Lake to the Air Force. My tour guide for the Nevada Test Site told me there were rumors that Area 51 had been traded to the Air Force for Tonopah, a large installation at the northwestern end of the Nellis Range. Yet according to the official DoE history of Tonopah, the site was surveyed by the Naval Air Special Weapons Facility at Kirkland Air Force Base and recommended in a report dated February 27, 1956.

The first appearances I found of the term "Area 51 camp" were in DoE documents from 1969 to 1970, assess-

ing ground motion and radiation levels after nuclear blasts
at NTS. Every time there was a nuclear detonation, the
Watertown personnel had to evacuate for weeks, which undoubtedly interfered with the flight test and training sched-
ules.

The secret air base has undergone several bursts of
growth during the past four decades. One buildup occurred
from 1960 to 1964, at approximately the same time that
stealth technology began to take off with research into new
radar absorbers such as carbon-fiber composites and high-
strength plastics. Another major influx of funding came in
the Reagan years, when the large runway was constructed.

We aren't sure exactly how much money has been spent
on Area 51 because it has been funded under so-called
black projects. Tens of billions of dollars have disappeared
into black-project budgets—and only a few members of
Congress have the clearance to know where and how the
money is being spent.

One thing is certain, there's a lot of black project money
being poured into Area 51 for the new research-and-
development aircraft—whether they are disc-shaped or bat-
winged stealths.

"Cammo Dudes" in Action

Seeing the "Cammo Dudes" in action gave new meaning
to the term "black project." I've been on tours of secured
areas—the Pentagon, Capitol Hill, the Nevada Test Site,
even a nuclear submarine—but this was security like I've
never seen before. Their silent efficiency was almost frightening. They even hide their radio communications—and
encryption is a costly and difficult process rarely under-
taken by the military.

The cameras on Freedom Ridge followed my movements as I climbed up the low hill on the other side of the
road, up dirt tracks fit only for a four-wheel-drive.

In response, the Jeep Cherokee finally began to move,
turning and driving up a well-maintained road to a lookout

post on the opposite hill. They were perhaps sixty feet away. Down in the wash between us were smaller versions of the warning signs, disappearing into the rugged land between the buttes.

My view into Area 51 was blocked by the mountain ridges to the west. I trained my binoculars on the Cherokee as one of the Cammo Dudes got out and uncovered a permanent binocular mounted on a tripod. I watched him watching me.

He was wearing gray pants and shirt that blended well with the desert, and his black gun holster was tied down to his thigh, the way SWAT teams and Special Forces do, so they can run after "violators."

Whatever they're hiding in Area 51, they certainly protect it well. One of the many secrets about Area 51 is exactly *who* runs the security force at the border. Best guesses say it's Wachenhut, the premier private security firm that works so closely with the CIA that it might as well be part of the Agency. But—no offense—these men were a notch above the typical Wachenhut employee.

The only time Glenn Campbell ever saw a Cammo Dude's ID was in August 1993, when one presented a card identifying him as a sworn and "compensated" deputy of the Lincoln County Sheriff's Department. A list of "Special Deputy Sheriffs" appears on the County Recorder, all entered and revoked on the same day, August 24, 1994. In all, Sheriff Dahl Bradfield deputized twenty-two men, supposedly beginning in 1989 shortly after he took office. That's more "special" deputies than the entire paid staff of the Lincoln County Sheriff's Department.

These men were sworn in by notaries in neighboring Clark County, with the records endorsed "DET AFFTC," which stands for Detachment–Air Force Flight Test Center. All twenty-two deputies listed their address as Pittman Station, a lonely post office substation on Boulder Highway. In early 1996, Campbell learned from the main postal center in Las Vegas that both Pittman Station and its zip code,

89044, had been decommissioned about "six or seven years ago."

It took several calls to reach Sheriff Bradfield in Lincoln County, who told me it was merely due to logistics—the distance between the sheriff's office in Alamo and the border of Area 51: "The reason we deputized them [the security force at Area 51] at that point was that they could only hold a suspect for thirty minutes. Then they changed the state regulation to one hour, and they didn't need to be deputized anymore." I asked if these special deputies were paid by Lincoln County, and Sheriff Bradfield said no. He also couldn't tell me who they did work for.

Since nobody seemed to know for certain, I looked in the most obvious place—the radio frequencies the security guards were using. Every nonfederal land-mobile radio service must be licensed by the Federal Communications Commission (FCC), while government agencies receive their authorization from the Interdepartmental Radio Advisory Committee (IRAC).

Frequencies are licensed to prevent interference for existing users. Those who illegally use a licensed frequency, particularly if it is a federal frequency, can receive stiff fines and prison sentences of up to ten years.

During my trips to Area 51, I've heard encrypted bursts over four of the five frequencies Campbell lists in the *"Area 51" Viewer's Guide*. I found all four in *Police Call* from Radio Shack (1996). Wachenhut frequencies wouldn't be listed in *Police Call* because private patrol and security companies must use the "Business Radio Services" from Radio Shack.

Four out of the five frequencies were registered to the Federal Emergency Management Agency (FEMA): 408.400, 418.050, 142.200, and 138.30. Frequency 170.500 was licensed by the Forest Service. On my first visit, I could see when the Cammo Dude in the Jeep raised his walkie-talkie and talked into it—at the same time, every time, the squelch of an encrypted transmission went over frequency 408.4.

So the Cammo Dudes are actively using FEMA frequencies. I couldn't help wondering: Where's the emergency?

I called the FEMA headquarters in Washington, D.C., and asked about frequencies in use at Area 51. I was immediately connected with Morrie Goodman, director of communications for FEMA. My conversation with Goodman was definitely one of the more highly charged encounters I had while researching this book. But then again, Goodman was preoccupied by a lot of things—"We've got so many disasters going on, tornadoes in Texas," he noted. But he took the time to make it very clear: "This communications director who knows everything about this agency doesn't know a thing about Area 51. Nor do we have anything to do with Area 51." Early in our conversation, Goodman also said, "I'm not allowed to talk about black projects—do you want me to get arrested?"

FEMA

The Federal Emergency Management Agency goes in after a flood or a hurricane and helps organize communities and charity assistance, making sure disaster victims are taken care of and necessary repairs are made. I couldn't put the two together—the silent, armed-to-the-teeth Cammo Dudes and FEMA, a benevolent government agency that gave me cheap apartment insurance while I lived in Manhattan.

But FEMA has been notoriously bad at its job. When Hurricane Andrew smashed into Florida, FEMA was accused of "dropping the ball" with disaster relief. The media and Congress finally looked into FEMA and discovered that the agency was spending twelve times more for "black operations" than for disaster programs.

According to a 1991 investigation by the General Accounting Office (GAO), the congressional watchdog unit, less than 10 percent of FEMA's staff (230 bureaucrats out of an estimated 2,600) were assigned full-time to preparing for major natural calamities such as storms or earthquakes.

Most of FEMA's personnel were occupied with plans for protecting the government during a nuclear attack.

Mark Farmer, a pilot and a former photojournalist for the U.S. Coast Guard, has photographed the Groom Lake air base and the surrounding area both from the ground and the air. Farmer is also one of the Interceptors—one of a loose network of military monitors who use the airwaves to spot secret aircraft. When I asked Farmer why FEMA frequencies would be used by security, he said nonchalantly, "I wouldn't be surprised if FEMA had a bunker at Area 51. It would make sense since it's protected by secrecy anyway."

"Underground facilities" play a large part in the mythology of the UFO phenomenon. Many of the rumors about Area 51 concern underground rail systems or subterranean complexes where alien technology is taken apart and examined. Bob Lazar claims that the underground hangars of S-4 go "through the small ridge of the mountain next to Papoose Lake."

FEMA certainly is known for its underground facilities. Mount Weather near Bluemont, Virginia, is only one of ninety-six shelters in the Federal Relocation Arc, serving leaders and critical personnel in North Carolina, Virginia, West Virginia, Maryland, and Pennsylvania. There are all kinds of rumors about the elaborate underground city at Mount Weather, including a battery-powered subway connecting numerous buildings, and an artificial lake.

Perhaps FEMA was also busy out at Area 51, and that's why the Office of Inspector General (OIG) gave the agency's effectiveness a universal thumbs-down during presidentially declared disasters in fiscal years 1989, 1990, and 1991. The OIG report concluded that FEMA didn't allocate funds to the states that needed them the most; instead, they used "various formulas, congressional direction, project proposals, and other techniques."

Though the FEMA budget has been drastically reduced (I lost my FEMA insurance in 1996 due to cutbacks), the Auditors' Report conducted by the OIG, on the fiscal year

1995 financial statements still wasn't satisfied with
FEMA's performance. By February 1997, FEMA had complied with only five out of the thirteen recommendations to
improve internal controls and ensure compliance with laws
and regulations.

I was reminded of the government's actions in the waste
lawsuit currently being fought over Area 51. On its official
website, under "Responsibilities of FEMA," the agency
states that it has precedence over other federal response
activities, "except where national security implications are
determined to be of a higher priority."

The words "national security" pop up with alarming frequency when officials talk about both Area 51 and UFOs.
I can understand the government wanting to keep its new
R&D craft secret, but why are tens of thousands of UFO
documents classified for "national security" reasons?

Executive Orders

When the waste lawsuit was in district court, the Air Force
Secretary, Sheila Widnáll, tried to circumvent the judicial
system by asking President Clinton to exempt Groom Lake
from "any federal, state, interstate, or local" environmental
laws. Clinton obligingly signed Executive Order 95-15 in
September 1995 issuing the exemption for one year. This
exemption continues to be renewed every year.

You hear a lot about executive orders from New World
Order conspiracy theorists and Patriot groups. Executive
orders, they maintain, are an unconstitutional presidential
power, yet they become law simply through publication in
the *Federal Register*. Congress is bypassed, therefore "we
the people" have no direct say in what becomes law. Congress also has no power to prevent martial law from being
declared, and according to Executive Order 11921, they
can't review the process for six months.

FEMA has been invested with a great deal of power
through executive orders. Just a few of the powers transferred to FEMA's Authority in 1979, to be put into effect

"in times of increased international tensions and economic or financial crisis," include:

- the National Security Act of 1947, which allows for the strategic relocation of industries, services, government, and other essential economic activities, and to rationalize the requirements for manpower, resources, and production facilities;
- the Act of August 29, 1916, which authorizes the Secretary of the Army, in time of war, to take possession of any transportation system for transporting troops, material, or any other purpose related to the emergency; and
- the International Emergency Economic Powers Act, which enables the President to seize the property of a foreign country or national.

In case you think executive orders aren't ever enacted, think again. President Andrew Jackson used executive orders to force the Cherokee Nation off its ancestral lands. The Cherokee fought the illegal action in the U.S. Supreme Court and won, but Jackson defied the Court's ruling, forcing the Cherokee to move in a journey now known as the Trail of Tears.

More recently, President Franklin Delano Roosevelt used Executive Order 9066 in December 1941 to place Japanese citizens of the United States in concentration camps. Their property was confiscated and when World War II ended, these Japanese families had to start all over again from scratch.

Perhaps the power of executive orders can be summed up most succinctly by arch-conservative activist Howard J. Ruff: "Since the enactment of Executive Order 11049, the only thing standing between us and dictatorship is the good character of the President, and the lack of a crisis severe enough that the public would stand still for it."

So what is FEMA doing out at Area 51? Even when there is no martial law in effect, FEMA offers "guidance"

to the Department of Defense and the National Security
Council (NSC) on issues of national security emergency
preparedness. FEMA could be authorized to provide security for Area 51 if the state government asks for help in
"an uncommon situation which requires law enforcement
assistance, which is or threatens to become of serious or
epidemic (large-scale) proportions, and with respect to
which State and local resources are inadequate to protect
lives and property of citizens, or to enforce the criminal
code."

Yet Margie Gunn, Lincoln County representative of the
Emergency Management Agency, told me that her county
hadn't requested emergency aid. Because it can be difficult
to get the FCC to issue new frequencies rapidly, Gunn figures federal agencies just work those things out among
themselves. Especially when, as Gunn said with a laugh,
"Area 51 doesn't exist, you know, except in everyone's
minds."

FEMA and UFOs

A key government study completed in 1953 by the Robertson panel concluded that UFOs were much more a threat
to the "orderly functioning of the protective organs of the
body politic" than to national security. This was supported
by the 1960 Brookings Institute Report for NASA, which
concluded that the discovery of extraterrestrial life could
have a "disastrous impact on society."

These studies indicated that people would panic and civil
unrest would ensue if aliens landed on Earth—a scenario
right out of the H. G. Wells story "War of the Worlds"
(1898). It was this belief in the potential for disasterlike
conditions that led the authors of *Fire Officer's Guide to
Disaster Control* to include a new chapter on UFOs in their
most current, 1993 edition.

The weighty *Fire Officer's Guide* is used by fire and
police departments across the United States. It is published
by the Delaware State Fire School and made available

through the Fire Engineering Book Service, which features it in its catalog as "An essential publication for those persons involved in emergency planning, management, response, and government operations."

The authors, William M. Kramer, Ph.D., and Charles W. Bahme, J. D., relied heavily on their own research and experiences when writing the UFO section, concluding:

Hence, as we near the year 2000 and move beyond, any comprehensive disaster plan should address the potential for panic and other deleterious effects that might befall a populated area when unexplainable phenomena occur. We will see, as we continue our discussion in this chapter, that widespread blackouts, communication disruptions, and other potentially disastrous conditions have been linked directly to UFO sightings.

Kramer and Bahme claim that power failures associated with UFOs took place in Brazil in 1957–59, in Italy in 1958, and in Mexico in 1965. They also quote the Operations and Training Order issued by the Inspector General of the Air Force on December 24, 1959, emphasizing the seriousness of UFOs: "Unidentified Flying Objects—sometimes treated lightly by the press and referred to as 'Flying Saucers'—must be rapidly and accurately identified as serious Air Force business. . . ."

But it was personal conviction that led these two authors to include the detailed section on UFOs in a manual for government employees, including reported shapes, history, secrecy, UFO hazards, and a recommendation for emergency action when confronted by a UFO.

Bahme's belief in the danger of UFOs harked back to the "Los Angeles Air Raid of 1942," which he personally witnessed:

All the fire fighters saw in the sky were the 15 or 20 moving "things" which seemed to change course at great speed apparently unaffected by the flak from bursting shells all around them. Rumors that one had been shot down were never verified, nor was the explanation that these zig-zagging invaders were weather balloons ever taken seriously.

Kramer and Bahme admit that "some fire chiefs have little confidence in disaster plans, especially those dealing with UFOs or enemy attack." Yet they counsel that "a good plan, good leadership and adequate resources" will inevitably save lives in any disaster.

When it comes to emergency preparedness, both the U.S. Fire Administration and the Federal Insurance Administration are under FEMA's jurisdiction. Under FEMA's Integrated Emergency Management System (IEMS), local fire jurisdictions are integrated with other emergency activities for disaster response.

So while I had Morrie Goodman, director of FEMA communications, on the phone, I asked if FEMA has any contingency plans for aliens landing in the United States. Goodman said his interest in UFOs is purely for their "entertainment value," but he added that when he was being fully briefed four years ago on entering his position, he had asked whether FEMA dealt with UFOs. Goodman says they told him to "get real" and moved on the serious issues at hand.

I asked if FEMA had officially approved the 1993 version of *The Fire Officer's Guide to Disaster Control*, as was reported in the January 1995 issue of *Omni Magazine*. But Goodman insisted, speaking very slowly so I wouldn't miss a word, "FEMA does not now or never has as far as preparedness, response and recovery, or any other arena, dealt with the subject of UFOs."

Secrecy at Area 51

Nobody knows for certain whether UFOs are being kept at Area 51 for research and development purposes. But there's no denying the deadly seriousness of government secrecy.

It's exemplified by a little catchphrase used by employees from the Nevada Test Site—where, incidentally, Area 51 employees are told to say they work. This phrase was repeated by FEMA spokesman Bob Blair when *Time* magazine asked about the underground complex at Mount Weather: "I'll be glad to tell you, but I'd have to kill you afterward."

I returned to Area 51 in June 1997 with my father, Bob Wright, and my partner, Kelly Beaton, the same month *Popular Mechanics* printed a cover story that Area 51 had moved. We already knew from the picture on the second page that Jim Wilson, the science editor, hadn't gotten within spitting distance of Area 51. He was shown standing in a vast desert valley in front of a cattle guard locked with padlocks, and therefore he concluded: Area 51 has moved.

Popular Mechanics has a real interest in UFOs; another recent cover story was entitled "Flying Saucers Are Real," based on Bob Lazar's testimony. The most recent Area 51 article noted that "Bob Lazar . . . claims the government moved the crashed flying saucer he worked on at the S4 site to a more secret location."

When we arrived at the border of Area 51, we did find some changes. The signs now announced: NO TRESPASSING, U.S. AIR FORCE INSTALLATION, as if you have simply stumbled across the boundary of the Nellis Range. Now in order to see signs that say USE OF DEADLY FORCE AUTHORIZED you have to hike some distance along the border. I had to applaud the good PR move that removed that stinging phrase from the main entrance.

We saw another carload of tourists arrive while we explored the area, but as we returned we scared them off. The Cammo Dudes didn't appear until we pulled back about a quarter of a mile and parked on the outermost buttes. I had just cracked open my door, camera in hand, when we heard the sound of rotors.

A Pave Hawk helicopter seemed to rise up from the ravine to the north, appearing out of nowhere. The side of the helicopter was open and a man in desert camouflage leaned out, looking through a piece of equipment—possibly a camera—he aimed in our direction. The helicopter dipped to within forty feet of our car, rocking us with the downdraft and raising a cloud of dust. It forced me to break off taking pictures to close the door, then the helicopter flew over and we heard on frequency 126.650, "staying on the perimeter of the Range."

If that wasn't enough, a Jeep Cherokee blasted out of Area 51—this one with a red and blue light-bar on top and a government license plate on the front. It shot past us going sixty—a piece of cake on the beautifully graded Groom Lake road.

As we followed, listening to their encrypted transmissions to the sheriff's department on 139.00, I laughed at the *Popular Mechanics* article and tossed it in the back. Not only was Area 51 alive and kicking, but it was still quite effectively guarding its secrets. But I bet the Air Force brass were congratulating themselves on how many hundreds of thousands of people would believe what they read in that national magazine.

Like all of my research, the UFO phenomenon persistently tried to hide its secrets. But as my forays into Area 51 certainly proved, we may not know exactly what's going on, but there's far too much evidence that *something* is happening to continue to ignore it.

So let's peel back the layers of secrecy and see what's hidden within the UFO phenomenon, using the secret government base at Area 51 as the UFO Rosetta stone.

CHAPTER 2

The History of UFO Sightings

What we will do here is to present evidence that UFO's are a global phenomenon which may have persisted for many thousands of years.

THIS AUTHORITATIVE quote was taken from Section 33.2 of the United States Air Forces Academy textbook *Introductory Space Science,* Volume II, Department of Physics. This textbook was used by the Air Force Academy at Colorado Springs from 1968 until fall 1970, when the thirty-third chapter, "Unidentified Flying Objects," was reduced by half, from fourteen to seven pages.

The UFO chapter was pulled shortly after the media got hold of the textbook, notably the *National Enquirer,* which at that time claimed to have the largest circulation of any weekly paper in America. In an early October 1970 issue, the *Enquirer* headlined with "AIR FORCE ACADEMY TEXTBOOK WARNS CADETS THAT UFO'S MAY BE SPACECRAFT OPERATED BY ALIENS FROM OTHER WORLDS."

I found both versions of the space sciences textbook posted on the Computer UFO Network (CUFON), and the original was on ParaNet Information Services, where Don Ecker of *UFO Magazine* transcribed the text sometime in the late eighties. Since this textbook was written by the Air Force after it had just spent twenty years as the only official investigator of UFOs (during Project Blue Book, 1948–1969), then arguably this textbook presents the government's "expert" opinion.

Colonel James F. Sunderman, director of information for the USAF Academy in Colorado, supplied copies of both versions of Chapter 33. In Sunderman's "letter of reply" dated November 4, 1970 (also posted on CUFON), the colonel offers the official explanation that the chapter was changed "to coincide with the findings of the Condon Report," published in January 1968.

Ancient UFOs

The space sciences textbook includes pictorial evidence supporting the theory of extraterrestrial visitations throughout human history:

> Only 8,000 years ago, rocks were sculpted in the Tassili plateau of Sahara, depicting what appeared to be human beings but with strange round heads (helmets? Or "sun" heads on human bodies?).

Archeologists usually refer to the paintings at Tassili n-Ajjer in southern Algeria as prehistoric "masked figures." Though there is evidence that the people of the Sahara influenced the cultures of both the Nile Valley and West Africa, there is no stylistic similarity between the "masks" in Tassili art and those from West Africa.

Scholars are not certain of the meaning of these paintings because they still haven't deciphered the hieroglyphic language engraved on the rocks next to them. Dating these figures is difficult even with radiocarbon techniques, yet they are roughly divided into several periods ranging from the beginning of human occupation at Tassili, around 5500 B.C. when the Sahara was much wetter, continuing sporadically until the fifth century B.C.

The faceless (aniconic) figures are found in both the early and middle periods. The smaller figures engraved in shelters are believed to be contemporary with the oldest paintings in Tassili. Either before or shortly after these cave paintings were made, an enormous "masked" figure was painted on the side of a cliff. This large figure is nearly eighteen feet high, outlined in dark purple and shaded with broad planes of color. It has a helmet-type device that encircles the head and rests directly on the shoulders.

This large figure was dubbed "the Great God Mars" by critic and art historian André Lhote in his 1950 *Treatise on Figure Painting.* The figure is unusual, resembling the large animal paintings in size, while the form is the same as many smaller faceless figures that have been found among the thirty thousand rock paintings and engravings.

Another ancient figural representation resembling the modern-day conception of a "gray alien" can be found at Glenn Campbell's Ufomind website. It is also in Seton Lloyd's *The Archaeology of Mesopotamia, Revised Edition* (1984).

This figure was found in an Ubaid grave at Eridu, dated approximately 5,500–4,000 B.C. The style is consistent with other Ubaid sculptures in the slanted eyes and conical head, and according to a message posted by Terence Moran, the extension of the head was usually fitted with a bitumen headdress. Yet this figure is unusual in that most were females while this one is clearly male.

Since figural representations can be interpreted according to personal bias, the best examples of ancient UFO sightings and alien contact are found in texts. Coincidentally, the Mesopotamian civilization also offers the first mention of "gods" who traveled from the stars in ships, impressing humans with their terrible weapons before returning to the sky. These stories are part of the earliest known written records in the world, the cuneiform texts and tablets of the Sumerians, dating back to the third millennium B.C.

Linguists have been unable to prove the relationship of the Sumerian language to any other known language. Apparently the stories evolved from a long tradition of oral compositions with mnemonic aids built into the internal rhythms. In form, they are similar to hymns or laudatory myths of great deeds.

The space sciences textbook cites another ancient group of "storyteller" legends from India which were eventually gathered in manuscript form in the *Book of Dzyan*. These stories describe a small group of beings who came to Earth "many thousands of years earlier in a metal craft which orbited the Earth several times before landing." The Academy textbook quotes at length from the *Book of Dzyan*:

> Separation did not bring peace to these people and finally their anger reached a point where the ruler of the original city took with him a small number of his warriors and they rose into the air in a huge shining metal vessel. While they were many leagues from the city of their enemies, they launched a great shining lance that rode on a beam of light. It burst apart in the city of their enemies with a great ball of flame that shot up to the heavens, almost to the stars.

Another ancient sighting was analyzed by the government study in 1969 which became known as the Condon Report (for more information, see Chapter 3). The Condon Committee took a great deal of time investigating an Egyptian papyrus that contained an account of a sighting that took place at the court of Thutmose III (c. 1504–1450 B.C.).

This papyrus belonged to Egyptologist Professor Alberto Tulli, and according to the translation of the hieroglyphs by Prince de Rachewiltz:

> . . . it was found a circle of fire that was coming from the sky . . . it had no head, the breath of its mouth had a foul odor. Its body was one rod long and one rod wide. It had no voice. . . . Now after some days had passed, these things became more numerous in the sky than ever. They shone more in the sky than the brightness of

the sun, and extended to the limits of the four supports of the heavens. . . .

Efforts to track down the papyrus and confirm the authenticity of this translation have been unsuccessful. During the Condon Committee's investigation, they received a letter from Dr. Walter Ramberg, scientific attaché to the U.S. embassy in Rome, who queried the inspector to the Egyptian Vatican Museum, Gianfranco Nolli. Ramberg reported back that Professor Tulli had died and his belongings had been "dispersed among heirs, who may have disposed of the papyrus as something of little value."

When the historical context of the reign of Thutmose III is examined, there is an intriguing correlation to modern UFO sightings, which have been documented to come in "waves" around large-scale wars. Thutmose III engaged in a great deal of war, extending the borders of his Egyptian kingdom with elaborate military campaigns that conquered all of Syria and reached deep into the Sudan.

The Condon Report made comparisons between this Egyptian sighting and passages found in the Book of Ezekiel from the Bible. The logic of the Condon Committee's arguments is difficult to follow, especially when the investigators attempt to make a vague case for plagiarism. The report waffles between concluding that the verses from Ezekiel derived from the ancient Egyptian manuscript, and conversely, that someone could have faked the papyrus based on the biblical passage.

While the authenticity of the papyrus can't be verified, nevertheless, there is a striking similarity to Ezekiel's description of his visions. By the river Chebar, recorded in Ezekiel 1:13, Ezekiel saw that "In the midst of the living creatures there was something that looked like burning coals of fire, like torches moving to and fro among the living creatures; and the fire was bright, and out of the fire went forth lightning."

The Book of Ezekiel is also referred to in the Air Force Academy textbook, which cites various biblical passages that could be interpreted as contact with UFOs and/or alien beings:

> And even more recently, in the Bible, Genesis (6:4) tells of angels from the sky mating with women of Earth, who bore them children. Genesis 19:3 tells of Lot meeting two angels in the desert and his later feeding them at his house. The Bible also tells a rather unusual story of Ezekiel who witnessed what has been interpreted by some to have been a spacecraft or aircraft landing near the Chebar River in Chaldea (593 B.C.).

St. Anthony, the Egyptian founder of Christian monasticism in the third and fourth centuries A.D., also claimed to have met a strange creature in the desert. According to Jacque Valleé's *Dimensions* (1988), when St. Anthony approaches the "manikin" with the "hooded snout, horned forehead, and extremities like goat's feet," it claims:

> "I am a mortal being and one of the inhabitants of the Desert whom the Gentiles deluded by various forms of error worship under the names of Fauns, Satyrs and Incubi. I am sent to represent my tribe. We pray you in our behalf to entreat the favour of your Lord and ours, who, we have learnt, came once to save the world, and whose sound has gone forth into all the earth."

These ancient passages illustrate the ways that people interpret what they see in terms of their own culture. Ancient observers did not have the concepts and terminology to describe complex mechanical objects or the strange appearance of extraterrestrials. To St. Anthony, a helmeted figure could have been seen as a "hooded snout" and "horned forehead," while the goat's feet could refer to the booted feet of an alien astronaut.

The psychologist Carl Jung pointed out that the UFO phenomenon is a mythology as complex as any other in our history. Jung explored the psychology of UFOs in 1959 when he wrote *Flying Saucers: A Modern Myth of Things Seen in the Skies.* If UFOs are indeed a myth, an interpretation of some intangible desire or human longing, then these myths should recur throughout human history. The Roman historian Sallust, who critically examined the origins of myths in the first century B.C., concluded, "These things never happened: they always are."

Ufologists often point to the numerous myths of gift-giving gods and the sudden rise of civilizations around the world as proof of early beneficial contact with alien beings. These mythological "bringers of civilization" are similar in form to the Greek god Prometheus, the hero who stole fire from the gods and gave it to man. The Greeks also speculated on the idea of life beyond our own world—not just gods living in the sky, but other beings in other environments distant from ours. This philosophical speculation on other worlds appears in ancient Chinese texts, as well as in Greek works by Pythagoreans in the fifth century B.C., and by the atomists Democritus and Epicurus in the fourth century B.C.

This civilizing influence is a key attribute of Nommo, the primal being among the Dogon in Mali, Africa. Nommo is said to have come from the sky bringing fire and the first fruits to earth. Before returning to the heavens, Nommo also gave the Mali a unique astronomical knowledge. The Dogon people knew of an unknown companion star to Sirius (commonly known as the Dog Star) long before it was discovered by modern astronomers. Even today, the Dogon are an extremely metaphysical culture with much more of their social organization tied to the creation myth than most other African tribes.

On the other side of the world, also looking to the skies were the people of Nazca living on the southern coast of Peru from about 500 B.C. to 900 A.D. This pre-Incan civilization is known for its beautiful multicolored pottery, decorated with stylized figures of people, birds, and animals.

It is in the Palpa Valley that their best-known creations can be seen: the Nazca Lines. These lines and figural outlines were dug into a level strip of land running nearly thirty-seven miles down the narrow valley. In 1952 the first scientific excavations took place and additional series of parallel lines appeared. Some crossed inexplicably while others seemed to be "rubbed out" to form giant wedge shapes.

In the wildly popular *Chariots of the Gods?* (1968), Erich von Daniken proposed that these lines were actually runways for ancient astronauts. Yet von Daniken's attribution of almost every ancient monument and ruin to alien innovations has been soundly rejected by scholars.

Since these lines can't be properly viewed from the ground, many archaeologists agree that they were meant to be viewed from the air. How the artists got into the air is another matter. In *Ancient Inventions,* Peter James and Nick Thorpe present evidence gathered by the International Explorers Society of Miami that the Nazca Indians constructed tight-weave cotton balloons that carried them into the sky so they could direct the creation of the enormous birds and monkeys.

Huge figures like the ones at Tassili n-Ajjer and Nazca can be found in many locations around the world among indigenous populations. Even the North American Indians created large figures, such as the ones in the Mojave Desert between Earp and Blythe, California. Ancestors of the Colorado River Indian tribes created these large-scale stick-figures, which seem to be aimed at viewers in the sky. One appears to be wearing a helmet, very much like an ancient representation of an astronaut.

Premodern UFOs

During the European Renaissance, science began the long and arduous process of displacing the scriptural authority of the Church. In the early sixteenth century, the Protestant Reformation created a schism in the Western world, weakening the power of the pope. Then came Copernicus' theory that the sun rather than the earth was the center of the solar system, and humanity's conception of the universe has never been the same.

When people could finally conceptualize planets as heavenly bodies that were similar to the earth, they naturally began to consider whether those other planets were also inhabited. The moon was the first logical site for people to look for new civilizations. Astronomer Johannes Kepler was one early proto–science fiction writer who wrote *Somnium* (*Dream*, 1634). John Wilkins also immortalized the existence of extraterrestrial civilizations in *The Discovery of a World in the Moone* (1638).

Two generations later, life on other planets was championed by writers such as Bernard le Bovier de Fontenelle in *Entretiens sur la pluralité des mondes* (*Conversations on the Plurality of Worlds*, 1686), and astronomer Christiaan Huygens in *Cosmotheoros* (1698). These imagined otherworldly environments were usually populated by men and animals similar to those on earth, though Huygens did state that though the aliens have hands and feet and stand upright, "it follows not therefore that they have the same Shape with us."

One of the most renowned interpretations of alien civilizations is found in Jonathan Swift's *Gulliver's Travels* (1726). Swift used the differences between man and aliens to satirize the failings of contemporary society. Yet UFO researchers have compared Swift's floating city of Laputa to the mammoth alien "motherships" regularly seen in modern sightings. Swift describes this "flying island" as "exactly circular" and powered aloft by a "loadstone of prodigious size in shape resembling a weaver's shuttle."

Scientific theorizing led to speculations on how "airships" could fly. A beautiful engraving from 1709 is reprinted in *The Curious Lore of Precious Stones* (1913), available through the Sourcebook Project of Maryland, a motherlode of new and ancient information on the frontiers of science. The engraving of an airship is in a book on precious stones because it was once believed that coral agates possessed the "magnetic power" that could keep a vessel aloft. The classic flying saucer shape of the airship is augmented by clusters of coral agates on the bottom, magnetically repelling the craft into the air.

An even earlier pictorial representation of UFOs flying through the air comes from a Renaissance woodcut (1566) of a view of the city of Basel, Switzerland. The figures in the foreground look up and point to the sky, which is filled with round black and white globes. The Air Force Academy textbook admits that "many documented sightings occurred throughout the Middle Ages, including an especially startling one of a UFO over London on 16 December 1742."

Now I wouldn't consider 1742 to be the "Middle Ages," but it is a specific date and place that the USAF identifies as a legitimate sighting. The UFO chapter also includes an incident that took place in the tenth century in Lyons, France, in which "three men and a woman supposedly descended from an airship or spaceship and were captured by a mob. These foreigners admitted to being wizards, and were killed."

The Archbishop of Lyons wrote a ninth-century Latin manuscript, *Liber contra insulam vulgi opinionem*, describing the stoning of the three men and a woman who had "fallen" from a ship in the sky. The Archbishop explained that this animosity occurred because the French peasants believed in a "certain region called Magonia from whence come ships in the clouds."

The next major conceptual shift came with the Industrial Age in the nineteenth century, when mechanical devices routinely performed miraculous deeds. Human technology lent credibility to the appearance of objects in the air that could hover and move quickly through the sky.

Along with the technological strides, Darwin's theory of evolution changed man's view of himself. The first writer to suggest the possibility that aliens could be completely different from us was Camille Flammarion in his nonfiction work *Real and Imaginary Worlds* (1864). In his fictional work *Lumen* (1887), Flammarion imagined life in the form of plants that could speak and think. Two years later, in

Urania (1889), he proposed that reincarnation could allow an individual's "lifespirit" to move from one physical form to the next after death.

Usually alien civilization was shown as very distant from our world, with the human protagonist traveling to meet cooperative, and sometimes amorous, aliens. This popular theme has recurred throughout modern history: the French writer J. H. Rosny presented a love affair between a human and a six-eyed tripedal Martian in *Les navigateurs de l'infini (The Navigators of Infinity,* 1925). Nearly forty years later, Robert Heinlein would write *Stranger in a Strange Land* (1961), featuring Valentine Michael Smith, a human raised by Martians to possess utopian ideals and a marvelous acceptance of a variety of human sexual expression.

This beneficial concept of alien life took a dramatic turn in the Victorian era. Victorian society repressed individuality, and fear of the unusual or abnormal was united with an anxiety about the approaching century—the same sort of superstitious millennium fever our own culture is currently experiencing.

Much like today, nineteenth-century anxiety unleashed an interest in paranormal phenomena. Henry James and Sir Arthur Conan Doyle are just two famous examples of the scores of writers who created melodramatic tales capturing the darker regions of the imagination.

H. G. Wells's "The War of the Worlds" (1898) depicted Martians invading Britain with their flying machines and terrible weapons. "The War of the Worlds" became the archetypal story of the "alien invasion"—a resoundingly popular theme throughout twentieth-century science fiction.

Wells found his inspiration in the real-life stories of sightings known as the "airship wave" of the late nineteenth century. The first airship sighting is said to have taken place in southern California in 1896, with many other sightings across America and around the world soon following.

One sighting was documented in the February 2, 1897 issue of the *Omaha Bee*. This article was reprinted in the

UFO Roundup (1997), and contains an account of a UFO sighting in Hastings, Nebraska, 160 miles southwest of Omaha: "Several Hastings people report that an air ship, or something of the kind, has been sailing around in the air west of this city."

This "air ship" was first noticed the previous fall when it was seen floating about five hundred feet above the ground. Then in January the "air ship" returned and was sighted in several different locations. It had "the appearance of an immense star, but after closer observation the powerful light shows by its color to be artificial."

The reporter faithfully describes the appearance and movements of the UFO:

> At 9:30 last Monday night [January 25, 1897] the large glaring light was seen to circle around for a few minutes and then descended for about 200 feet, circling as it traveled at a remarkable speed for about two miles and then slowing up it circled for fully 15 minutes, when it began to lower and disappear as mysteriously as it had made its appearance. . . . A close watch is being kept for its reappearance.

In a second article on February 5, 1897, the *Omaha Bee* reported that the UFO had been sighted again, this time by people returning from a prayer meeting in Inavale. This tiny farm town is just forty miles (sixty-four kilometers) south of Hastings, near the Kansas state line.

Ironically, The USAF Academy textbook recounts as true one of the first UFO hoaxes, in the form of a "sworn statement" made on April 21, 1897, by "a prosperous and prominent farmer" named Alexander Hamilton from Le Roy, Kansas. The statement includes the fact that "his cattle were attacked at about 10:30 P.M. the previous Monday" and describes how Hamilton, his son, and his tenant:

> . . . grabbed axes and ran some 700 feet from the house to the cow lot where a great cigar-shaped ship about 300

feet long floated some 30 feet above his cattle. It had a carriage underneath which was brightly lighted within and which had numerous windows. Inside were six strange looking beings jabbering in a foreign language.

Supposedly, when the beings became aware of Hamilton and the others, they shined a bright searchlight on the farmer. The power appeared to come from a turbine wheel (about thirty feet in diameter) located under the craft:

> The ship rose, taking with it a two-year old heifer which was roped about the neck by a cable of one-half inch thick, red material. The next day a neighbor, Link Thomas, found the animal's hide, legs and head in his field. He was mystified at how the remains got to where they were because of the lack of tracks in the soft soil. Alexander Hamilton's sworn statement was accompanied by an affidavit as to his veracity. The affidavit was signed by ten of the local leading citizens.

This hoax by Hamilton is still often claimed as the first record of UFO cattle mutilation. The core details are the same: a bright light that approaches a distant area and mangled cattle are found the next day. Yet the day before Hamilton claimed his heifer was taken, an estimated three thousand people in Cripple Creek, Kansas, saw an object shimmering in the sunlight nearly a mile away.

Thousands of airship sightings were reported during this time—some were undoubtedly dirigibles created by contemporary inventors, and some were hoaxes yet others remain unexplained. The airship wave ended in April 1897, according to Paris Flammonde in *UFO Exist!* In the June 1897 *Scientific American,* an article dismissed the thousands of observations that took place over the past year as "creations from the brains of imaginative persons."

The next major UFO wave witnessed by civilians around the world would take place exactly fifty years later, in 1947.

Modern UFOs

The modern era of UFO sightings is characterized by the active involvement of scientists who began investigating the phenomenon. As early as 1896, Konstantin Eduardovich Tsiolkovsky, a pioneering scientist in rocket and space research, published an essay on communication with inhabitants of other planets. That same year, Tsiolkovsky also published "Exploration of Cosmic Space by Means of Reaction Devices," his seminal work on aeronautics.

In 1928, Tsiolkovsky wrote a largely neglected treatise, "The Will of the Universe: Unknown Intelligent Forces," which supported the extraterrestrial theory of UFOs:

A mass of inexplicable phenomena have been recorded in history and literature. The majority of them can undoubtedly be classified with hallucinations and other delusions, but does this apply to all such phenomena? Now that the possibility of interplanetary travel has been proven, man should show greater consideration for such "incomprehensible" phenomena. I believe that some such phenomena are not illusions, but real proof of the presence of unknown intelligent forces in outer space.

For most of his long scientific career, Tsiolkovsky carefully considered the evidence for the existence of aliens and why these aliens had not made their presence more widely known on earth. As reported by biophysicist Mark Milchiker in *SPUTNIK*, the monthly digest of the Soviet press, Tsiolkovsky scribbled a note on a letter from a student, A. Yudin of Tomsk, two years before he died in 1935: "Attempts of higher beings to help us are possible, because they continue to be made to this day. We, people, do not try to convince animals of the irrationality of their life. The distance between us and perfect beings is hardly any less."

At the turn of the century, American astronomer Percival Lowell offered seemingly scientific proof of the reality of alien civilizations. Lowell was not the only astronomer who agreed with Giovanni Schiaparelli's descriptions of *"canali"* he had observed on Mars, yet many people misinterpreted the Italian word to mean "canals" rather than "channels." According to Lowell, these canals were artifacts constructed by the intelligent inhabitants of Mars.

Lowell financed his own observatory in Arizona and began distributing drawings of the canals he observed on Mars, faithfully capturing many of the patterns made by the giant canyons and volcanoes only vaguely discernible on the surface through nineteenth-century telescopes. Lowell proclaimed that the patterns were an enormously complex water-distribution system that allowed the Martians to continue watering their farms on an increasingly arid world.

Lowell's misinterpretation of the evidence is a common problem throughout the history of the UFO phenomenon. Because individual sightings can be argued or disproved, some people believe that the entire subject of UFOs is a waste of time. Yet evidence can't be so easily dismissed. Witness testimony is used in our courts of law to prove guilt or innocence, but the problem lies in questioning the witness in a manner that elicits the facts rather than an interpretation of those facts.

Modern research presents us with more than enough witness testimony of the UFO phenomenon to winnow the facts from the chaff. With a grant from the Maryland-based Fund for UFO Research (FUFOR), Jan Aldrich is presently coordinating "Project 1947," a two-and-a-half-year, worldwide volunteer effort to reexamine UFO press clippings from the year 1947. Over five thousand newspapers from all over the world are being screened for UFO reports, as are libraries, historical societies, universities, and archives.

Aldrich first became interested in UFOs in the seventh grade when he witnessed the unusual phenomenon of ball lightning. As a retired military meteorological officer and historian, Aldrich started Project 1947 as historical research into the beginning of the modern UFO era. The project will document how ideas about UFOs developed, and will establish a solid collection of official UFO documents, articles, and personal accounts to be published in the Project 1947 volumes.

According to Project 1947, several established UFO waves took place in the early twentieth century. From 1908 to 1910, there was another worldwide airship wave, and from 1912 to 1913 in Britain there was the "Phantom Airship Scare." As always, these documented sightings are described in terms that agree with contemporary technology—that of dirigibles and air balloons.

One document supplied by Project 1947 is a letter to ATIC (Air Technical Intelligence Center) at Wright-Patterson Air Force Base in Ohio, dated April 11, 1952, from a former studio manager for De Frenes & Company Motion Picture Studios, Philadelphia. The witness, Mr. Harrison, approached the studio to find out the cost of producing an animated film about a strange object he had seen in the sky nearly thirty years earlier.

The alleged sighting took place on August 4, 1917, in Philadelphia. The studio manager wrote down what Mr. Harrison had told him as "an instance of the odd type of people one runs into in the motion picture business." Mr. Harrison's theories on what he had seen took a decidedly religious turn as he speculated it may have been a "mystic Morse Code" or "a manifestation of the Holy Grail." Mr. Harrison's sighting is described by the studio manager as follows:

> In mid-afternoon of August 4, 1917, this Mr. Harrison had been standing at the window of one of the upper floors of an office building in Philadelphia. There were a certain amount of clouds in the sky, but the sun was shining. High in the sky he saw a series of bright glittering objects. They were arranged in a pattern as drawn below.

Though Mr. Harrison never saw the phenomenon again, the sighting apparently had a strong impact on him. The

studio manager was struck by the fact that Harrison had
been trying to interpret what he had seen for the past thirty
years. Yet this sort of life-altering impact is common
among people who observe UFOs.

Diaries and autobiographies provide excellent documentation of early UFO sightings. Nicholas Roerich, a famous
Russian painter and Buddhist researcher, traveled for four
years through India, Tibet, Mongolia, and China in the late
1920s. There is a museum dedicated to Roerich's work in
New York City, complete with Internet site.

A quote from Roerich's diary "Altai-Himalaya," dated
August 5, 1926, describes:

> Something remarkable! We were in our camp in the Ku-
> kunor district not far from the Humboldt chain. In the
> morning about half past nine some of our caravaneers
> noticed a remarkably big black eagle flying above us.
> Seven of us began to watch this unusual bird. At the
> same moment another one of our carvaneers remarked,
> "There is something far above the bird." And he shouted
> his astonishment. We all saw, in a direction from north
> to south, something big and shiny reflecting the sun, like
> a huge oval moving at great speed. Crossing our camp
> this thing changed in its direction from south to south-
> west. And we saw how it disappeared in the intense blue
> sky. We even had time to take field glasses and saw
> quite distinctly an oval form with a shiny surface, one
> side which was brilliant from the sun.

One 1920s incident of physical interaction with a UFO
can be considered a prototype EME (electromagnetic effect) report in which a UFO sighting coincides with mechanical trouble. In *Fate Magazine,* October 1973, Aaron
C. Stern of Pine, Colorado, describes a UFO encounter that
took place in August 1928, witnessed by his father and
himself. Just after leaving their home in Tulsa, Olkahoma,
fifty miles west of the city, their Willys Knight car started
to miss and backfire. Stern asserts:

As I started to look under the hood, suddenly the whole area was illuminated by the brightest light I have ever seen. It flashed by about 150 feet overhead. It was primarily a white light but as it faded it seemed to burst into many colors like a fireworks spectacle. Then darkness closed in again. Dad and I stood like statues—speechless. Then we both blurted almost simultaneously. "What was that?"

Stern described how they both "stood there trying to understand what had occurred" for the next fifteen to thirty minutes. Apparently they had been stunned by the appearance of the UFO. When he had recovered somewhat, Stern didn't bother trying to tinker with the engine. He simply turned the key and it started immediately. They completed their journey with no further trouble from the car.

There are numerous accounts of EME contact with UFOs, yet few people take the time to have their equipment checked after the encounter for radiation or indications of the effect. The engineers of the Condon Committee reported that the only way a vehicle could be stopped was by a strong magnetic field which would leave residual magnetism.

The number of reported sightings declined during the 1930s—the pre–World War II years were difficult due to the worldwide economic depression and the tensions from the rising power of Nazi Germany. Escapism was clear in the popularity of pulp sci-fi magazines. Some continued to explore the Wellsian theme of alien invasion, throwing in the innovative twist that humans invade the aliens' home world, as in P. Schuyler Miller's "Forgotten Man of Space" (1933). Other pulp sci-fi writers presented their audience with convincingly horrific alien monsters in their stories, such as John W. Campbell Jr.'s "Who Goes There?" (1938) and A. E. van Vogt's "Black Destroyer" (1939).

The other prominent alien theme in the early twentieth century was space opera or planetary romances, memorably created in the Barsoom series of stories by Edgar Rice Burroughs. Burroughs wrote about exotic alien princesses who conveniently fell in love with the heroes who rescued their entire race from malevolent monsters. A more serious exploration of this theme can be found in Raymond Z. Gallun's "Old Faithful" (1934), in which humans overcome the biological differences between themselves and a Martian, eventually reaching an understanding of their intellectual equality.

Cooperation and communication with alien races underwent a marked shift in emphasis during World War II. In van Vogt's "Co-operate or Else!" (1942), a man and an exotic alien are stranded on a strange planet during an interstellar war, and they are forced to work together in order to survive. A similar yet more hesitant groping for an understanding is portrayed in Murray Leinster's story "The Ethical Equations" (1945), which concerns man's first contact with aliens and the importance every action assumes when one is trying to establish friendly relations.

Things changed again with World War II, the first aerial combat war. During the war, thousands of UFOs were witnessed by airmen on both sides of the fighting. Like the early airship and ghost ship appearances, these sightings came in distinct waves, in 1942 and 1944–45.

According to Project 1947, the name "foo-fighter" was invented at the end of World War II. During the war, pilots filed reports in numerous unit histories, operations, and intelligence documents citing observations of gremlins, kraut fireballs, jets, rockets, and even vertigo. In most cases the term "foo-fighters" was not used, but the phrase was eventually adopted from the popular "Smokey Stover" comic strip: "Where there's foo there's fire."

Pilots weren't the only witnesses. The radar plotters at the Argus 16 Combat Intelligence Center at Tarawa recorded foo-fighters, according to an article by Jerome Clark and Lucius Farish in the *International UFO Reporter,* Spring 1975:

On April 1944 a "bogey," the blip of an unknown object, was tracked moving at the then incredible speed of

700 miles per hour. When the radar operators had determined there was nothing wrong with their sets, they had no choice but to conclude that it was a supersonic Japanese plane. Of course, it wasn't, since after the war American intelligence experts found that the Japanese had no such fighter.

In the *Herald Tribune,* a story on foo-fighters on January 3, 1945, unsuccessfully attempted to find a geophysical explanation for the anomalous objects:

Induction is suggested by the reports from Allied airmen, that the foo-fighters keep up with their planes at fixed distances, regardless of plane speed, changes in speed or changes in direction. Electrical induction of some sort would explain such marvelous synchronization. Nothing else that is well known would explain such perfect timing. . . . Induction, however, fails completely to describe what happens when a fire-ball zooms upward, leaving its plane. Apparently the balls fly paths thousands of feet away from the planes.

There are literally hundreds of reports of sightings made during the war or soon after, when the American government officially began investigating UFOs. No conclusive explanation was ever found that accounted for the elusive foo-fighters.

The UFO Wave of 1947

Many ufologists date the beginning of the modern UFO era to June 24, 1947, when fire-control equipment salesman Kenneth Arnold sighted "a formation of very bright objects" while flying over the Cascade Mountains of Washington State. Captains Brown and Davidson from Hamilton Field investigated Arnold's case almost three weeks after the fact, and they found Arnold to be a man of character and integrity.

The interviewers who finally arrived to take Arnold's statement remarked on his bitterness that it had taken so long for someone from the military to talk to him. Arnold's report was nearly lost in the official shuffle of hundreds of sightings that occurred during the six-week-long UFO wave that summer; meanwhile Arnold's sighting was mentioned in the press just about every day until the first of July.

The June 25 issue of the *Chicago Daily Tribune* quoted Arnold in a page one story:

"The first thing I noticed was a series of flashes in my eyes as if a mirror was reflecting sunlight at me. . . . I saw the flashes were coming from a series of objects that were traveling incredibly fast. They were silvery and shiny and seemed to be shaped like a pie plate. . . . What startled me most at this point was . . . that I could not find any tails on them.

"I counted nine of them as they disappeared behind the peak of Mount Rainier. Their speed was apparently so great I decided to clock them. I took out my watch and checked off one minute and 42 seconds from the time they passed Mount Rainier until they reached the peak of Mount Adams. . . . All told the objects remained in view slightly less than two minutes from the time I first noticed them."

On July 12, 1947, Arnold sent drawings of the objects to Wright-Patterson Air Field along with his report. The drawings show an object that is rounded at the front with slightly flattened sides, coming to a point at the rear. Two years later in the "Project Saucer" press release, Arnold described them as "flat like a pie pan and so shiny they reflected the sun like a mirror."

Bill Bequette, a reporter with the *East Oregonian* newspaper, recalled that Arnold described the objects moving "like a saucer would if you skipped it across the water," and when he placed his story on the AP wire, he inadvertently yet indelibly nicknamed UFOs "flying saucers."

When the AP story appeared nationwide on June 26, additional UFO stories began to come out. During the next week, skeptical opinions of the existence of UFOs were presented by Howard Blakeslee, Associated Press science editor, and an official "not interested" statement was released by the Army Air Force spokesman in Washington, D.C. (this was prior to the formation of the Air Force as a separate department).

There were numerous sightings that took place on the July Fourth weekend. According to Jan Aldrich of Project 1947, there was a sighting by a Captain Smith, a United Airlines pilot. The Coast Guard photographed a UFO, and some National Guard and private fliers organized air patrols to search for discs.

After July 7, hoaxes began to appear in response to the offers of "reward money" for a real flying saucer. There were also an increasing number of journalistic spoofs on the flying saucer craze. The report of the Roswell, New Mexico crash appeared nationwide in newspapers on July 9, often coupled with the official debunking story issued at General Ramey's press conference that it was really a "weather balloon" (for more information, see Chapter 6).

As Aldrich concluded, based on Project 1947 research, "By the 11th of July, the widely reported stories were of the hoax discs in Hollywood and Twin Falls (sort of the Coup de Grace of press coverage). From 12–15 of July, press accounts rapidly fall off."

Foreign reports of saucers continued to receive some press coverage, and sightings from around the world lasted well into the fall of 1947. The AP carried an article from Denmark on October 28, 1947:

A flying bottle is the newest object to squeeze into Denmark's firmament, already crowded with reported flying balls, flying discs, saucers, and fireballs. The newspaper *National Tidende* reported today that a bottle-shaped object with a tail of fire whizzed past a farmer's wife, Mrs.

Carl Hansen, her daughter and a maid of Neorreby, Funen, Denmark when they were out in their yard.

Throughout history, people have instinctively ridiculed the unexplainable or ignored the unknown, and as in the summer of 1947, this tends to facilitate the suppression of UFO reports. Yet it was the first time that government officials were forced to take action because of a UFO wave. In America, Project Sign was created under Army Air Force jurisdiction to investigate UFOs. Thus, Kenneth Arnold's sighting and the UFO wave of 1947 can be said to have initiated the age of government investigations into flying saucers.

CHAPTER 3

Government Investigations of UFOs

WHEN UFO sightings during the summer of 1947 continued for weeks without explanation, the media questioned Army Air Force officials as to whether they were testing any new types of planes. The AAF protested that they had nothing capable of speeds that fast or able to perform the maneuvers that had been described—and they certainly didn't have nine such aircraft, as pilot Kenneth Arnold had reported.

Thus the American government was faced with the possibility that a foreign country had superior technology. Both the military and intelligence communities undoubtedly felt compelled to investigate. The Army Air Force Intelligence Agency established Project Sign in 1948 as the official UFO investigative unit, followed by Project Grudge from 1949 to 1952, renamed Project Blue Book from 1953 to 1969. Project Blue Book was run under the auspices of the Air Technical Intelligence Center (ATIC) and later fell under the jurisdiction of the Foreign Technology Division.

Dr. J. Allen Hynek, former head of the Optical Satellite Tracking Program at the Smithsonian Astrophysical Observatory, was chosen to become the project's scientific consultant. Dr. Hynek worked with Project Blue Book for the next twenty years, until investigations ceased in 1969.

During Hynek's decades-long contact with the UFO phenomenon, he gradually changed from a skeptic into a believer. A few years after Blue Book closed, Hynek founded the civilian UFO organization the Center for UFO Studies (CUFOS), which is still in existence today, dedicated to the research and analysis of the UFO phenomenon.

Project Blue Book is generally considered to be a half-hearted effort on the part of the Air Force that was both understaffed and underfunded. According to Dr. Hynek, the Air Force program functioned more like a public relations office than a scientific investigation. Letters and reports from the general public often went unanswered and uninvestigated. Press reports were barely looked at before being thrown away.

Even so, from the summer of 1947 until December 19, 1969, Air Force representatives gathered 12,618 official case reports of UFOs, defined by the Air Force as "any aerial object or phenomenon which the observer is unable to identify." Later Hynek corrected the definition of a UFO to "Any airborne object, which by performance, aerodynamic characteristics or unusual features does not conform to any known aircraft or missile type, or which cannot be positively identified as a familiar or known object."

As the historical research shows, eyewitness testimony can be tricky. Visual perception is inevitably interpreted according to an individual's cultural beliefs. Yet in general, sightings can be classified in four categories:

1. Visual sightings in the daytime
2. Visual sightings at night
3. Radar sightings
4. Physical evidence (radiation burns on skin or indentations in the ground)

The most reliable reports consist of two or more independent witnesses. This helps rule out sincere yet misguided interpretations of vivid dreams or hallucinations of UFOs or alien contact. After interviewing hundreds of people and analyzing thousands of sightings reports, Hynek concluded in *The UFO Experience* (1972) that "the most coherent and articulate UFO reports come from people who have not given much thought to the subject and generally who are surprised and shocked by their experience."

Even the most objective observer can be fooled by tricks of the eyes, mirages, or hallucinations. Reflections from windows and eyeglasses can superimpose images. Optical defects often turn point sources of light into what appears to be a saucer-shaped object. Fixed points of light, such as the planet Venus, can seem to move when viewed without a clamped telescope or a sighting bar. It's also difficult to estimate visual distance because judgments are made based on the *assumed* size of the object.

Radar readings, while more reliable, also can confuse physical objects with atmospheric phenomena. False radar echoes come from electronic interference, reflections from ionized layers and clouds, and even regions of high humidity.

When Francis Ridge looked into Blue Book's numbers, I trusted his opinion. Ridge is a thirty-seven-year veteran of UFO research, the moderator of the Close-Encounters electronic mailing list, and currently working full-time on the Lunascan Project, gathering sightings and evidence of "fast walkers" or, in NORAD terminology, "Uncorrelated Lunar Objects," which seemingly move over the moon. In the 1960s, Ridge belonged to the civilian UFO organization NICAP (National Investigations Committee on Aerial Phenomena), which actively investigated sightings.

Ridge points out that Blue Book had a certain system, with "three categories for all sighting groups: known, probable, possible. You would have been amazed to see what the statistics looked like if you lumped the known and probable together."

In all, Ridge figured that 22.39 percent of the reported sightings fell into the "possible" range. The combined percentage of known/probable for balloons was 6.56 percent, as compared to the 11.95 percent that were only considered "possible balloons." Out of 14.20 percent of misidentified astronomical bodies, only 6.80 percent were known or probable stars and/or planets. The other percentages have similar breakdowns, and nearly one fourth of the reports weren't analyzed for "lack of proper data."

When E. J. Ruppelt, an engineer, took over Project Blue Book in 1951, his investigators gathered an immense amount of data during his two-year tenure. But every time Ruppelt presented evidence from reliable witnesses, backed by radar readings and increased radiation counts at the sites of UFO sightings, the Air Force consultants replied "the data still aren't good enough."

In the middle of his term as director, Ruppelt investigated green fire balls that were seen at Los Alamos Labs. The scientists and technicians there speculated that the balls were probes "projected into our atmosphere from a 'spaceship' hovering several hundred miles above the earth." Ruppelt commented:

> Two years ago I would have been amazed to hear a group of reputable scientists make such a startling statement. Now, however, I took it as a matter of course. I'd heard the same type of statement many times before from equally qualified groups.

In 1956, Ruppelt published his own book on the UFO phenomenon, *The Report on Unidentified Flying Objects*. Ruppelt made it clear he leaned toward the ET hypothesis of UFOs, though as director of Blue Book, his appraisal wasn't nearly as sensational as Donald Keyhoe's series of dramatic UFO books (Keyhoe was later the director of the civilian UFO group NICAP).

Ufologists routinely point to the lack of government support for the Blue Book in its later years. During Ruppelt's term, Project Blue Book listed 26.94 percent of the reports as "Unknowns." By 1969, of the 12,000-plus cases studied, only 701, about 6 percent, were now classified "unknown." By the end, Project Blue Book was doing everything they could to explain away sightings. As Francis Ridge explained:

> In the S. Illinois case [Wayne City, August 1963] E-M effects on a car chased by a UFO, Blue Book flew in the three Air Force physicists (one of which was the Blue Book Director, himself, Hector Quintanella). There were quite a few sightings and witnesses. The explanations were: the planet Jupiter; then a refueling operation. I think this is where the "buy one, get one free" started.

Hynek himself was ultimately disillusioned by his years spent as scientific consultant to Project Blue Book. Shortly before his death, he stated, "I can safely say that the whole time I was with the Air Force, we never had anything that resembled a really good scientific dialogue on the subject."

The Washington Wave of 1952

The most dramatic modern UFO sightings comprised the Washington Wave of 1952, when UFOs appeared over the Capitol in Washington, D.C. The Cold War was heating up, and not only was America in the midst of the Korean War (from June 1950 to July 1953), but the country would detonate its first H-bomb on November 1, 1952.

It started on July 13, when a Ground Observer Corps spotter in Baltimore sighted a UFO. Among other sightings, a National Airlines plane, en route to National Airport, observed a blue-white ball of light hovering west of Washington, D.C. The next day, a Pan American Airways plane observed six glowing red, circular objects approaching from below the aircraft.

Nearly a week later, on July 19, the movements of the strange lights in the sky between 11:40 P.M. and 5:00 A.M. were recorded by air-traffic controllers at Washington National Airport, and confirmed by visual observations of in-

coming flight crews. Francis Ridge describes how Senior
Controller Harry G. Barnes notified the Air Defense Command:

> When he got back to the main scope the objects had
> separated. Can you imagine what went through these
> men's minds? A cluster of unidentified targets drops in
> out of nowhere, then stops, then fans out to prohibited
> flying areas! Two were over the White House, another
> was near the Capitol.

Barnes contacted Andrews Air Force Base, across the
Potomac in Maryland. Air Force radar operators at the AFB
weather tower tracked ten UFOs for fifteen to twenty
minutes. The objects approached the runway, scattered,
made sharp turns and reversals of direction. A Capital Airline pilot was vectored toward the object and tracked it at
130 mph before it abruptly shot off into space. At the same
time, the object disappeared from the radar scope within
one sweep, indicating near instantaneous acceleration to
speeds over 500 mph.

A week later, on the night of July 26, UFOs once again
appeared over the capital. Ruppelt claimed in *The Report
on Unidentified Flying Objects* that UFO targets appeared
on ARTC radar at National Airport and civilian pilots saw
glowing white objects on four occasions: a United Airlines
pilot near Herndon, Virginia; two CAA pilots over Maryland; and a National Airlines pilot near Andrews AFB at
1,700 feet saw a UFO "flying directly over the airliner."

The Air Force Command Post was notified of unidentified radar targets and two F-94 jet interceptors scrambled
from New Castle AFB, Delaware, to investigate. Major
Dewey Fournet (Project Blue Book officer in the Pentagon)
and Lieutenant Holcomb (Navy radar and electronics
expert) arrived at Washington National's ARTC Center radar room in time to observe "7 good, solid targets."

According to the timeline of the D.C. Wave put together
by Richard Hall, current chairman of the Fund for UFO

Research and a former director of the civilian UFO organization NICAP, the Pentagon Blue Book officer "observed Holcomb check on temperature inversions, but they were minor and could not explain what was going on. He so advised AF Command Post, requesting interception mission."

One F-94 pilot claimed he made visual contact and appeared to be gaining on the target. Hall states that both F-94 and UFO were observed on radar and when the F-94 pilot sped up, the UFO disappeared both visually and from radar. The pilot remarked about the "incredible speed of the object."

According to *The UFO Controversy in America,* by Temple University historian David Jacobs, "So many calls came into the Pentagon alone that its telephone circuits were completely tied up with UFO inquiries for the next few days."

The USAF called one of the largest peacetime press conferences to date and tried to pass off the incidents as "temperature inversions." But the "temperature inversion" story fell apart under the abundant expert testimony that weather conditions were not conducive to inversions on the nights in question, and that the blips were completely unlike normal ground echoes.

The press conference was headed by the director of Air Force intelligence, Major General John Samford, and Major General Roger Ramey, chief of the Air Defense Command. Ramey even tried to deny that jet interceptors had been scrambled to attempt interception; this is the same General Ramey who had announced five years earlier that the Roswell crash was a "weather balloon."

Apparently no photographs of the Washington sighting were ever taken, yet radar controllers who followed the movements at Andrews AFB confirm that there was a large orange sphere hanging over the base. The press, including a reporter and photographer from *Life* magazine, observed the blips on the radar scope in National's ARTC, but they were ordered from the room when the jets were scrambled.

The Washington Wave of 1952 remained one of the "unknowns" in the Blue Book files. That was all the public knew until a National Security Agency analysis from 1968 was declassified and released through the Freedom of Information Act. This analysis is entitled "UFO Hypothesis and Survival Questions," and it discusses the Washington, D.C. sightings under the heading "#5. UFOs Are Related to Intra-terrestrial Intelligence." In this NSA document, the D.C. sightings are considered to be "well documented" and they "strongly support" the view that UFOs are indeed of extraterrestrial origin.

The Robertson Panel

According to the official history, the Washington Wave prompted the National Security Council to request that the CIA investigate the UFO phenomenon in order to "determine if the existence of UFOs would create a danger to the national security of the United States."

In reality, the CIA fabricated the NSC request as a cover for its own interest in the UFO phenomenon. This was proved by declassified documents obtained in the late seventies by Ground Saucer Watch (GSW) of Phoenix, Arizona, when the organization filed through the Freedom of Information Act (FOIA). GSW received a copy of a 1952 memorandum from CIA director Walter Bedell Smith that was sent *to* the National Security Council, stating the CIA's belief that

> a broader, coordinated effort should be initiated to develop a firm scientific understanding of the several phenomena which are apparently involved in these reports, and to assure ourselves that [they] will not hamper our present efforts in the Cold War or confuse our early warning system in case of an attack.

Thus the Robertson panel was convened in Washington, D.C., on January 14, 1953. It was headed by Dr. Harold P.

Robertson, director of the Weapons Systems Evaluation Group for the Secretary of Defense, and consisted of some of the best scientific minds of the day. Members included nuclear physicist Dr. Luis Alvarez, who would later win the Nobel Prize; Dr. Samuel Goudsmit of the Brookhaven National Laboratories; and astronomer Dr. Thornton Page with Johns Hopkins University, and later, NASA.

The Robertson panel heard evidence on UFOs that was presented by the Blue Book project and Air Force investigations. In all, about twenty UFO reports and films of only two UFO sightings were examined. Barely twelve hours later, the Robertson committee felt they had suitably absorbed the previous six years of UFO investigations.

The panel concluded that unidentified flying objects were not a direct physical threat to national security and "that the continued emphasis on the reporting of these phenomena does, in these perilous times, result in a threat to the orderly functioning of the protective organs of the body politic."

This alleged threat consisted of "the clogging of channels of communication by irrelevant reports," the danger of false alarms, and most insidious, "the cultivation of a morbid national psychology in which skillful hostile propaganda could induce hysterical behavior and harmful distrust of duly constituted authority."

The Robertson panel can hardly claim to have taken a scientific approach—it is irresponsible to make definitive recommendations on *anything* after only twelve hours of consideration. As Lawrence Fawcett and Barry J. Greenwood point out in their 1984 book, *The UFO Cover-Up,* the Robertson panel briefly discussed one case from Tremonton, Utah, in 1952, that Navy analysts had concluded was an "unknown" after *one thousand* hours of investigation.

Clearly, the Robertson panel was a propaganda tool for the CIA rather than a serious investigation. Indeed, the panel concluded:

We suggest that these aims may be achieved by an integrated program designed to reassure the public of the total lack of evidence of inimical forces behind the phenomena, to train personnel to recognize and reject false indications quickly and effectively, and to strengthen regular channels for the evaluation of and prompt reaction to true indications of hostile measures.

Since the Robertson panel's recommendations were classified, the American public wasn't aware that they were about to be hit with a change in the official spin on the coverage of UFO sightings.

One of the suggestions was tailor-made for the CIA—that the two major UFO research groups existing at the time, the Aerial Phenomena Research Organization (APRO) and Civilian Saucer Intelligence, should be "watched because of their potentially great influence on mass thinking if widespread sightings should occur."

Meanwhile, sightings reported by military witnesses continued, and some people began to speak out based on years of expertise in direct observations. Navy Rear Admiral Delmer S. Fahrey, formerly head of the Navy's guided missile program, stated at a press conference in Washington, D.C., on January 16, 1957, that "there are objects coming into our atmosphere at very high speeds. No agency in this country or Russia is able to duplicate at this time the speeds and accelerations which radars and observers indicate these flying objects are able to achieve." As reported in *The New York Times* the next day, Fahrey said he also believed "an intelligence" directed the objects "because of the way they fly. They are not entirely actuated by automatic equipment. The way they change position in formations and override each other would indicate that their motion is directed."

Despite a growing conviction among those closely exposed to the UFO phenomenon, reports of sightings dropped significantly in America after the implementation of the Robertson panel's recommendations. Thereafter, this official policy would be scrupulously followed by the Air Force.

The Brookings Institute Report

The next major study took place in 1960, when NASA contracted with the Brookings Institute to consider, among other things, the possible effects of contact with extraterrestrial beings. The agency's one hundred-page report, prepared at a cost of $86,000, was for NASA's committee on beings-in-space.

The Brookings Report theorized that alien artifacts might someday be found on the moon, Venus, or Mars, adding, "While the discovery of intelligent life in other parts of the universe is not likely in the immediate future, it could nevertheless, happen at any time."

The Brookings Report even went so far as to designate those "most devastated groups" as scientists and engineers. The report encouraged the government to withhold information about alien beings from the public because the discovery could have a disastrous impact: "Societies sure of their own place have disintegrated when confronted by a superior society, and others have survived even though changed."

A once-secret National Security Agency (NSA) document from 1968 entitled "UFO Hypothesis and Survival Questions" reinforced the paranoid mind-set among the intelligence community:

Often in the past, a technological superior people are also possessors of a more virile or aggressive culture. In a confrontation between two peoples of significantly different cultural levels, those having the inferior or less virile culture, most often suffer a tragic loss of identity and are usually absorbed by the other people.

UFO researchers often repeat this tired adage that "superior technological societies destroy the less advantaged society." It makes me wonder why people don't pay more attention to history. The "more advanced" civilization doesn't always win—the repeated sack of Rome by Germanic tribes is just one example. There couldn't have been a more loose-knit, motley group of people, yet they managed to waltz right into the heart of the greatest empire on earth and burn their most sacred shrines and treasures to the ground—more than once.

Consider more modern examples: The Germans were the most technologically and scientifically advanced people on the face of the Earth when they launched World War I. But the Germans lost both that war and the next one. And in Vietnam, the Americans were clearly the technological superiors, yet they were fighting a losing battle from the first day they arrived. There is no rule of thumb when it comes to predicting the victor in any encounter—not on the grounds of intelligence, technology, passion, or even strength.

This fear of conquest by a superior civilization comes from the context in which the Robertson panel was convened. General paranoia was one of the hallmarks of the Cold War, leading inevitably to the McCarthy congressional hearings, which tried to uncover "card-carrying Communists" among army officers, bureaucrats, and civilians.

American officials had to take it seriously when leading scientists claimed that the discovery of life on other worlds could cause the collapse of our civilization. No wonder the government simply decided to follow the recommendations of the Brookings Report and the Robertson panel and to try to soft-pedal the theory that there were aliens flying over our cities. The crime is that we are still being governed by those baseless anxieties that established the government's UFO policy four decades ago.

Not everyone believed these blatant propaganda moves. The *Yale Scientific Magazine* in April 1963 summed up the situation this way:

Based upon unreliable and unscientific surmises as data, the Air Force develops elaborate statistical findings which seem impressive to the uninitiated public unschooled in the fallacy of the statistical method. One must conclude that the highly publicized Air Force pronouncements based upon unsound statistics serve merely to misrepresent the true character of the UFO phenomena.

The Condon Report

After twenty years of investigating UFOs, Project Blue Book was increasingly under attack by elected representatives. John W. McCormack, Speaker of the House of Representatives of the United States, said in January 1965, "I feel that the Air Force has not been giving out all the available information on the Unidentified Flying Objects. You cannot disregard so many unimpeachable sources."

The public was no longer satisfied with explanations of "birds in flight" or "reflections from windows against haze in the sky." Hynek made an infamous off-the-cuff remark when a glowing, football-shaped UFO was witnessed in 1966 by the local civil-defense director, along with eighty-seven female students at a college in Hillsdale, Michigan. Hynek's comment that it could have been "ignited swamp gas" was mocked by the media and provoked a national outcry.

To save its reputation, the Air Force agreed to an outside review of Blue Book's files. In 1966, it commissioned a two-year study that funded *half a million dollars* to the University of Colorado at Boulder to complete an investigation.

The tone of the Condon Committee was set by its director, physicist Edward Condon, a well-respected scientist with impressive credentials as the director of the National Bureau of Standards, and president of the American Association for the Advancement of Science. Condon had already made up his mind the day after his appointment as head of the committee, and he was quoted in an interview by the Denver *Rocky Mountain News* as saying that there was "no evidence" of "advanced life on other planets."

Many government insiders knew the Condon Committee was nothing more than a publicity ploy long before the study was completed. This was confirmed by a leaked memo to university administrators from Robert Low, assistant dean of the graduate school. In this memo, Low asserted that "the trick would be, I think, to describe the project so that to the public it would appear a totally objective study but to the scientific community would present the image of a group of nonbelievers trying their best to be objective but having an almost zero expectation of finding a saucer."

One of the staff members Condon fired for leaking the Low memo to the press was team psychologist David Saunders. Saunders immediately cowrote a book on his stint at the University of Colorado project entitled *UFOs? Yes! Where the Condon Committee Went Wrong* (1968). Saunders didn't have proof of CIA involvement, but he knew enough to warn on the last page of his book, "The Central Intelligence Agency is around, everywhere."

The CIA connection to the Condon Report was finally confirmed in the early 1980s, when under the FOIA, a CIA memo from February 23, 1967, was released. This memo discusses Dr. Condon's visit to the National Photographic Interpretation Center, run by the CIA. According to Lawrence Fawcett and Barry J. Greenwood in *The UFO Cover-up*, the points that were clearly established included:

a. Any work performed by NPIC to assist Dr. Condon in his investigation will not be identified as work accomplished by the CIA. Dr. Condon was advised by Mr. Lundahl to make no reference to CIA in regard to this work effort. Dr. Condon stated that if he felt it necessary to obtain an official CIA comment he would make a

separate distinct entry into CIA not related to contacts
he has with NPIC.

The CIA agency, NPIC, agreed to perform work of a
"photogrammetric nature" such as measuring objects in
photographs supplied by Dr. Condon. By using NPIC to
technically analyze images of UFOs, Dr. Condon was accepting the judgment of the CIA rather than that of an independent scientific entity.

There is no doubt that Project Blue Book reported directly to the intelligence community throughout its existence. In the Fall 1966 issue of the classified publication
Studies in Intelligence, there was an article entitled "The
Investigation of UFOs" by Hector Quintanella, Jr., then
head of Blue Book. Quintanella discussed the Socorro case,
a New Mexico sighting on April 24, 1964, reported by Sergeant Lonnie Zamora of the Socorro Police Department.
The site was immediately investigated by a Sergeant
Chavez, who discovered "marks and burns."

In reviewing the case, Quintanella states in a paragraph
under "Diagnosis: Unsolved":

There is no doubt that Lonnie Zamora saw an object
which left quite an impression on him. There is also no
question about Zamora's reliability. He is a serious officer, a pillar of his church, and a man well versed in
recognizing airborne vehicles in his area. He is puzzled
by what he saw, and frankly, so are we. This is the best-
documented case on record, and still we have been unable, in spite of thorough investigation, to find the
vehicle or other stimulus that scared Zamora to the point
of panic.

The "Scientific Study of Unidentified Flying Objects,"
better known as the Condon Report, was released in January 1968. In all, thirty of the ninety-one cases that were
analyzed remained unidentified. The report was nearly a
thousand pages long, far too much for anyone to easily

wade through. Conveniently, Condon's conclusions were placed at the beginning, stating that "further extensive study of UFOs probably cannot be justified in the expectation that science will be advanced thereby."

The Condon Report also summarized the committee's opinion of the extraterrestrial hypothesis: ". . . we found that no direct evidence whatever of a convincing nature now exists for the claim that any UFOs represent spacecraft visiting Earth from another civilization."

Dr. James E. McDonald, adviser to the National Science Foundation, the Office of Naval Research, and the National Academy of Sciences, criticized the results of the Condon Report at his July 1968 Symposium on Unidentified Flying Objects, submitted to the House Committee on Science and Astronautics:

> The sheer bulk of the Report, and the inclusion of much that can only be viewed as "scientific padding" cannot conceal from anyone who studies it closely the salient point that it represents an examination of only a tiny fraction of the most puzzling UFO reports of the past two decades, and that its level of scientific argumentation is wholly unsatisfactory.

While McDonald called the UFO phenomenon "one of the greatest scientific problems of our time," his opinion was contrary to contemporary scientific opinion. The Condon Report was immediately endorsed by the National Academy of Sciences—despite the fact that the academy didn't independently check the findings.

Nearly thirty years after the results of the Condon Report were issued, the *Society for Scientific Exploration* published a 1996 essay by P. A. Sturrock from the Center for Space Science and Astrophysics. Sturrock concluded,

> The overview shows that most case studies were conducted by junior staff; the senior staff took little part, and the director took no part, in these investigations. The

analysis of evidence by categories shows that there are substantial and significant differences between the findings of the project staff and those that the director attributes to the project.

However, at the time of the release of the Condon Report, the nation was undergoing social upheaval and violent protests over the growing American involvement in Vietnam. People had more important things to worry about than the unsolved mystery of UFOs.

But one need only look at one vital statistic that lies at the heart of the Condon Report: the scientists concluded that 15 percent of the UFOs they studied were unknowns. This figure is 9 percent higher than that found by the Blue Book Project. In most scientific studies, this would seem to indicate that *more* is going on than had been previously assumed. Yet instead of calling for additional investigation, the Condon Report recommended that investigations cease.

With very little fanfare, the Secretary of the Air Force, Robert C. Seamans, Jr., announced the closing of Project Blue Book at a press conference on December 17, 1969. Seamans insisted that the continuance of Project Blue Book "cannot be justified either on the ground of national security or in the interest of science."

However, the real reason for the termination of Project Blue Book was discovered in an Air Force memo dated two months earlier, on October 20. This memo, signed by Brigadier General C. H. Bolender, recommends the end of Blue Book because it wasn't receiving the important reports anyway: "Reports of unidentified flying objects which could affect national security are made in accordance with JANAP [Joint Army Navy Air Force Publication] 147 or Air Force Manual 55-11, and are not part of the Blue Book system."

As Fawcett and Greenwood point out in *The UFO Cover-up,* sixteen attachments that once accompanied the JANAP 147 document are no longer in the Air Force files: "Blue Book was little more than an exercise in public relations. The really significant reports went somewhere else. Where did they go? That's what we would like to know."

The O'Brien Committee

Just before the Air Force initiated the two-year Condon Committee study, the USAF Scientific Advisory Board created an ad hoc committee to review Project Blue Book. This study became known among a limited circle as the O'Brien Committee.

The Computer UFO Network (CUFON) posted the 1966 "Special Report" of the O'Brien Committee in all three versions—Sanitized, Unsanitized, and the Archives text. Usually the Air Force extracts a partial quote from the Special Report's Conclusions and Recommendations, citing only the first sentence of the following paragraph:

> In 19 years and more than 10,000 sightings recorded and classified, there appears to be no verified and fully satisfactory evidence of any case that is clearly outside the framework of presently known science and technology. Nevertheless, there is always the possibility that analysis of new sightings may provide some additions to scientific knowledge of value to the Air Force. Moreover, some of the case records which the Committee looked at that were listed as "identified" were sightings where the evidence collected was too meager or indefinite to permit positive listing in the identified category. Because of this the Committee recommends that the present program be strengthened to provide opportunity for scientific investigation of selected sightings in more detail and depth than has been possible to date.

So here is an eminent panel of scientists privately recommending—just prior to the convening of the very-public Condon Committee—that the subject of UFOs deserved a more "scientific investigation." This is a powerful endorsement of the worthiness of UFO research, especially when you consider that one of the members of the panel was Dr. Carl Sagan, a renowned skeptic of the extraterrestrial theory of UFOs.

The O'Brien Committee suggested that "a few selected universities" could provide "scientific teams" to investigate sightings of UFOs. They pointed out the necessity of including a physical scientist on this team, "preferably an astronomer or geophysicist familiar with atmospheric physics." They also indicated the need to have these teams in close proximity to Air Force Systems Command.

The final recommendation of the O'Brien Committee was that "one university or not-for-profit organization should be selected to coordinate the work of the teams . . . and also to make certain of very close communication and coordination with the office of Project Blue Book."

This agrees with the final paragraph of the conclusion of the original Chapter 33 of the Air Force Academy space sciences textbook dated 1968:

> A solution to the UFO problem may be obtained by the long and diligent effort of a large group of well financed and competent scientists, unfortunately there is no evidence suggesting that such an effort is going to be made. However, even if such an effort were made, there is no guarantee of success because of the isolated and sporadic nature of the sightings. Also, there may be nothing to find, and that would mean a long search with no profit at the end.

The military had learned its lesson with Project Blue Book—investigating the UFO phenomenon was a public relations nightmare. The CIA was already conducting covert investigations, so the logical choice would be to assign a scientific investigation to go "underground" where it wouldn't matter if years passed with little progress.

According to numerous declassified memos, most of the defense and intelligence agencies were connected in some way to UFO investigations, including international groups such as NORAD and NATO. In Britain, the Ministry of Defense continues to maintain a UFO desk, most memorably run by Nick Pope, author of *Open Skies, Closed Minds* (1996). In North America, the only official and fairly complete records of UFO sightings, other than Project Blue Book, were maintained in Canada.

Coincidentally, just after the Condon Committee gave its recommendations, the Canadian UFO files were transferred from the Canadian Department of National Defense to the Canadian National Research Council. This was at approximately the same time that Brigadier General Bolender sent the memo stating that the important sightings weren't going to Blue Book—and, what do you know, Bolender was the U.S. deputy director of development.

So I turned to agencies responsible for research and development.

NASA

If any coordination on the UFO phenomenon were to be done, NASA (the National Aeronautics and Space Administration) should be right on top of the list. It would have been a natural progression from Project Blue Book, which had most recently been under the jurisdiction of the Aerospace Technical Intelligence Center (ATIC).

NASA is a civilian space agency, established in 1958 to coordinate and direct aeronautical and space research in America. But you might be surprised at the scope of their studies. NASA's Earth Sciences Directorate at Goddard Space Flight Center in Maryland works closely with FEMA on national disaster issues, offering to help—along with SCSC (the Scientific and Commercial Systems Corporation)—assist FEMA through their Earth Alert System (EAS).

NASA has scores of projects and a flexible army of "lifer" scientists who shift from one compartment to the other depending on the need. Though NASA isn't a federal agency, its research and development personnel often have high security clearances in order to actively cooperate with the CIA, NSA, NRO, and other federal agencies on issues of national security. The offices of NASA include: Aeronautics and Space Transportation Technology, National Reconnaissance Office, Space Flight, Mission to Planet Earth, Life and Microgravity Sciences and Applications, Small and Disadvantaged Business Utilization, Space Science, and Space Access and Technology.

NASA's involvement with "extraterrestrial exposure" began in July 1969, six months before Project Blue Book was closed. According to Title 14, Section 1211 of the *Code of Federal Regulations*, adopted just before the Apollo moon shots, the NASA administrator has jurisdiction in determining "extraterrestrial exposure" of "all NASA manned and unmanned space missions."

There was no public debate about this code—it was stuffed in with a bunch of other codes that were approved in one large batch. NASA spokespeople have claimed this popularly called "ET Law" was established because of

(a) NASA policy, responsibility and authority to guard the Earth against any harmful contamination or adverse changes in its environment resulting from personnel, spacecraft and other property returning to the Earth after landing on or coming within the atmospheric envelope of a celestial body; and (b) security requirements, restrictions and safeguards that are necessary in the interest of national security.

The state of "extraterrestrial exposure" is defined as any person, property, animal, or other form of life or matter who or which has either directly touched or come within the atmospheric envelope of another celestial body.

The code doesn't restrict NASA's power to only American-made vehicles, or for that matter, to manmade vehicles. Absolute power is granted to the NASA administrator to determine with or without a hearing whether a person or object was exposed. Anyone exposed extraterrestrially could be placed under quarantine, which couldn't be broken even by court order. The code also called for a $5,000 fine or one-year imprisonment to anyone who willfully violated this regulation.

Since this code also extended to anyone who was touched directly or was in close proximity to someone extraterrestrially exposed, it has been interpreted by some ufologists as a way to silence witnesses of ETs. Though the code was apparently rushed onto the books to protect humanity against any adverse alien contact, six months later the Air Force could interpret that NASA was covering the situation, both in terms of national security and research, and therefore Blue Book could be closed.

Ufologists made the ET law public knowledge, and there are people who still quote it today. But Title 14, Section 1211 was removed from the *Code of Federal Regulations* in April 1991. The summary stated that the code had served its purpose and was "no longer in keeping with current policy."

When I called the NASA newsroom at Johnson Spaceflight Center near Houston, John Lawrence recalled that "virus life was an active discussion" in the late sixties, and he said the code "was for the express purpose of quarantining the Apollo astronauts when they came back from the moon." He even described how the quarantine community consisting of astronauts and observers kept growing over the ensuing months as more people were accidentally "extraterrestrially exposed."

There is certainly precedent in human history for the deadly consequences of an "alien" virus. In the Middle Ages, the Black Death, which slaughtered more than a third of Western Europe, was due to bubonic plague imported from China. A tragic modern example is the transmutation of the HIV virus from the animal population in Africa. Now loose in human society, it continues to kill worldwide. Would an alien virus be any different?

Lawrence said the ET law had likely been removed from the books through a built-in termination date, typical among federal codes. When I asked why alien viruses were no longer a concern, particularly when NASA was finally talking about returning samples from other planets, Lawrence said, "We don't have any active programs to bring back samples. But there is a lot of impetus in the community because of the evidence of life on Mars and conditions on the moons of Jupiter. Something like this will come back on the books. It would be reckless not to."

I wasn't convinced that there was much danger from alien viruses surviving on one of the inhospitable planets in our solar system, but Lawrence surprised me by saying, "One of the Apollo missions went and found some fungus on one of the early unmanned probes we sent to the moon. The assumption is the probe got contaminated under construction—even though it was in clean rooms—and that's where the fungus came from. But the fact that even a terrestrial fungus could grow on the moon is amazing."

The ET law is just the beginning—after all, NASA would inevitably deal with extraterrestrial matters because it's their people and their vehicles on the front lines. In every angle of the UFO phenomenon I subsequently investigated, the top-quality research was being done by NASA employees—albeit in an "unofficial" capacity.

Richard F. Haines, a perceptual psychologist and chief of the Space Human Factors Office at NASA's Ames Research Center in California, has actively researched pilots' reports of UFOs. He compiled AIRCAT in the late 1980s, a computerized catalog that lists more than three thousand UFO sightings by aviators over the past forty years. His latest book was published in 1994, and Haines is looking for help in computerizing more of his data (see Chapter 8).

Another NASA scientist, Paul Hill, worked on the cutting edge of research and development in mechanical engineering and aeronautics at Langley Research Center from 1939 to 1970. For nearly twenty years, Hill claimed he served as the "unofficial" clearinghouse for UFO reports at NASA, collecting and analyzing sightings for physical properties, propulsion possibilities, and dynamics from

UFO information that was "passing through" the government agency (see Chapter 10).

Even prior to the establishment of the ET law in 1968, NASA had already studied UFOs in the Brookings Institute study in 1960. And the House Committee on Science and Astronautics held a symposium on the UFO phenomenon six months *after* the Condon Report. James McDonald put forth his opinion that "twenty years of public interest, public puzzlement, and even some public disquiet" demanded efforts to clarify this "scientific mystery."

After Project Blue Book closed, NASA seems to always have the official word on UFOs. Thornton Leigh Page, research astrophysicist at the Lyndon B. Johnson Space Center, NASA, even wrote much of the official word on "Unidentified Flying Objects" in the 1984 *Encyclopaedia Britannica* (the 1984 section was cut by one quarter in the 1997 version). Dr. Page was a member of the 1953 Robertson panel, and coauthor, with Carl Sagan, of *UFO's: A Scientific Debate* (1972).

In the 1984 *Britannica* essay, Page stated that several "groups of American scientists" believed the UFO phenomenon warranted further study. His recommendation was to proceed with two different studies: analyzing reported sightings, and performing statistical analysis of the psychological and sociological patterns of sightings.

Page also recommended that "hard data" should be systematically collected by networks of cameras or radar sets. This would eliminate the questionable reliability of eyewitnesses, and could be "associated with studies of meteors, auroras, or other atmospheric phenomenon." Page adds, "The National Aeronautics and Space Administration [NASA] operates several artificial satellites equipped with optical TV cameras that radio image-data to ground-based receivers. Two sets of satellites record cloud patterns for weather prediction, and they might detect bright, high UFOs."

Certainly, the best evidence of tangible objects in our atmosphere comes from radar networks operated by the civilian entity, the U.S. and Canadian aviation administrations, and by the military in NORAD (North American Air Defense Command). Together, they track every moving object in the sky, regularly recording "uncorrelated objects." All that is needed is a specially programmed computer and a team devoted to the task of sorting through the tapes for patterns and anomalous readings. But a project of this scope would require a sizable government grant.

NASA *should* be running a UFO investigative project, just as the French agency CNES (National Center for Space Research) runs SEPRA (Service for Assessment of Atmospheric Reentry Phenomena) in Toulouse, France. SEPRA is funded by the French government and has been studying UFO sightings for years, conducting investigations at the request of the gendarmerie or other public bodies, and employing rigorous scientific methods.

SEPRA's figures claim that only 1 percent of sightings are hoaxes. In 20 percent of the reports, a "rational conclusion" is reached, with another 40 percent inconclusive because of lack of data, but evidence suggesting a rational conclusion. The other 40 percent are uncertain.

As M. Robert Galley, French minister of defense, said in a radio interview by Jean-Blaude Bourret in February 1974, "I must say that if listeners could see for themselves the mass of reports coming in from the airborne gendarmerie, from the mobile gendarmerie, and from the gendarmerie charged with the job of conducting investigations, all of which reports are forwarded by us to the National Center for Space Studies, then they would see that it is all pretty disturbing."

President Jimmy Carter promised in his Presidential campaign that if he was elected he would look into UFO reports. True to his word, Carter's science adviser recommended that a small panel of inquiry be formed by NASA to see if there had been any "significant findings" since the Condon Report. As reported in Richard C. Henry's "UFOs and NASA" in the *Journal for Scientific Exploration*, "Five months later, NASA responded to that recommendation by proposing 'to take no steps to establish a research activity in this area or to convene a symposium on the subject.' "

Theoretically, any information NASA or government agencies hold on UFOs should be available through de-classified documents. However, ufologists are finding that records are difficult to get. Since the inception of the FOIA in 1966, it has consistently been fought and challenged by government agencies every step of the way. But to find out more about that, we have to look into the history of government secrecy and black projects.

CHAPTER 4

Government Secrecy and Black Projects

VICE ADMIRAL Roscoe H. Hillenkoeter, the first CIA director in 1947, later joined the civilian UFO organization NICAP. Hillenkoeter signed a statement to Congress on August 22, 1960, which said, in part: "It is imperative that we learn where the UFOs come from and what their purpose is."

UFOs were a real problem for the American government. The military couldn't admit that they didn't know what UFOs were because then their competence to guard our skies would be questioned. Officials were also held accountable for the tax dollars being spent on investigations that yielded no positive conclusions.

The answer, as usual during the Cold War, was secrecy. Even during the early UFO projects Sign and Grudge (1948–52), the intelligence community was already conducting their own covert investigations. An Office of Special Intelligence (OSI) memo concerning "Unidentified Aircraft" or "Unidentified Aerial Phenomena" was sent to the director of the FBI in 1949, emphasizing, *This matter is considered top secret by Intelligence Officers of both the Army and the Air Forces.*

The official CIA policy statement on "Responsibility for Unidentified Flying Objects" was declassified more than twenty years after it went into effect in February 1956. The policy statement assigns responsibility for holding UFO reports to the Applied Science Division (ASD) of the CIA's Office of Scientific Intelligence (OSI).

The ASD judged whether the raw reports could provide information on "foreign weapons research and development." Reports that weren't useful in this regard were forwarded to the "Fundamental Sciences Area," where they were investigated for potentially useful "foreign science developments."

Apparently the OSI wasn't merely content with examining raw reports. The declassified OSI "Summary of Aerial Phenomena in New Mexico," 1950, describes how the OSI was actively researching the UFO phenomenon. OSI hired Land-Air to establish observation posts in the vicinity of Vaughn, New Mexico, "for the purpose of photographing and determining the speed, height and nature of the unusual phenomena referred to as green fireballs and discs."

According to Jan Aldrich, coordinator of Project 1947, there is a file of UFO reports at National Archives II which were found at Wright-Patterson Air Force Base after the transfer of UFO reports to the National Archives:

These reports, less than one hundred in number, run from 1951 to the early 1960s. They are not very remarkable. However, most of them have their routing documents attached. Routinely, UFO reports were sent to the CIA and other agencies in multiple copies and a few times even to the Australians, British, and Canadians.

The Air Force may have routed UFO reports directly to the CIA because of the covert nature of the CIA's U-2 reconnaissance program. The CIA was authorizing stealth flights into the Soviet Union, so obviously the agency was particularly interested in sightings that occurred in the areas of its operations.

Freedom of Information Act

In July 1975, Ground Saucer Watch (GSW) of Phoenix filed under the Freedom of Information Act for CIA documents related to UFOs. The CIA took over eight months to respond with a "brief history" of their investigation of the UFO phenomenon, and then issued the following denial: "At no time, prior to the formation of the Robertson Panel and subsequent to the issuance of the panel's report, has the CIA engaged in the study of the UFO phenomenon. The Robertson Panel Report is the summation of the Agency's interest and involvement in this matter."

Ground Saucer Watch engaged the CIA in a protracted legal battle and eventually proved the CIA was lying. Almost nine hundred pages of CIA UFO-related documents were eventually released to Ground Saucer Watch through the efforts of Peter Gersten, legal consultant to both GSW and CAUS (Citizens Against UFO Secrecy).

GSW's use of the Freedom of Information Act marks an important milestone in UFO research. The FOIA was signed into law in 1966 by a Democratic Congress under President Lyndon Johnson. In the best spirit of American democracy, the FOIA allowed the public access to all but the most highly classified government records. Nine categories of information were originally exempted from release, including documents containing information on national security and foreign policy.

But citizens' requests to government agencies resulted in the release of very few documents until the midseventies. You might be surprised to find out that President Nixon was the first to review the secrecy process, imposing time limits on agencies receiving FOIA requests and reducing fees for the search and reproduction of documents. The courts were also given the power to judge whether specific documents fell under FOIA guidelines. President

Carter contributed next to opening the doors of government secrecy, even allowing documents to be released containing details about civilians living near the atomic bombs that had been set off at the Nevada Test Site in the 1950s and 1960s.

Yet the process of acquiring documents from government agencies was erratic—some known documents have never been released, while others were readily available. With simple FOIA requests, the FBI handed over nearly two thousand pages to CAUS and to Dr. Bruce Maccabee. On the other hand, NORAD notified CAUS that they would be charged a $250,000 search fee to obtain the files they had requested.

The FOIA has facilitated the release of tens of thousands of UFO documents that were previously classified. Yet there are many UFO documents the American government refuses to declassify because of "national security." Thus we have the ultimate paradox: how can national security still be an issue when the government claims UFOs are not extraterrestrial and they pose no threat?

The declassified documents that were released prove at least two things:

1. UFOs have been sighted over U.S. military and other government facilities since World War II.
2. Government officials have been monitoring the UFO phenomenon, yet they still have no definitive answer for what UFOs are.

The secrecy policies in effect today were mostly established during the last decade of the Cold War, such as Executive Order 12356, signed by Ronald Reagan, eliminating response time limits. Now searches routinely take as long as two years, and the fees have gone back up again.

Then President Clinton released a memorandum in October 1993 which stated in part: "The Act [FOIA] is a vital part of the participatory system of government. I am committed to enhancing its effectiveness in my Administration.

... I therefore call upon all Federal departments and agencies to renew their commitment to the Freedom of Information Act, to its underlying principles of government openness, and to its sound administration."

Clinton's Executive Order 12958 requires a mandatory declassification of almost everything over twenty-five years old. Now the trouble is getting government agencies to comply with this order.

Paul McGinnis will tell you how hard it is to get information on Area 51 through the FOIA. McGinnis has been pursuing the Air Force and the CIA for several years, trying to obtain documents related to Groom Lake, or as the DoE puts it, the "strategic areas northeast of the Nevada Test Site." The CIA told McGinnis he would have to "seek judicial review" under the FOIA to get material on the U-2 program in the 1950s and 1960s.

According to McGinnis, the Air Force would "neither confirm nor deny" responses on his FOIA case seeking Aircraft Landing Authorization Request forms for all foreign aircraft that have landed at Groom in the past five years. The Air Force added, "Any other response would reveal currently and properly classified information or factual circumstances which are exempt from disclosure."

McGinnis's next option is to sue the government under the FOIA in federal district court in order to force release of the documents on Groom Lake. In an open letter to Sheila Widnall, then Secretary of the Air Force, dated July 13, 1996, McGinnis discusses the various evasion tactics taken by the Air Force to avoid releasing information, concluding:

As a U.S. taxpayer, I feel that I am getting ripped off by the Air Force and its classified military spending. Based on my research, and my political activities trying to reform these programs so that there is some accountability to the American public, I now believe that you are a corrupt public official, and there are few or no legitimate national security interests that are served by the Air Force actions described above.

Black Projects

Area 51 is funded by money allocated to so-called black projects. Officially known as Special Access Programs (SAPs), these classified projects are protected under Title 10 of the *U.S. Code,* Section 119. That means that currently, only four people in the entire Congress know where *billions* of dollars are being spent.

During the 1995 Air Force investigation of the Roswell incident, one of the conclusions was that:

> If the Air Force recovered some type of extraterrestrial spacecraft and/or bodies and was exploiting this for scientific and technological purposes, then such a program would be operated as a SAP. SAF/AAZ, the Central Office for all Air Force SAPs, has knowledge of and security oversight over all SAPs. SAF/AAZ categorically stated that no such Special Access Program(s) exists that pertain to extraterrestrial spacecraft/aliens. . . .

Whether the military is hiding UFO discs or a new unmanned reconnaissance spy plane at Groom Lake, they are spending U.S tax dollars—a large percentage of our GNP—without being accountable to American taxpayers. Despite assurances to the contrary, it would be easy for the government to hide anything it wanted, even evidence of UFO investigations, within secret black projects because SAP information is classified from the moment it is gathered.

We already know the government has repeatedly lied to the American public in order to maintain the secrecy of Area 51. The Las Vegas Sectional Aeronautical Chart, published by the National Oceanic and Atmospheric Administration for navigation purposes, shows none of the Groom Lake landing strips, aircraft hangars, or government buildings.

However, a "Landing Strip" is clearly marked across the Groom Lake bed on the Bureau of Land Management (BLM) U.S Geological Survey map of the Pahranagat Range Quadrangle, dated 1978. I asked one of the BLM employees at the Las Vegas office if anyone had ever officially asked them to remove the road indications and landing strip, but the man just laughed and said, "Nobody pays any attention to what BLM does."

Apparently the only ones being fooled are the American public. For decades, foreign satellite photos have monitored the expansion of the Area 51 complex, noting everything down to the last tin-sided shed. The Russians will even sell you one of their satellite images of Groom Lake for around $5,000.

Government secrecy is a serious issue to the Federation of American Scientists (FAS), the oldest organization dedicated to ending the arms race and avoiding the use of nuclear weapons. FAS was founded in 1945 by members of the Manhattan Project. The distinguished Board of Sponsors—which includes half of America's living Nobel laureates—engages in research analysis and public education on a broad range of science, technology, and public policy issues.

FAS knows plenty about the abuses of and fit uses for government secrecy. The Manhattan Project was a massive undertaking that was largely successful at remaining a government secret during wartime, *when secrecy was necessary*. In spite of employing tens of thousands of people, using a sizable percentage of the electrical output of the nation, and spending outrageous amounts of money constructing unique facilities in the midst of wartime shortages, the Manhattan Project managed to secretly create and deploy the atomic bomb.

FAS now helps uncover government abuses through its "Project on Government and Secrecy." Whether the government agrees or not, the American public is gradually becoming aware of the worst abuses inherent in our system. The National Reconnaissance Office was kept secret from everyone—even while it was being funded billions of dollars. It wasn't until a building went up in the center of Washington that people began to look up and say, hey, where did that come from?

FAS estimates that operations at the Groom Lake base cost at least one billion dollars per year. But that's only a drop in the bucket, according to a May 1997 *Time* article by Mark Thompson. Thompson writes, "In March 1997, the Pentagon submitted a proposal on behalf of the U.S military to Congress to spend a total of $415 billion over the next 35 years. That's as much as was spent in the defense buildup of the 1980s."

This continuing expenditure was justified by General Joseph Ralston, vice chairman of the Joint Chiefs of Staff, who pointed to more than six thousand warplanes that were "potential threats" to America. Yet these so-called threats included aircraft that belong to our allies: Britain, France, and Canada. Any eight-year-old would agree there's not much danger there, and in response Representative Curt Weldon (R-Pa.), who chairs the House Committee on National Security's research and development panel, stated unequivocally, "We haven't been given a threat that warrants these programs."

Try telling that to the intelligence community, responsible for the lion's share of our nation's budget. In the *Defense Daily* for December 19, 1996, the chairman of the Senate Intelligence Committee, Senator Richard Shelby, signaled that he would oppose the declassification of the total intelligence budget, because it would "just open the intelligence community up for criticism and assault by those who don't understand its mission and don't want to."

Yet the White House specifically stated that the 1997 intelligence budget could be safely declassified. Shelby's reasoning also violates Executive Order 12958: "If there is significant doubt about the need to classify information, it shall not be classified."

Senator Shelby's defense of the classification of the black budget indicates that secrecy is now being manipulated and used as a propaganda tool rather than reserved for vital issues of national security.

Manipulating the Media

Terry Hansen explored the effects of government secrecy in his 1995 essay, "The Psychology of Dreamland: How Secrecy Is Destroying Public Faith in Government and Science." Hansen found that "For most Americans, all they know is what they read in the newspapers or see on TV, and if they don't read about or see UFO reports, then they effectively cease to exist."

In the mid-1970s, Hansen interviewed James Mc-Campbell, an engineering physicist and author, who concluded that UFO news stories were being suppressed. When Hansen asked about lack of American press coverage of sensational UFO-related developments in France, McCampbell responded:

> I think that the principal sources of information in the media are controlled, at least by pressure from the government, to keep information concerning UFOs out of general circulation.

The lack of media coverage of UFOs is in keeping with the recommendations of the CIA's Robertson panel and NASA's Brookings Institute Report. Consider the best radar-documented UFO wave, in November 1975, when UFOs appeared over Canadian and North American military and strategic defense bases. On November 11, a message was sent to NORAD units in North America, summing up the "numerous reports of suspicious objects." The commander in charge of NORAD dismissed some of these objects (at Loring and Wurtsmith) as helicopters, but he added, "I have also expressed my concern to SAFOI that we come up soonest with a proposed answer to queries from the press to prevent overreaction by the public to reports by the media that may be blown out of proportion.

To date efforts by Air Guard helicopters, SAC helicopters and NORAD F-106s have failed to produce a positive ID."

NORAD is clearly concerned about finding the right "proposed answer" to the media because of the seriousness of the reports. Their tactic worked because the unusual lighted objects were labeled "unidentified helicopters" in most of the local presses, and were ignored nationwide. But why wasn't there a mention of them in *The New York Times* or *The Washington Post*? After all, "unidentified helicopters" were flying over our most sensitive nuclear weapons installations—surely that was worth a brief comment?

The true extent of the 1975 radar documentation of the UFOs was not known until CAUS received the NORAD logs through the FOIA. These documents offer no explanation for the sightings, which were considered to be a definite threat to national security within the highest levels of both the Canadian and U.S governments.

It's not uncommon for government officials to engage in passive media manipulation, discouraging or ridiculing news reports that interfere with their goals. Some have speculated that this explains the media silence in the United States on the infamous Belgium Wave in the late 1980s. The only notice was a brief dismissive article in *The Wall Street Journal* on October 10, 1990, entitled "Belgium Scientists Seriously Pursue a Triangular UFO."

Yet the Belgian air force and government documented the UFO sightings and shared their results with civilian investigators and the public. Antonio Huneeus, UFO journalist and coauthor of *Best Available Evidence*, called it "Breaking Down 'The Wall' of UFO Silence" when major European publications began covering the sightings. Yet the officials of NATO, Great Britain, and the rest of the European Union remained comparatively closed-mouthed.

Rumors and reports suggested that the triangular UFOs were black-project aircraft originating in the United States. As late as August 1996, when NASA announced the unveiling of LoFLYTE, an ultracomputerized hypersonic aircraft capable of Mach 4 speeds (one mile a second), the

Belgian news and *Sunday Times* speculated that LoFLYTE was the craft that had been sighted. Aside from the fact that the aircraft was experimental in 1996, five years after the initial wave ended, the size is far too small at only eight feet four inches.

Nick Pope also dismisses the suggestion that the "Black Triangles" sighted all over western Europe are secret military craft. Pope was in a position to ask the Americans because he was in charge of investigating UFO sightings for the Ministry of Defense in Great Britain from 1991 to 1994. But American officials denied having anything to do with the sightings.

Pope, like Hynek, experienced a slow conversion during his years of investigating UFOs. Pope concluded that the black triangles seemed to involve technologies considerably more advanced than our own, and that some were indeed extraterrestrial in origin. In his 1996 book *Open Skies, Closed Minds,* Pope summed up the descriptions submitted to the gendarmerie, as well as the incidents the gendarmerie personally witnessed, which were backed by radar lock-ons:

A high proportion of witnesses saw these lights in a triangular formation on the underside of a huge craft which hovered over villages and towns at low altitudes and was very clearly visible from the ground. The speed of the triangle varied: some reports spoke of 30–40 mph—slow even for a car; others described a hovering motion followed by a disappearance at incredibly high speed, several times faster than a jet.

Pope noted the astonishing coincidence between the Great Britain Wave of 1993 and the Belgian Wave of 1990—both took place in the last days of March, exactly three years apart:

Newspaper reports of incidents occurring that night would run on 1 April, the day when every national and many provincial papers carry an April Fool story. Who was going to take these stories seriously? Predictably, only the UFO community ran articles and asked questions, and followed up as best they could. The public at large just smiled wryly over their breakfast cereal.

Project FT (Project Flying Triangle) was organized by Victor J. Kean, Omar Fowler, and Ron West in 1995 to coordinate efforts to record and analyze data gathered by a network of civilian UFO groups and individuals on the current sightings in the United Kingdom. In 1995, Project FT received reports of 1,586 Flying Triangles, similar to those responsible for both the Belgian and the British waves. Kean explained in his April 1997 report on Project FT:

Analysis of the data reveals that, no matter where the FT was seen during any particular working period (WP)—Sunset to following Sunrise—it invariably visited one of the UK's nuclear power stations (NPS). This occurred during some 80% of all WPs during which the FT was observed. On some occasions the FT was observed in the proximity of more than one NPS during the same WP.

In September 1995, the Belgian minister of defense didn't mince words when he was asked about the UFOs: "These incidents were and still are being treated with the utmost seriousness. We gave chase but could not begin to keep up in the F-16s. Perhaps we will never fully fathom this mysterious business, but we continue to try."

The two F-16 fighters brought back evidence of triangular UFOs in the form of radar tapes and fifteen photographs showing acceleration speeds from 170 mph to 1,100 mph in two seconds. Yet the only real coverage the Belgium sightings received in America was in the tabloids, right next to the "I Was Impregnated by an Alien" stories.

Other than spoofs and sensationalism, the UFO phenomenon has been consistently avoided by major American publications and TV networks. The first indications of a break in the media silence came in the mid-nineties, when there was a remarkable increase in the number of UFO documentaries shown on educational cable networks such as Discovery and The Learning Channel.

The media "blackout" on UFOs was never more clear than in the matter of the sightings over Phoenix on March 13, 1997. Thousands of witnesses, including pilots and air traffic controllers, saw large lights hovering in the air at various times throughout the night. At least a dozen videotapes were shot from various angles, and many people reported seeing a triangular or "boomerang-shaped" aircraft moving over the city. It was reportedly as long as several football fields.

These sightings received only sporadic local coverage, and much of it was devoted to the theory that the lights were flares dropped during Air Force exercises over Goldwater Firing range, 85 miles southwest of Phoenix. As one concerned citizen stated at a town meeting in Tempe, Arizona, in late March, "Why do I feel like coverage is so thin? It seems like there is a media blackout going on here."

Months later, on June 18, the media floodgates were suddenly opened by a report on the "Phoenix Lights" carried in *USA Today*. The story was lightly mocked that evening by Tom Brokaw on the "NBC Nightly News," but it was enough to launch the subject nationwide. As Tom King, Arizona director of Skywatch International, stated in *UFO UpDates* on June 19: "You can't turn on the TV or radio anymore without hearing about the March 13 Arizona sightings. The media coverage is heavier than coverage after the sightings originally happened. Why?"

CNN's report suggested that the delay was caused by "researchers still sorting out hundreds of witness accounts." The CNN website carried amateur video of lights in the sky, and an interview with witnesses—Tim Ley, who called himself a "polite skeptic" before his sighting, along with his wife Bobbi and their son Hal. The family witnessed the triangular craft passing right overhead—it was so large that the other side was several blocks away. Yet Bobbi Ley told CNN reporter, John Hook, "It didn't seem threatening. . . . When it was right overhead and we couldn't hear a sound, it was like you're just awestruck."

Also on June 19, the Associated Press carried Governor Fife Symington's announcement (made during a lunch break from his federal fraud trial) that he had ordered a state probe into the "mysterious lights." At a press conference a few hours later, Symington showed up with his chief of staff wearing a rubber "gray alien" mask and claimed he had been "just kidding." As Tom King reported on *UFO UpDates*, "He turned the entire event into a joke. It pissed off all the news reporters who thought they had a good scoop for taxpayers, and UFO witnesses."

After the initial rush of reports, on June 22, MSNBC aired a segment on the UFO phenomenon. It included video of the Phoenix Lights, concluding the report with the statement that the local Air Force base claimed they didn't drop flares that night.

I called Luke Air Force Base in Arizona, and spoke to Lieutenant Colonel Mike Hauser in Public Affairs, who insisted, "We never made any official statement regarding flares that night. Luke's F-16s don't carry the parachute flares that float down slowly, we only carry the illumination flares—and we didn't drop any of those that night." Hauser also made it very clear that Luke AFB wasn't going to investigate the sightings, as per Air Force policy. The latest explanation is that the flares were dropped by Air National Guard units 175th Wing and 104 fighter squadron visiting from Baltimore, Maryland.

The next day, the evening news in San Francisco reported that a similar "boomerang-shaped" craft had been spotted over Area 51. Then just as fast as the UFOs had resurfaced in the news, months after they were sighted, they disappeared from the media again.

Area 51 Land Grab

It takes a different kind of story to grab the attention of the major media. Bob Lazar's claims of "I was hired to help back-engineer a flying saucer" got hardly a yawn of acknowledgment from the mainstream media in the late 1980s. Yet it was altogether different when the Air Force initiated procedures in 1993 to seize 3,900 acres adjoining Groom Lake, attempting to close down the last two public viewing sites of their secret air base at Area 51.

This wasn't the USAF's first illegal seizure of land—in 1984 it initiated the seizure of 89,000 acres of public land surrounding the high-security test-flight facility. According to the official Air Force record, "In 1988 the U.S. Congress withdrew the Groom Range Addition to the Nellis Air Force Range as a security and safety buffer zone between public lands administered by the BLM and the NAFR complex." Yet when the land seizure was investigated by a congressional committee, an Air Force spokesman simply claimed that the Air Force had the authority to take the land but would not reveal the source of that authority or the reason for doing so in an open session.

Ten years later, the Air Force tried to seize a critical 3,900 acres it had missed in a surveying error. Part of this BLM land, dubbed "Freedom Ridge," is a low butte that was easily accessible by foot or four-wheel-drive. In the proposed Withdrawal Amendment and Environmental Assessment for the Freedom Ridge/White Sides land withdrawal, the land needed to be withdrawn because:

> The USAF subsequently discovered that two areas adjacent to this buffer zone provide viewing of military activities on this portion of the NAFR. Public viewing of military activities (which has often included illegal photography of range activities) has increased during the past few years, necessitating the diversion, postpone-

ment, or cancellation of missions to prevent a compromise of national security.

These reasons were presented only *after* the period of public commentary was over, and none of the local activists who were fighting the withdrawal had a chance to directly address the logic or legality of the action. Glenn Campbell actively networked to raise awareness of the Air Force land seizure, and he helped turn the fight into a popular media event. As Campbell said in his electronic newsletter, *The Groom Lake Desert Rat:*

It was common knowledge at the time that a land seizure was coming, and I knew that the name [Freedom Ridge] was important to help define the battle. I tried putting a lot of different words together, and Freedom Ridge is the one that stuck. We would fight to the death to save it! The real victory for me was when I heard the Cammo Dudes call it Freedom Ridge on the Radio.

National news crews began to arrive to cover the story. They recorded the controversial public hearings held in Las Vegas, releasing sound bites such as "This issue is the withdrawal of freedom, not just Freedom Ridge, but freedom."

The Air Force excused its actions, claiming it was "for the public safety and the safe and secure operation of activities." The inevitable result, according to Campbell:

Had the Air Force stated the real purpose of the withdrawal—to keep eyes off Groom Lake—and maybe given some journalists a tour of the base cafeteria, there would have been not nearly so much hoopla. The American public is still patriotic enough that it will usually support national defense when offered at least a plausible explanation, but the absurd nonexistence of the Groom base, mitigated only by vague AF press releases about possible "facilities" in that vicinity, made the taxpayer feel he was being ripped off and gave rise to endless perceived conspiracies.

Fuel was added to the fire when a Lincoln County sheriff's deputy seized equipment from an ABC News team on assignment near the border of Area 51 in April 1994. According to the *Las Vegas Review Journal,* the deputy was responding to complaints made by Air Force security officers. The seized tapes and equipment were later returned, but the media doesn't like it when the government interferes with them.

A few months later, when Lincoln County sheriff's deputy Sergeant Doug Lamoreaux tried to seize videotapes taken by a news crew from KNBC-TV of Los Angeles, Glenn Campbell was arrested for "obstructing a public officer." The news crew had interviewed Campbell on Freedom Ridge, and despite the claims of reporter Chuck Henry and camera operator Julie Yellen that they didn't film the restricted base itself, Sergeant Lamoreaux ordered them to turn over the tapes.

Campbell described the reasoning used for the search and seizure in the *Desert Rat:*

Lamoreaux then said that, since the crew would not turn over the tapes voluntarily, he would seize them without a warrant. Lamoreaux claimed that the crew had pointed the camera at his vehicle as he approached them on Freedom Ridge—a charge the crew denied. He said that since this was also in the general direction of the base, his viewing of this action constituted "probable cause" for the seizure of the tapes. He said that a Supreme Court ruling, which he could not name [*Ross v. U.S.*], gave him the authority to seize such "contraband" from a vehicle without a warrant.

When Lamoreaux approached the car, Campbell reached in and pushed down the automatic lock for the door on the other side. Lamoreaux arrested Campbell and proceeded to search the crew's vehicle without permission or a warrant. He seized all the recorded videotapes in their possession. The crew were released while Campbell was handcuffed and taken to the Lincoln County Sheriff's Substation in Alamo for booking.

Seizure of film and videotapes is an ongoing problem in Lincoln County. On June 18, 1997, Campbell stated for the record:

> No one has *ever* got their film back—except ABC News on one occasion, and KNBC got one cassette of five back. No one, including them, has *ever* been notified that their film is not coming back. Not me or anyone. I have written the Sheriff several times regarding the film. Never a reply. The Sheriff, when you can find him, refers me to the D.A. The D.A. refers me to the Sheriff. (You know the drill.)

That's certainly true—I got shuffled around, and never was able to connect with the D.A. First I talked to Captain Gary Davis, the undersheriff of Lincoln County, and I pointed out that many people claim that their film has been taken and never returned. Davis said that each case was dealt with individually:

> It depends on the circumstances. The film has to be viewed by someone in the military to determine whether anything was seen. We are the ones who return it, usually. Once we turn it over to the Air Force police and they do what they have to do, normally the stuff comes back. If there's something there that shouldn't be there, it's blacked out. I don't know of anyone that was notified that it wasn't being returned. If someone hasn't gotten film back, then we would deal with it. .... To my knowledge all the film has been returned.

When I sent Campbell the transcript of the above paragraph, he bluntly replied: "Flat out lie. Davis knows everything in the department and directly approves the turning over of film to the AF."

In my phone conversation a couple of weeks later with Sheriff Dahl Bradfield, he agreed with Captain Davis, using almost exactly the same qualifiers: "As far as I know, most of the film has been returned back. Give us specifics and we could go through our records and figure out if individuals were questioned or detained and find out what happened to their film."

Glenn Campbell is already the first in line to take the sheriff up on that offer. If anyone else has not received their film or equipment back then they should pursue the matter—it's not just about a few pictures, it's about public accountability and due process of law.

For all the work performed by the Lincoln County Sheriff's Department, chasing down media crews and tourists who try to get a good look at Area 51, they are well compensated. According to a copy of a "quarterly invoice" from Sheriff Bradfield dated January 5, 1994, the department received $12,477.62 for "Law Enforcement services for the Nellis Air Force Range normally provided by the Lincoln County Sheriffs Department." That amounts to almost $50,000 a year for services, including investigations of "suspected or reported violations of law" and arrest of "persons suspected of committing violations of law." The sheriffs also provide "special assistance to the applicable on-site security force in case of emergency."

Basically, the sheriff's department serves as the interface between the public and the requests of the "appropriate authority" at Nellis. This allows the "on-site security force" to remain anonymous.

With anonymity, the Cammo Dudes also can avoid responsibility for their actions. In January 1994, when seven people visited Area 51 to have a picnic, they became lost and inadvertently crossed the boundary. According to *The New York Times Sunday Magazine,* Connie Ruiz and her party had traveled along a dusty trail to a turnaround point when they were suddenly surrounded: "They held us at gunpoint, searched our vehicles and detained us for approximately two hours before the Highway Patrol came. They never read us our rights."

Lincoln County Justice of the Peace Nola Holton sentenced each of the three trespassers who pleaded "no contest" to a $250 fine. Connie Ruiz and William Fitzgerald fought the charges, but later agreed to the D.A.'s plea bargain for a $100 fine in exchange for a "no contest" plea. But Justice Holton ignored the D.A.'s recommendation and fined them each a total of $600.

William Fitzgerald told the *Las Vegas Review Journal* that he and the others were placed in handcuffs and body chains: "We only got on the wrong road, for cryin' out loud. What is this, Nazi Germany? There was no reason to do what they did. That was overkill."

The Cost of Secrecy

The public received no prior warning that the Freedom Ridge/White Sides land withdrawal had been authorized until it was published in the *Federal Register* (60 FR 18030) on April 10, 1995. On the same day, Campbell discovered that orange marker posts and restricted-area signs had been placed along the new border of Area 51. Now the facility can only be seen from distant points like Tikaboo Peak, which requires a strenuous hike in order to view the base.

Two years after the land seizure, the Information Security Oversight Office reported to Congress that it cost an estimated $5.2 billion to maintain secrecy in 1996. The same office reported that in 1995 we had 21,871 "original" new top secret designations and another 374,244 "derivative" Top Secret designations. That's nearly 400,000 new secrets created at the top secret level alone—which is supposed to mean disclosure would cause "exceptionally grave damage to the national security." Is America really on such shaky ground?

Barely a month after the Oversight report, Senator Daniel Patrick Moynihan (D-N.Y.), chairman of a high-powered "U.S. Commission on Protecting and Reducing Secrecy," issued this commission's recommendations to Congress. Moynihan concluded, "It is time to reexamine the foundations of that secrecy system."

Senator Moynihan cited in his testimony a "most remarkable" letter received from George F. Kennan, professor emeritus at the Institute for Advanced Study in Princeton, New Jersey. Professor Kennan builds a "compelling case" for the proposition that much of our secrecy system is a result of trying to penetrate the obsessively secretive Soviet Communist regime of the Stalin era. As Professor Kennan writes:

It is my conviction, based on some 70 years of experience, first as a government official and then in the past 45 years as an historian, that the need by our government for secret intelligence about affairs elsewhere in the world has been vastly over-rated. I would say that something upwards of 95% of what we need to know about foreign countries could be very well obtained by the careful and competent study of perfectly legitimate sources of information open and available to us in the rich library and archival holdings of this country.

Senator Moynihan and Senator Jesse Helms introduced the Government Secrecy Act of 1997, cosponsored by Representatives Combest and Hamilton. This legislation defines "the principles and standards to govern classification and declassification, and establishing within an existing agency a National Declassification Center to coordinate responsibility for declassifying historical documents."

The Government Secrecy Act would limit classification to ten years, unless an agency head certifies that the information needs additional protection. Regardless, the information must be opened to the public within thirty years *unless* an agency head can show that the data are essential for national security or would do "demonstrable harm to an individual."

Senator Fred Thompson, chairman of the Committee on Governmental Affairs, stated at the Hearing on the Report of the Commission:

> For centuries, governments have been preoccupied with keeping secrets. Information is power and those that have access to it are powerful. Our democratic nation, however, is founded on the principle that the people are sovereign and must be trusted with the power of information if they are to make informed choices.

Yet Senator Helms in his statement felt "obliged to begin with a reiteration of the obvious," citing the "serious and long-term threats" from the usual "communist and anti-American regimes" as well as "new threats" that have arisen:

> Most alarming, perhaps, is the growing trend of espionage conducted not by our enemies but by American allies. Such espionage is on the rise especially against U.S. economic secrets. According to a February 1996 report by GAO, classified military information and sensitive military technologies are high priority targets for the intelligence agencies of U.S. allies.

Is this yet another instance of government officials groping for a reason to maintain and even increase secrecy? Economic espionage also is the subject of John J. Fialka's 1997 book *War by Other Means,* which attempts to make the case that China "has flooded the United States with spies." Yet the crimes that Fialka describes are minor or were actually committed against China, not the United States. Fialka also claims that Japan and Russia are dangerous thieves, stealing American research and patents and bettering their economy at the expense of America—yet the Russian economy was destroyed in the arms race and Japan's stock market recently fell to half its former mark.

In response to the Commission's report, Eleanor Randolph, for the *Los Angeles Times,* claimed that the Cold War's end and Internet access have joined to "aid forces of openness": "Although the Clinton administration has helped open many of the dustier archives, some of the most dramatic releases recently—such as the information about Nazi gold hoarded in Switzerland and some of the background data on the JFK assassination—are the result of congressional or media pressure."

Anyone who is concerned about government secrecy should write their senators and representatives, asking them to accelerate the free flow of government information from national agencies. Those Congressional terms are the only leverage that American citizens have to influence the direction of their government.

Terry Anderson, the former Associated Press reporter taken hostage in Lebanon in 1985, agrees that it's about time to change the level of secrecy in the United States. When Anderson filed FOIA requests with thirteen agencies after he was released in 1991 to get information on his own capture and detainment for his memoirs, he was frustrated by the complete lack of response:

> Given the natural inertia of the bureaucracy, these guys don't really have anything to win when they release documents. And they have a lot to lose if they release the wrong document and somebody starts screaming at them. They don't get bonuses for being open. They don't get patted on the back for being open, and without strong and sustained pressure from the public and this White House, they're not going to change.

CHAPTER 5

Disinformation

Y OUR EYES would water, sting, your throat would go
dry, and you felt like you were drug through a pig
pen, so to speak."

This is how one former worker in Area 51, known only
as "John Doe #1," spoke of his experience at the secret
base in an interview aired on "60 Minutes" in March 1996.
John Doe #1 described to Leslie Stahl how the workers
burned waste at Area 51, which caused a terrible skin con-
dition known as acute phototoxic dermatitis: "There's no
cure for it that I can find . . . [it's] cracking, bleeding. It
gets pretty scaly."

John Doe #1 maintains his anonymity because every one
of the one thousand civilian workers and two thousand military employees of the Groom Lake facility has signed a
security oath pledging to keep all information about the
base confidential.

But deaths and illnesses among workers who regularly
burned waste products at Area 51 caused five of them to
break their oaths. They claim they were injured from the
burning chemicals and highly toxic classified materials. If

their claims are true, then the administrators of Area 51 have broken environmental laws prohibiting open-pit burning of hazardous wastes.

The plaintiffs were formally granted anonymity by federal judge Philip Pro, to protect them against possible ten-year prison terms for talking about the operation of black projects at the base.

The six "John Does" were joined by Helen Frost, the widow of Robert Frost, who died of cirrhosis of the liver in 1989 at age fifty seven. An analysis by Peter Kahn, former member of the New Jersey Agent Orange Commission and a Rutgers University biochemist, found substantial quantities of dioxins and dibenzofurans in Robert Frost's fatty tissue. Kahn attributed this to industrial exposure, and he found other toxic chemical compounds he couldn't recall ever seeing in human tissue.

Frost was one of two workers who died exhibiting symptoms of cracking skin, respiratory problems, and dime-size open sores, which can be caused by exposure to cancer-causing chemicals. Another plaintiff, Walter Kasza, a sheet-metal worker at Area 51, died in April 1995 of liver and kidney cancer. His wife blames it on a decade of exposure to the burning waste.

The Area 51 workers were represented by Jonathan Turley, a George Washington University law professor who directs the Environmental Crimes Project at the university's National Law Center. Turley filed suit in federal court in the District of Columbia, naming U.S. Environmental Protection Agency Administrator Carol Browner as a defendant. This so-called EPA case claimed that Browner failed to inspect the base for compliance with the Resource Conservation and Recovery Act.

A second lawsuit was filed on August 15 1995, in District Court in Las Vegas, naming Defense Secretary William Perry, National Security Adviser Anthony Lake, and Air Force Secretary Sheila Widnall as defendants. This suit claims these officials willfully concealed hazardous waste violations.

The plaintiffs have filed a citizen's suit, authorized by Congress to vindicate public rights and interests. The workers aren't asking for millions of dollars in damages—they only want information to help them treat their health problems, ranging from skin lesions to cancer. And they want their medical bills paid. As Turley explained in a rare interview granted to "60 Minutes," no one is "absolutely sure" what the two men died from. "What I'm trying to find out is whether they did die because of this."

Groom Lake workers claim that nothing left the facility, according to Margaret A. Jacobs of *The Wall Street Journal,* reporting in February 1996. Everything else, including "office furniture, jeeps and leftover lobster and prime rib, was either burned or buried."

Yet when Turley asked if there was jet fuel at the Groom Lake facility (since workers claimed the waste was ignited with jet fuel), the government lawyers stated that "to admit or deny the presence of jet fuel at an air base would put American lives in danger." The same response was given when Turley asked whether ordinary house paint could be found on the premises. Certainly no national security issues are at stake in admitting that house paint was used at the base—but if paint was burned, that would violate environmental laws.

Yet the Air Force refuses to answer these simple questions, and Judge Pro consistently supported the military's secrecy campaign. The secretary of Air Force, Sheila Widnall, proposed the "mosaic theory," in which minor pieces of information could be combined to provide a foreign power with sensitive information. Theoretically, this mosaic would include the composition of Lockheed Martin's new electrochromic coatings, which will render stealth aircraft invisible even in daylight.

It was during a notorious closed hearing in June 1995 in Las Vegas District Court that Richard Sarver defended the military by claiming that all government facilities abide by the nation's environmental laws. This was contradicted by reports from a 1995 government task force which estimated that cleaning up hazardous waste at federal facilities, mostly military-related, would cost $234 billion to $389 billion.

The presence of hazardous waste at Area 51 was seemingly confirmed by the Environmental Protection Agency inspection that Judge Pro ordered that same year—the first time the Groom Lake facility had *ever* undergone a hazardous waste inventory. When Turley cross-examined the EPA spokesman in court, he said they would put "the facility" on the Federal Agency Hazardous Waste Compliance Docket. Since the docket is a list of federal facilities with hazardous waste, Turley pointed out, "Doesn't that mean you have hazardous waste?!" They replied, "Well, not necessarily . . ."

So Turley requested to see the hazardous waste inventory on Area 51, which by law is required to be open to the public. The only exemption can come from the president of the United States, and President Clinton granted the exemption. In his September 29, 1995 memorandum to the administrator of the Environmental Protection Agency and the secretary of the Air Force, the president stated:

> I find that it is in the paramount interest of the United States to exempt the United States Air Force's operating location near Groom Lake, Nevada (the subject of litigation in *Kasza* v. *Browner* [D. Nev. CV-S-94-795-PMP] and *Frost* v. *Perry* [D. Nev. CV-S-94-714-PMP] from any applicable requirement for the disclosure to unauthorized persons of classified information concerning that operating location.

This is the same president who two years earlier called on all government agencies to volunteer information according to the "underlying principles of government openness, and to its sound administration" inherent in the FOIA.

The government has never before invoked the national security privilege in order to shield itself from criminal liability. Indeed, Richard Nixon tested the limits of executive-branch power in his handling of Watergate—and the high court ruled that executive privilege can't be used to cover a crime. National security issues are intended to protect against courtroom disclosures of procedures for gathering intelligence secrets or military planning. But that doesn't seem to apply in this case.

The open-pit burning, which workers allege took place at least once a week in one hundred-yard-long, twenty-five-foot-wide pits, is a very serious crime punishable by up to fifteen years in prison and a $1 million fine. The Air Force—or whichever agency is ultimately responsible for Area 51—is clearly in the wrong in that it never had the required EPA inspections until 1995. Early in litigation, the military conceded that it never applied for a permit or manifest to exempt the operating facility at Groom Lake.

From all available evidence, the Air Force also didn't attempt to settle the workers' lawsuit in private. If it had, the Pentagon could have avoided public disclosure of the existence of the Groom Lake facility—as well as admitting that they had lied about it for the past forty years! They would also have been spared the extremely bad publicity of having allegedly created an environmental hazard.

Instead, the workers report that from the first day they approached the Air Force, they were treated with high-handed disdain. The Pentagon continued to impose extreme secrecy on the most mundane operating issues, and the military managed to get both the president and the judiciary to agree that the Department of Defense would have the last word.

The American people are faced with a strange contradiction—liberty and freedom are defended by individuals who operate within a totalitarian structure. In the military and intelligence communities, authority is supreme. As long as the chain of command is followed, and as long as military expenditures and policy are defended on the grounds of national security, then the rank-and-file soldiers and civil servants won't question the system.

Some conspiracy proponents claim that the Air Force

wanted to draw attention to Area 51 to hide the existence of secret activities taking place elsewhere. But as Glenn Campbell points out, once a government facility becomes as romanticized as Area 51, then military and UFO enthusiasts in the other fifty states inevitably start looking around for secret bases in their own backyards.

Campbell suggests an alternative explanation that is "even more frightening":

> Maybe there is NO ONE controlling our society. Maybe shit just happens. The real course of history could be pushed along by random winds that no one on earth has a handle on. For example, technology is not a democratic process. If someone invents a useful new device, like the light bulb, telephone or World Wide Web, it can spread throughout society almost overnight, and its effects upon our life on earth, both good and bad, can be far more profound than any act ever promulgated by Congress. At best, Congress will only react to the new idea after its effects are already obvious, but by then the process is usually unstoppable.

The Area 51 Security Manual

Professor Turley and his clients say they can prove the government violated the Resource Conservation and Recovery Act, the federal law regulating hazardous waste, without revealing any sensitive material. Turley introduced an unclassified security manual entitled *DET 3SP Job Knowledge* that was purportedly from Area 51. The Defense Department responded by retroactively classifying the security manual along with everything in Turley's office that quoted from it, including notes and legal briefs. The government lawyers even got a court order to "seal" Turley's office, preventing him from removing his own files or allowing students or other faculty members into his rooms. Yet Judge Pro refused to allow the manual itself to be placed under seal and considered part of the plaintiffs' case.

Mark Farmer, pilot and photojournalist who has spent years researching Area 51, told me in 1997 that he received the security manual four years earlier from an anonymous source. He sat on it for a while before giving it to George Knapp, news anchor at KLAS-TV in Las Vegas, Nevada. Campbell says he also received a copy of the manual from around the same time, "probably from the same source."

This security manual is posted on the Internet in several minor variations. It is a twenty-nine-page document that mainly deals with call signs for specific emergencies and maps of buildings labeled "AFOSI," "Graphics Room," and "Sam's Place (BAR/MWR Office)."

There doesn't seem to be anything remarkable about the security manual, except that it confirms minor points, such as naming Pittman Station, the same substation used by the former "Special Deputies" who patrol the border. On the last page, it provides the official cover story for employees: "For security reasons if a contractor is asked where he/she works, they will answer "E.G.& G. at the Test Site.""

Congressman Lee Hamilton (D-Ind.) publicly stated his opinion on the case as follows: "The Air Force is classifying all information about Area 51 in order to protect themselves from a lawsuit. I'm not personally prepared, to take the word of a person who has, or an entity which has a huge financial stake in the outcome here, that this information needs to be classified."

Congressman Hamilton also believes that "judges are often snowed by the national security establishment." He was proven right on March 6, 1996, when Judge Pro dismissed the lawsuit, ruling that pursuing the case risked "significant harm to national security."

At George Knapp's urging, KLAS-TV asked the court to make public the portions of the sealed record of the first trial that were unjustifiably classified. Judge Pro denied the motion at the time, but he did rule that once the proceedings were concluded, the Pentagon must open the trial records.

After much effort, KLAS finally received hundreds of pages—most of which were blacked out.

When I called Professor Turley, he said he couldn't discuss the case and referred me to briefs filed at the court of appeals in San Francisco. The one thing he did say was that he was currently owed $400,000 in outstanding legal fees. But he's not in any hurry—both Turley and his co-counsel have agreed to turn all their fees over to the center they run, the Environmental Law Advocacy Center.

I contacted the U.S. Court of Appeals for the Ninth Circuit, expecting resistance in a case bogged down in so much secrecy. But they immediately provided me with a service that copied the briefs filed for two of the cases. Before you know it, I had a three-inch stack of legal papers sitting on my desk.

There is an entire section on "Misrepresentations to the Public and Media" concerning the security manual in the plaintiffs-appellants brief against the U.S. Department of Defense and the U.S. Environmental Protection Agency. Air Force Colonel Tom Boyd issued a statement to the media claiming that the defendants had only "expressed an interest" in getting the security manual returned, and that "the government did not threaten or make any attempts to seize the document."

The appellate brief contends the government stated to counsel for the workers: "we refer you to 18 U.S.C. 793(e), which as you know prohibits unauthorized possession of national security information." Violation of the law cited is a felony offense, and the threat was backed up by the district court judge, who "echoed the potential for prosecution."

Next, it appears the government is trying to get around the anonymity issue. The government "Crimes Section" is now permitted by a 1996 court order to inquire whether workers are represented by Professor Turley. If the anonymity of the workers is compromised, then they are open to the penalties inherent in having broken a security agreement: jail time and heavy fines.

In Turley's summary of the argument for *Frost* v. *Perry,* he contends that the court ruled in favor of the government on every substantive motion brought by plaintiffs. "In doing so, the court massively expanded the government's authority in using the privilege. The court specifically ignored compelling evidence that the privilege was being used for purely tactical purposes."

These Area 51 lawsuits are significant because constitutional experts say the case could ultimately go to the Supreme Court to test the limits of executive-branch power. On January 8, 1998, in an opinion by Judge Pamela Ann Rymes of the 9th U.S. Circuit Court of Appeals, she writes, "The government may use the state secrets privilege to withhold a broad range of information."

"I've got two dead clients," Turley concluded in the interview with Stahl and "60 Minutes."

> I've got other people who are ill, and I've got defendants who committed crimes. They know they committed crimes. So do I. And so does the court. And the question is, whether they are going to be held accountable. Because ultimately, that is what this case is about. Whether there is something unique about the United States government that either makes it accountable or exempt from its own laws.

"Misinformed or Intentionally Misleading"

The district court committed both "factual and legal errors," Turley contends in the reply brief of *Frost* v. *Cohen,* requiring a reversal of the decision. The defendants were ordered to release the transcript from the secret June 20, 1995 hearing, but even when they didn't comply, the court denied a second motion from the plaintiffs.

In their reply, the government defended its actions, claiming it had "complied with the court's January 22, 1996, order." But Turley insists, "This response is either grossly misinformed or intentionally misleading. . . ."

Disinformation is the word for this sort of deliberate misleading of the public. It is the reverse of information, in that it contains significant factual errors buried in plausible statements.

Disinformation can be as simple as denying the existence of the Aurora, a secret R&D Aircraft, because that isn't its proper code name. Steve Douglass one of the Interceptors and an Aviation journalist, commented on government lies in his Internet essay "Chasing Aurora and Other Black Unicorns": "Aviation journalists will agree, that the Pentagon has lied about covert projects before. In particular the existence of the F-117 was denied by military officials many times before finally revealing it to the public in 1989."

As for UFOs, there's the CIA's repeated denial of involvement in UFO investigations. The CIA still hasn't offered an explanation for why it lied about its involvement or why it continues to classify UFO-related documents due to "national security" issues. Perhaps the best explanation comes from Gerald K. Haines' 1997 official CIA report, "A Diehard Issue: CIA's role in the Study of UFO's, 1947–90," which admits the CIA knew that many "UFO" sightings were really sightings of the U-2 and the SR-71 Blackbird reconnaisance flights.

Disinformation often employs an exaggeration of the facts, and can sometimes rise from unintentional embellishment by government employees who leak the truth about their agency's involvement in research and development of UFO information. All it takes is the addition of a little circumstantial evidence stated as fact, and disinformation is born.

For example, Victor Marchetti, the former executive assistant to the deputy director of the CIA, wrote about rumors he had heard within "high levels" of the government in an article in *Second Look* magazine (May 1979). These rumors included tales about the crash and recovery of UFOs along with the bodies of "little men." Marchetti believed that CIA attempts to whitewash the UFO phenomenon have all the classic earmarks of a cover-up.

Though Marchetti clearly states that he never saw conclusive evidence that UFOs were alien vehicles, other investigators repeat his rumors as fact. Only a year before Marchetti's book was published, Jesse Marcel had come forward with renewed claims of the crashed flying saucer near Roswell, New Mexico. Suddenly Roswell rose from the ashes where it had lain dormant for over thirty years (more on that in Chapter 6).

The difficulty in mounting a deliberate disinformation campaign limits its use to the most critical situations. British intelligence efforts during World War II proved the effectiveness of disinformation, when the D-Day invasion force reached Normandy without the knowledge of German intelligence. As Anthony Cave Brown writes in *Bodyguard of Lies* (1975), "Deception was the province of the LCS [London Controlling Section], and its special assignment was to plant upon the enemy, along the channels open to it through the Allied high command, hundreds, perhaps thousands of splinters of information that, when assembled by the enemy intelligence services, would form a plausible and acceptable—but false—picture of Allied military intentions."

Some ufologists argue that if aliens are regularly visiting earth and interacting with our government, then that would be a critical matter worthy of a large-scale disinformation campaign. The government was certainly given a good reason to hide the existence of aliens in NASA's 1968 Brookings Report and the Cold War–era Robertson Report, the first to suggest that knowledge of ETs would "induce hysterical behavior and harmful distrust of duly constituted authority."

Thus, some UFO researchers speculate that the government knows aliens exist, and is conditioning us to accept the idea through movies such as Steven Spielberg's *ET* (supposedly made with the cooperation of government officials). In order to facilitate the calculated release of information, carefully prepared "leaks" help spread the word about the existence of aliens.

Richard Boylan, Ph.D., a member of CSETI (Center for the Study of Extraterrestrial Intelligence), is also an avid supporter of government conspiracy theories. Boylan often discusses the so-called Aviary, a group of "government insiders" identified by another conspiracy theorist, William Moore, who claims these officials are employed to manipulate the public's perception of ETs.

Boylan was conducting UFO abduction research when the California Board of Psychology took his license in August 1995, due to seven counts of gross misconduct. A superior court judge ruled that Boylan would never get back his license to practice psychology. According to a report from KCRA-TV in Sacramento, California, the judge said that Boylan's conduct was outrageous, but that his UFO story was "simply irrelevant."

In a letter to *ORTK Bulletin* in August 1995, Boylan claimed, "a former Air Force Major, now a malpractice lawyer," and ". . . former Air Force Colonel Bruce Ebert, and president of the Board of Psychology, pursued these complaints, even though in the meantime the ex-clients had abandoned their complaints, and had written letters to the Board of Psychology stating that they had no further interest in pursuing their complaints."

A few months later, in early 1996, Boylan posted an exposé on the Internet that claimed his insider contact (known as Beltway throat) had passed on rumors from a member of the Aviary. Along with a prediction of alien contact in April 1997, the rumors included one that "Christ was an ET," and supposedly high-level officials feared that knowledge of ETs might shake the Christian world to the point that Christians wouldn't take "direction from their governmental leaders, thus leading to social chaos."

As George Wingfield wrote when he reposted Boylan's rumors on the Internet in April 1997, "Like so much else that we receive on the Net these days, it is fiction rather than fact, or, in other words, pure bullsh*t."

Majestic-12

There has been an ugly rise in the number of former government employees releasing false information in order to profit from the interest in UFOs. Some do it simply for the attention they get from the hard-core believers in the UFO community. But most make money—mainly through speaking fees from conventions and universities, or by writing a book.

Barry Greenwood refuses to accept that the government actively generates disinformation or employs "disinformation agents." The most effective disinformation comes from individual government employees, he says, either active or retired. These informants usually support the theory that the government is covering up alien contact and is in possession of alien technology. As CUFOS (Center for UFO Studies) puts it, "For the most part, individuals who have claimed knowledge of secret alien bases or secret UFO projects have proven to be unreliable witnesses; therefore, their statements must be considered cautiously until there is reliable and independent verification of their claims."

Claims are one thing—government documents are quite another. Ufologists spent a decade trying to figure out if the Majestic-12 documents were genuine, and today, most of the serious researchers agree that they are fake. The experience led Greenwood to conclude, "MJ-12 did immense damage to document research. Now I look at anything written about UFOs and I say, is that for real?"

The "original" MJ-12 document was dated November 18, 1952. It is in the form of a briefing for incoming President Dwight D. Eisenhower, including a report on the recovery of a crashed UFO and alien bodies in New Mexico. MJ-12 also revealed that a "covert analytical effort" had been established to investigate the matter, headed by Air Force General Nathan Twining and Dr. Vannevar Bush.

The MJ-12 document made its debut on the broadcast of "The UFO Experience," first aired in November 1982.

The director, Jamie Shandera, announced she had received a roll of 35mm film from an anonymous source that contained images of the briefing document—as if someone had photographed it on the sly.

MJ-12 was allegedly made up of high-level government officials committed to concealing the reality of alien visitations. The individuals listed—Hillenkoetter, Bush, Forrestal, Twining, Vandenberg, Bronk, Hunsaker, Souers, Gray, Menzel, Montague, and Berkner—have all been linked to UFO research or the debunking of UFO research. Significantly, none of these men was alive at the time to confirm or deny his involvement.

Some investigators still believe that the MJ-12 documents are proof of the existence of a "covert analytical effort" much like the British LCS. Stanley Friedman researched the MJ-12 document and even received a research grant of $16,000 from the Fund for UFO Research. Friedman leans toward accepting the MJ-12 documents as genuine, or perhaps, highly sophisticated disinformation prepared by the intelligence community. Friedman has published books based on his research, one coauthored with Don Berliner, *Crash at Corona* (1992).

Friedman's latest book, *Top Secret Majic,* contains references to an alleged Majestic-12 operations manual, entitled *Extraterrestrial Entities and Technology, Recovery and Disposal.* Under the Extraterrestrial Technology Classification Table, listing the different items such as "Aircraft," "Powerplant," and "Living entity," the "receiving facility" listed for most of them is "Area 51 S-4."

There's one problem—the date on the Majestic-12 operations manual is April 1954. In researching the Department of Energy's database, I learned that was over a year before construction was begun on the "Watertown" facility.

So if the Majestic-12 documents are fake, who is responsible? William Moore at first claimed he had been chosen by MJ-12 to make disclosures to the public about alien beings. Then Moore publicly confessed at the 1989 MU-

FON, Mutual UFO Network, symposium in Las Vegas that he had lied about being a "controlled informant."

Moore was certainly involved in the matter right from the beginning, including passing disinformation to Paul Bennewitz. Sergeant Richard Doty in turn supplied Moore with information about the "Aviary."

According to Barry Greenwood, the real culprit was Sergeant Doty, an OSI agent for the Air Force who first embellished reports on sightings in New Mexico submitted by Paul Bennewitz. As Greenwood told me, "Doty has a history of faking government documents. Eventually the government knew what was going on, but I can't say what they knew when. Doty approached Peter Gersten looking for a job with CAUS, even though it was just a bunch of us working together. But he offered inside government information in exchange for a job."

The members of CAUS had always suspected the documents were "too good." The Bennewitz report by Doty appeared just as Fawcett and Greenwood were completing their book *Clear Intent* (which was later released as *The UFO Cover-up*). The Bennewitz report was included, along with the author's reservations about the fact that an OSI agent had "volunteered" the documents in a startling contradiction of Air Force policy.

Even when the *National Enquirer* investigated Doty's claims, it was unable to come up with a shred of supporting evidence. Doty was demoted to a position in charge of the mess hall, and he left the Air Force altogether.

Sadly, Paul Bennewitz suffered a complete mental breakdown because of Moore and Doty's manipulations. Bennewitz is only one casualty of UFO disinformation—a worsening situation that should be taken seriously. As the 1968 National Security Agency analysis "UFO Hypothesis and Survival Questions" concluded:

Rarely have men of science, while acting within their professional capacities, perpetuated hoaxes. . . . If UFOs, contrary to all indications and expectations, are indeed

hoaxes—hoaxes of a world-wide dimension—hoaxes of
increasing frequency, then a human mental aberration of
alarming proportions would appear to be developing.
Such an aberration would seem to have serious implications for nations equipped with nuclear toys—and
should require immediate and careful study by scientists.

Conspiracy Theories

The problem with increased government secrecy is that reporters are forced to rely on leaks to get their information.
This leads to a rise in unsubstantiated rumors and the conviction that "the truth" is hidden somewhere deep inside
Washington's mountain of classified documents. Or as Paul
McMasters, First Amendment expert at the Freedom Forum
in Virginia, puts it, "The government's obsession with secrecy creates a citizens' obsession with conspiracy."

A disturbing CNN/*Time* poll released in June 1997
shows that 80 percent of Americans think the government
is more likely to be hiding knowledge of the existence of
extraterrestrial life forms than telling the truth in its latest
Roswell report. Yet only 54 percent of the respondents believed that intelligent life exists outside Earth!

Conspiracy theories are at an all-time high since the
1950s. Probably no sitting president has been so vilified.
Kennedy was dead before the stories about Marilyn and
mob ties became popular myth, but Clinton has been repeatedly associated with scandalous rumors, from women
to Whitewater. Paula Jones's case of sexual harassment
went right to the Supreme Court, and was well covered by
the mainstream media the entire way.

Conspiracy theories aren't just annoying—they have
deadly consequences. The Waco incident in February 1993,
when the Branch Davidian complex burned to the ground
right in front of the FBI, helped feed the conspiracy paranoia of the militia group that blew up Oklahoma's federal
building.

So why would the American government allow UFO

disinformation to continue, when it is officially discouraging belief in the existence of the UFO phenomenon? James Oberg, a "contractor" for NASA and a UFO skeptic, believes that the government is simply using the rumors of UFOs to hide its covert aircraft exercises. If tourists are busy pointing to the sky shouting *UFO!* then people are less likely to look for other explanations.

Oberg points to the Soviet Union's "no comment" attitude about UFO reports during the 1970s and 1980s, because such reports masked military operations conducted at their own version of Area 51, the ultrasecret Plesetsk Cosmodrome. Oberg conceded to Dennis Stacy, in his six-part series on "Six Decades of Government UFO Cover-Ups" published in *Omni Magazine* in 1994, "Could a similar scenario occur in this country? It's conceivable. On the other hand, should our own government take an interest in UFO reports, especially those that may reflect missile or space technology from around the world? Sure. I'd be dismayed if we didn't."

When I checked the Air Force Academy's space sciences textbook, there was only a brief dismissive statement under "Secret Weapons": "A few individuals have proposed that UFO's are actually advanced weapon systems, and that their natures must not be revealed. Very few people accept this as a credible suggestion."

Even before the CIA report admitting using UFO stories as cover for its stealths and spyplanes, many respected military observers agreed that most UFO sightings were really black-project aircraft. Mark Farmer told me, in May 1997 "The government is passively manipulating the public by not stamping out UFO rumors at Area 51."

When UFO claims are exaggerated, there's a backlash of disbelief, leaving many people tempted to dismiss the entire phenomenon as "delusions" or "mirages." As Terry Hansen wrote in his Internet essay, "Psychology of Dreamland" in 1995:

One suggested reason would be to suck civilian UFO investigators into accepting the authenticity of MJ-12 and then obliterate their credibility with the media and scientific world by exposing the document as a hoax. After all, a similar thing seems to have occurred back in the 1950s following publication of a book about a crashed UFO and alien bodies called *Behind the Flying Saucers* written by Frank Scully. Was history about to repeat itself?

Some ufologists, such as Norio Hayakawa, agree that there are no UFOs, yet that the government encourages rumors of ETs. But Hayakawa points to a much bigger threat in the "New World Order," which some people claim is poised to take away our civil liberties.

Hayakawa is the former Southwest Regional Director for the Civilian Intelligence Network, a Los Angeles–based network of civilian researchers who investigate and analyze the American government's covert activities. According to Hayakawa's homepage, GroomWatch, he is convinced that

a secret international network of elitists "cabal" (ever since 1947, "coincidentally" or not, just one year prior to the time of modern-day re-establishment of the State of Israel) has been preparing to stage a phony extraterrestrial event in the very near future (perhaps as early as 1998—the year of triple 666? And also "coincidentally" the 50th Anniversary of the modern-day re-birth of Israel).

Usually the agencies alleged to be involved in this "satellite" or "shadow" government are the top people in charge of various combinations of the CIA, NSA, FEMA, and/or the United Nations. As Hayakawa puts it, the government is manipulating the "alien connection" to Area 51 for its own advantage, to frighten the public into accepting a bureaucratic takeover.

Many of the senior UFO researchers don't believe there is a complex government conspiracy under way. After more than three decades in the field, James Moseley, editor of *Saucer Smear*, the trade paper for ufologists, asserts:

> I don't believe any of the (UFO) landings. I don't believe in Roswell. Certainly people are seeing things in the sky that we can't explain, but I don't think we have any proof they are aliens. . . . I don't think the government does, either. The government . . . is so horrendously incompetent and disorganized that they are incapable of covering their own tracks, much less a mystery of this magnitude.

Robert Todd agrees. The Pennsylvania researcher was an early participant in CAUS and is currently the editor of the sporadically published newsletter *Spot Report*, released with Barry Greenwood's newsletter *Just Cause*, now known as the "UFO Historical Review."

Todd tends to be rather contemptuous when tearing apart other ufologists' research. Todd was also interviewed about government cover-ups by Dennis Stacy, and stated:

> The UFO community won't be satisfied until the government admits it's behind a vast cover. Is there a lot of material still being withheld? Without a doubt. But does that prove the government is engaged in a massive conspiracy, or that it's merely a massive bureaucracy? I can't state this strongly enough: I don't believe there's a cover-up at all.

After thirty-two years researching UFOs, Barry Greenwood sounds like he's suffering from a profound disillusionment. You probably would be too, after researching a "nonexistent" phenomenon that's been documented with obsessive secrecy by the government. As Greenwood explained, "When the subject was still developing, there was no way to avoid that the ET theory was a possibility. It was a reasonable hypothesis, then, but now you can't trust what's being reported anymore unless you see it from the original source."

The government's attitude toward the UFO phenomenon has been highly inconsistent, which is why Dennis Stacy, editor of the *MUFON UFO Journal,* wrote his six-part series on the government cover-up for *Omni.* As Stacy found, "One night UFOs constitute a threat to the national security; the next they are merely part of a public hysteria based on religious feelings, fear of technology, mass hypnosis, or whatever the prevailing psychology of the era will bear."

Cults as a Consequence

On April Fools Day 1997, the Pentagon once again denied that it had anything to do with UFO investigations. According to the AP wire, Pentagon spokesman Kenneth Bacon gave the usual Air Force statement about the conclusions of the Condon Report, and when asked about the possible existence of UFOs, Bacon said the U.S. government "cannot substantiate that they exist."

This most recent denial from the Air Force was prompted by the suicide of thirty-nine members of the Heaven's Gate cult in a rented Rancho Santa Fe mansion in March 1997. The group members killed themselves because they believed their souls would be transported to eternal life on a spaceship following the Hale-Bopp comet. Marshall Applewhite, the leader of Heaven's Gate, claimed to be in contact with a greater, more powerful entity. Historically these entities used to be known as "gods," but the members of Heaven's Gate believed that ultra-advanced aliens were their salvation.

Thus, the extraterrestrial theory of UFOs has become entangled in the growing New Age movement, taking on increasingly mystical and religious properties as people are forced to interpret their own experiences. The confusion will only get worse as "leaders" vie with one another, claiming they know the truth about UFOs.

The irony is, the government could supplant such self-proclaimed prophets by becoming the guiding authority on the UFO phenomenon, accepting the enigma while funding serious scientific studies. The government could release the information that already exists—data that has been gathered, analyzed, and recorded by national agencies. Otherwise, disinformation will continue to breed more disinformation and paranoia will only build.

Applewhite and his followers are nothing new—they have been around a long time in one form or another, first as "HIM," for Human Individual Metamorphosis, and later as "The Total Overcomers." They always believed that they would leave earth in a UFO, following the resurrection of Applewhite (known as "Do") and his wife, Bonnie Nettles ("Ti"), who died in 1985. Much of this is described in Jacques Vallée's excellent book *Messengers of Deception* (1979).

Amy Hebert had her own encounters with Applewhite's followers which she posted on UFO Updates in April 1997. Hebert describes how she was at first skeptical about their claims, but later had a change of opinion:

> The Arkansas Overcomers were the most intelligent, open, friendly and caring group of people I'd ever met. I wanted to take them all home with me and keep them. Now whether this was due to some cult "brainwashing" techniques or some unsatisfied need within myself, who knows? They seemed to have found what they wanted in life and wanted to share everything with others.

Rumors of an approaching alien ship were started by an amateur astronomer from Houston, Chuck Shramek. Shramek photographed a "Saturn-like object" (SLO) near the Hale-Bopp comet on November 14, 1996. Additional observation would have proved the object was a star that was misidentified in his Megastar computer software, but he wasn't able to observe it for another week.

Meanwhile, the photograph was publicized by Art Bell on "Coast to Coast," a nationwide radio talk show. Ufologists Lee Shargel, Courtney Brown, and others quickly confirmed that it was an alien spaceship and that the comet signaled the aliens' imminent arrival.

Applewhite, along with several Heaven's Gate members, visited Shargel at a book-signing promotion for his new book, *Voice in the Mirror*, not long before their suicide. According to Shargel, who spoke as a guest on ABC's "This Week" on March 30, 1997, the cult believed that his book contained a message from the aliens to them. Shargel wouldn't say whether he personally ever had an experience with aliens.

Yet earlier in March, the *Sun Sentinel* in Coral Springs, Florida, announced that the jacket of Shargel's novel was dishonest. Shargel lied when he stated that he has a Ph.D. from Northeastern University, and that he was employed by NASA on the Hubble Space Telescope project. When confronted with his lies by the newspaper, Shargel responded, "Bad publicity still is publicity. As long as they get the spelling right, S-H-A-R-G-E-L, that's all I care about."

The Heaven's Gate website outlined the group's belief that the Hale-Bopp comet was a marker indicating that the time had come "to leave this world." Their suicide was planned weeks in advance, with cult members traveling—as was typical of them, in a large group—to visit Sea World, Mexico, northern California, and Oregon. They even went to Las Vegas, some say drawn to a public meeting to discuss Area 51.

By the time of the comet's nearest approach to earth, the alien UFO companion theory had been debunked and few people continued to believe a spaceship was approaching earth. Yet the Heaven's Gate members were already committed to their course of action, admitting on their website, "Whether Hale-Bopp has a companion or not is irrelevant from our perspective. . . ."

After the mass suicide, the media focused on the irrationality of the members' beliefs, while UFO groups quickly tried to distance themselves from Heaven's Gate, labeling them a religious cult. Yet even cults can be based on respected beliefs—the Reverend Jim Jones led the mass suicide of nine hundred people in the Guyana jungle in 1978, while adhering to the tenets of the Disciples of Christ, a respected and widely supported Protestant church.

More ufologists should be pointing to the government as an accomplice, allowing disinformation campaigns to run wild when they could easily debunk charlatans and those who claim to have inside government information. Governments won't change on their own, and as one cautious official told me, "To admit that we have no information on a specific subject could imply that we do have information on related topics."

The mass suicide is proof of the harm that comes from allowing the UFO phenomenon to remain unexplained. Applewhite's extremism led him to castrate himself in a quest for androgyny, and other members of Heaven's Gate did the same. Then they followed him into death.

After studying Applewhite's cult for three years, Amy Hebert concluded:

The Heaven's Gate cult is not just a bizarre anomaly to be dismissed and forgotten. They are part of the Zeit-geist, a sign of the times we are living in. They are human beings who want to be something more than human. Rather than improve the human species as a whole, they seek only the transcendence of their individual souls. We must ask ourselves in what ways we, as a society, prompted or promoted the events which led 39 people to leave this classroom called "Earth" and seek alternative experiences to life.

CHAPTER 6

Roswell

"A S FAR as I know, an alien spacecraft did not crash at Roswell, N. M., in 1947. . . . If the United States Air Force did recover alien bodies, they didn't tell me about it either, and I want to know," President Clinton is quoted as saying, in the "gossip" section of the New York *Daily News* (December 18, 1995). So now, apparently, it's official—everyone wants to know the truth about Roswell.

Roswell was only the first of a series of reports of crashed saucers in Arizona, New Mexico, Nevada, Texas, and northern Mexico. The first and most famous crash site lies eighty-five miles northwest of Roswell, a small town east of the Sierra Blanca mountain range, on the plains of southeastern New Mexico. The site is between Corona and Ramon, south of highway 247.

Mac Brazel found the strange metal strewn across land on a sheep ranch belonging to J. B. Foster. After an unknown length of time had passed, Brazel contacted Sheriff George Wilcox, who notified the Roswell Army Air Field.

Major Jesse Marcel, intelligence officer, and Captain Sheridan Cavitt, Counterintelligence Corps (CIC), returned to Foster Ranch with Brazel to gather up some of the wreckage. Marcel later said he was notified by Wilcox on July 7, 1947, and that they went out to the ranch that same day and saw debris "scattered over an area about three quarters of a mile long and several hundred feet wide."

The next day, an Army command press release was issued and carried in an article that appeared on the front page of the local *Roswell Daily Record*. That same afternoon, the Associated Press released the following announcement:

> The many rumors regarding the flying disc became a reality yesterday when the Intelligence Office of the 509th Bomb Group of the Eighth Air Force, Roswell Army Air Field, was fortunate enough to gain possession of a disc through the cooperation of one of the local ranchers and the sheriff's office of Chaves County.... Action was immediately taken and the disc was picked up at the rancher's home. It was inspected at the Roswell Army Air Field and subsequently loaned by Major Marcel to higher headquarters.

There's been some dispute about who authorized the press release from Roswell Air Field. Was it the base commander, Colonel William Blanchard, as Lieutenant Walter Haut, public information officer claimed? Or was the Roswell paper correct when it identified Major Marcel as the releasing authority?

This press release was reprinted around the world, even while the Army command hurried to retract the claim that a "flying saucer" had been recovered. At a press conference in Fort Worth, Texas, on July 8, Brigadier General Roger Ramey, commander of the Eighth Air Force base, posed with some blackened debris he called a "weather balloon." Major Marcel was also at the press conference, having flown in from Roswell.

The military proceeded to cordon the crash-site area while they retrieved all of the wreckage. Traditional accounts of the Roswell crash and the recovery say that the debris was taken to Roswell Army Air Field and eventually flown by B-29 and C-54 aircraft to Wright Field, later Wright-Patterson Air Force Base, in Dayton, Ohio. The Center for UFO Studies (CUFOS) says further press coverage was restricted and that "Public interest faded, and the Roswell event became a part of UFO folklore, with most ufologists accepting the official government version of the story."

Witnesses

The story remained buried until it was revived in 1978, when Jesse Marcel began to comment publicly on the strange debris he had recovered near Roswell. Marcel asserted that a flying disc really had crashed, and that the press conference he had participated in had been a cover-up by Army Air Force officials to satisfy the press and pacify the public.

Reporter Johnny Mann accompanied Marcel to Roswell in 1980 to interview him about the UFO crash. Mann examined the picture of Marcel posing with debris and reportedly said, "Jess, I gotta tell you. This looks like a weather balloon." According to Mann, Marcel replied, "That's not the stuff I found on the ranch."

Marcel never claimed that alien bodies were among the wreckage, but he continued to his dying day to insist that the wreckage was "not of the Earth." Marcel also described "small square or rectangular beams" and tinfoillike material that couldn't be broken or burned.

Once Marcel came forward, other witnesses immediately began to speak up, corroborating his story. A chunk of the witness testimony, twenty-six of over one hundred people who have now come forward to tell what they saw or know, was collected on a videotape entitled *Recollections of Roswell,* available from the nonprofit Fund for UFO Research.

FUFOR offers an answer to why these witnesses waited thirty years before coming forward: "Some of the witnesses say they were told at the time by military personnel that they and members of their family would be killed if they ever talked about what they had seen."

All we have is testimony—none of these witnesses can offer any hard evidence that the strange debris was from an alien craft. There are also conflicting claims that the saucer really crashed on the desert west of I-25, on the plains of St. Agustin about 180 miles west of Roswell. According to Barney Barnett, he and a group of student archaeologists from the University of Pennsylvania found a metallic, disc-shaped object on July 3, 1947. Among the wreckage were the bodies of dead humanoids the size of children.

Over the years the number of saucers that crashed and the body count has varied depending on the witness or researcher. Since there are no documents or hard evidence, the Roswell case comes down to eyewitness testimony. This has caused the search for the truth of the decades-old case to blossom into a complex phenomenon in its own right.

Nearly a dozen full-length books have been written on the Roswell case, describing detailed investigations or inside information. Despite government denials, well-known ufologists such as Kevin Randle, Jerome Clark, and Stanton Friedman basically agree that there was a crash of an alien craft outside of Roswell, New Mexico, during the first week in July, 1947.

In the CUFON interview dated September 1995, Michael D. Swords, Ph.D., one of the most respected ufologists, summed up:

Roswell continues to look like a story which builds rather than disintegrates—the others go nowhere so far. But if Roswell is real, then the question is answered. If so, however, only a very few persons would likely know of it, not "the government" in any large sense.

The International Roswell Initiative was begun as a serious grassroots movement by Kent Jeffrey, Joachim Koch,

and Hans-Juergen Kyborg, and was soon sponsored by the
UFO Research Coalition (CUFOS, MUFON, and FUFOR).
The IRI has collected over twenty-five thousand signatures
on its Roswell Declaration, requesting an executive order
to declassify any government-held information on Roswell
or the UFO phenomenon in general:

> If, as is officially claimed, no information on Roswell,
> UFOs, or extraterrestrial intelligence is being withheld,
> an Executive Order declassifying it would be a mere
> formality, as there would be nothing to disclose. The
> Order would, however, have the positive effect of setting
> the record straight once and for all. Years of controversy
> and suspicion would be ended, both in the eyes of the
> United States' own citizens and in the eyes of the world.

Government Explanations

Representative Steven Schiff (R-N.M.) was the first to get
a significant admission from the government on the Roswell incident. Schiff announced in a *Washington Post* article in January 1994 that he first requested information
about Roswell from the Department of Defense. When he
was unable to get an answer, he then asked the General
Accounting Office (GAO) to search for any documents that
referred to Roswell: "Generally, I'm a skeptic about UFOs
and alien beings, but there are indications from the runa-
round that I got that whatever it was, it wasn't a balloon.
Apparently, it's another government coverup."

He was right. The Office of the Secretary of the Air
Force responded in 1995 with "The Roswell Report: Fact
vs Fiction in the New Mexico Desert," admitting that the
Army/Air Force command had lied to the public. After
nearly forty years of claiming that a weather balloon had
crashed, the Air Force now explained that "the material
recovered near Roswell was consistent" with top-secret
Project Mogul. Mogul was a special series of balloons

carrying acoustic microphones to detect radioactive debris from Soviet nuclear explosions.

The national media published the Air Force report. In *The New York Times*, William J. Broad defended the Air Force's deception, calling it "a white lie."

The problem is that it can't be verified by government documentation. The USAF report declared that the lack of documents proved there had been no unusual activity in the area of Roswell: "There were no indications and warnings, notice of alerts, or a higher tempo of operational activity reported that would logically be generated if an alien craft, whose intentions were unknown, entered US territory."

Then the GAO released its report on the 1947 Roswell incident, under the noninflammatory title "Records Management Procedures Dealing with Weather Balloon, Unknown Aircraft, and Similar Crash Incidents." The final report consisted of an eight-page letter to Congressman Schiff with nine pages of appendices. The GAO only briefly commented on the Air Force study and offered no evidence to support the Air Force Project Mogul balloon hypothesis.

The GAO found only two documents on Roswell, both from 1947: an FBI teletype reporting that an object resembling a high-altitude weather balloon with a radar reflector had been recovered near Roswell, and an Air Force report that noted the recovery of a flying disc that was later determined by military officials to be a radar-tracking balloon. As for the rest of the documentation on the Roswell debris, the GAO stated that "although some of the records concerning Roswell activities had been destroyed, there was no information available regarding when or under what authority the records were destroyed."

There aren't even any documents from the Roswell air base. According to the *IRI Bulletin* #3 (August 9, 1995), "Most significant is that the outgoing messages from Roswell Army Air Field (RAAF) for the period from October 1946 through December 1949 were destroyed without authorization. Those messages would most probably have contained the key to what really occurred at Roswell in 1947." W. G. Seibert, an archivist at the National Personnel Records Center, explains the lack of documents in his report to the GAO. Seibert says that records "at or below wing level" should have been destroyed after two years.

When I asked Barry Greenwood whether this was reasonable, he tended to agree. "It's likely they did destroy it. There's regulations covering the destruction of certain classified materials. They keep it on file six months, then they have the option of destroying it. The documents manager would be required to destroy it."

Without supporting documents, the Air Force's Mogul hypothesis rested on the testimony of those involved in the Mogul project—their recollections of the events backed up by project notes and personal diaries. In order to make sure all the relevant testimony was submitted, the Air Force released all personnel who were interviewed from their security oaths.

The major witness for the Mogul case is Charles B. Moore, one of three surviving Project Mogul scientists. Moore had been a New York University graduate student when he worked on the Mogul Project—which was so secret that he told James Moseley editor of *Saucer Smear* that he didn't know its name until Robert Todd notified him during the course of his investigation in 1992.

As reported in the January 1995 issue of *Skeptical Inquirer,* Moore helped rig the long train of up to two dozen neoprene sounding balloons, totaling more than six hundred feet in length. The acoustic microphones and radar reflectors and batteries packed in black boxes hung from ring attachments. Moore helped launch Flight 4 on June 4, 1947, and they traced it as far as Arabela, New Mexico, only seventeen miles from where the debris was found.

Moore later used National Weather Service wind data provided by Kevin Randle to simulate the probable paths of the known launches—Flights 5 and 6, which landed near Roswell. His results indicated that Flight 4 could have landed at the crash site at the Foster ranch.

Ironically, Moore had his own UFO sighting on April 24, 1949, while tracking one of his balloons near Arrey, New Mexico (about fifty miles west of White Sands Missile Range). Moore and his team saw a large elliptical UFO moving at high speed, which Moore watched through his theodolite, a surveying instrument consisting of a telescope mounted to swivel both horizontally and vertically.

When the UFO dropped between the men and a distant mountain range, they estimated its size at about one hundred feet by forty feet. The UFO then shot straight up and faded from sight about sixty miles overhead. This case was reported in detail in the 1952 *Life* magazine article, and remained one of Project Blue Book's unknown cases.

Moore's latest contribution to the UFO field is a book published in July 1997, joining the rest of a jostling crowd of Roswell/UFO books released to coincide with the fiftieth anniversary of the crash at Roswell. Moore is one of three coauthors of *UFO Crash at Roswell: The Genesis of a Modern Myth.*

It seemed that the Mogul hypothesis would be the last word from the Air Force on the Roswell crash, when in an unexpected move, the USAF issued a new report in June 1997. "The Roswell Report: Case Closed" was written by Air Force Captain James McAndrew.

The Air Force more or less stood by its Project Mogul explanation for the wreckage near Roswell. "Case Closed" mainly addresses "lingering questions" from the witnesses who claim to have seen alien bodies. Based on a review of its records and interviews with witnesses, the Air Force maintains that "activities which occurred over a period of many years have been consolidated and are now represented to have occurred in two or three days in July 1947."

Among the report's more startling conclusions was that the alien bodies observed in the New Mexico desert "were probably anthropomorphic test dummies that were carried aloft by U.S. Air Force high-altitude balloons for scientific research."

These blue dummies dressed in flight suits were dropped

from the balloons and examined for the effect of the impact. It's likely the Air Force put out their report to coincide with the Roswell anniversary, but in the midst of the revelries, on July 5, the AP wire carried a statement from Lieutenant Colonel (Ret.) Raymond A. Madson, who says he doesn't agree with the latest Air Force explanation of what occurred in Roswell.

Colonel Madson worked with high-tech crash test dummies in the 1950s. The dummies were clearly stamped with labels identifying them as Air Force property, and the Air Force even publicized a $25 reward to local residents around Alamogordo so they would return the dummies to the base. Madson stated there's no way the dummies would be confused with the aliens described in rumors arising from the Roswell incident: "The dummies were not covered up or hidden (when transported), and there was no security in the dummy drop phase of the experiments."

Jerry Clark of the Center for UFO Studies (CUFOS) told MSNBC, "Because the evidence for alien bodies is intriguing but evidentially thin, I think it's odd that the Air Force felt it had to explain these reports. It just seems an exercise that undercuts itself. . . . When you do this, you're going one step toward explaining that something extraordinary may have happened."

Debating Roswell

Even the Roswell skeptics think the USAF has gone too far with their latest report. Karl Pflock believes "Case Closed" was simply rushed into publication to counter the fiftieth-anniversary hoopla over Roswell. On MSNBC, Pflock said, "People who want to believe in Roswell, as well as the people like myself who are convinced that Roswell was something mundane . . . will find it laughable."

Pflock was the first to reveal the Mogul project explanation in April 1994 in his report "Roswell in Perspective." Pflock is a former CIA briefing officer and chairman of NICAP's Washington, D.C. subcommittee during the late

1960s and early 1970s. Pflock's research was based in part on a grant from the nonprofit Fund for UFO Research (Stanton Friedman also received a grant, and he supports the crashed flying saucer and alien bodies theory, while Pflock seriously doubts that a "real" flying saucer crashed at Roswell).

UFO researcher Robert Todd also independently discovered evidence that the Roswell material was the remnants of a Project Mogul launch. Todd found the same two documents referenced by the GAO: 000-Flying Discs—"Sign," "Grudge" 1947–50, and MX-1011—"Rockfish," "Mogul" Projects Acoustical Research 1946–50, which he describes in his *Cowflop Quarterly* of July 1996. The GAO report stated that in 1973 these classified correspondence files were destroyed along with an entire floor of the National Personnel Records Center in St. Louis.

In December 1996, *Just Cause* covered the just-released Project Sign/Project Grudge files, totaling nine hundred pages of new material on the USAF's early UFO investigations, 1948–49. Greenwood concludes that as late as June 1948, "high level thinking" tended toward viewing UFOs as "largely being experimental, low aspect ratio aircraft" instead of alien ships:

> At this time we would have had the Roswell "vehicle" for about a year. If we already knew that UFOs were alien and had the proof, why this tremendous amount of wasted energy chasing high-altitude reports? Wouldn't the Air Force's Director of Research and Development have had his hands full doing research on the in-hand alien vehicle instead of being concerned with sightings of distant objects which were often not clearly reported or which contained little useful detail for an engineer?

Some of the witnesses most closely involved are unsure of which explanation to believe. Walter Haut, the former press officer for the 509th Bomb Wing at Roswell AAF, issued the famous July 8, 1947 press release claiming a flying disc had been recovered. Haut never actually saw the debris, but until recently, he was among the true believers that a strange craft had crashed at the Foster ranch. He even helped found the International UFO Museum and Research Center in the heart of downtown Roswell.

Now recently retired from the International UFO Museum, Haut wonders if the debris could have been from Mogul. When Fox News interviewed Haut, he says that he found out a few days after the announcement that somehow "it was a screwup." In an article for the August/September 1992 issue of *Air & Space Smithsonian,* Frank Kuznik asked Haut what he remembered of that day when he was asked to write the press release. Haut replied that "It was not that big a production at that time, in my mind." When pressed by Kuznik that something as revolutionary as a "flying saucer" should have made more of an impression, Haut reminded him,

> Well, there were quite a few reports of flying saucers at that time. I had a multitude of hats I wore. I had all kinds of things to do. I asked my wife, when all this [the renewed interest in Roswell in the mid-1980s] started, "Do you remember me coming home and saying anything about it?"

Her reply, as he recalled, was no. Perhaps it was unremarkable because at the time, everyone was calling UFOs "flying saucers"—which didn't necessarily mean "alien aircraft."

The published ufologists, such as Stanton Friedman and Kevin Randle, continue to disagree with the official Air Force explanations. They point to supporting testimony for the crash of an alien craft provided by Major Marcel's son, physician Jesse Marcel, Jr.

Dr. Marcel claims to have been shown the debris by his father the night it was retrieved in July 1947. Only eleven years old at the time, Marcel remembers handling the material that his father had spread out on the kitchen floor.

In the mid-1990s, Marcel underwent hypnotic regression at the urging of Kent Jeffrey, one of the founders of the Roswell Initiative. Marcel's regression session was conducted by FBI hypnotist Neil Hibbler in Washington, D.C. Videotapes were made of the regression, but they haven't been released.

On the basis of these tapes, Jeffrey concluded that Marcel saw balloon debris—which, he says, was "a major disappointment for me." In an interview on KTVU-TV News in Oakland, California, in April 1997, Jeffrey explained, "I started out here in a quest for the truth. Unfortunately, that truth ended up to be different than I thought it might be and hoped that it would be."

In rebuttal, Marcel did an interview with the electronic newsletter *CNI News* on May 1, reiterating that the debris was not a balloon: "The [hypnosis] session was interesting, but it sure didn't change my mind. My recollections are the same."

Marcel says there are discrepancies between the material he saw and the materials used in the construction of Mogul balloons. He noted that "the foil they used on the [Mogul] radar target was paper-backed foil, and the foil I saw was not paper-backed." The "I-beams" were made of balsawood in the Mogul project, but the debris Marcel handled was completely different:

> It was very light, like balsawood, but I recall metal, not wood. I've built a lot of model airplanes out of balsawood, and I think I would recognize the difference. I'm going to stick to my memory. I remember these beams as metal and not balsawood.

Referring to controversial embossed symbols on a small "I-beam," identified as stylized flowers on adhesive tape, Marcel insists, "The figures that they used were on cellophane tape, which is about an inch wide. This is far larger than what I saw. . . . I looked at some of the drawings of the letters and flower-like images [from the Mogul tape] and I just don't recall anything close to that . . . it wasn't flower-like, it was more geometric designs."

In March 1997, Bob Shell posted a discussion he had with Dr. Marcel on UFO UpDates. When Shell asked about the Air Force theory that the crash was the Mogul Project, Dr. Marcel replied,

> I have felt and certainly still feel that the debris recovered in Roswell was a portion of an extraterrestrial probe. My thoughts about the Air Force involvement may stem from the fact that I am a trusting individual and am trying to "make excuses" for the Air Force and in particular Capt. McAndrew. I want to believe that these guys are really not in the loop to know what actually happened and they are going on a belief system that they will move heaven and earth (including distortion of fact) to foster that belief system.

Government Insider Claims

The most recent Roswell controversy concerns the claims of Colonel Philip Corso, once on President Eisenhower's National Security Council and former head of the Foreign Technology Desk at the U.S. Army's Research and Development Department from 1961 to 1963. Art Bell announced in early 1997 that Corso's book *The Day After Roswell* would be released—you guessed it—to coincide with the fiftieth anniversary of Roswell.

The book jacket claims this "landmark exposé" puts "a fifty-year-old controversy to rest," detailing the work of Lieutenant Colonel Philip Corso, who was in command of

> the dismantling and appropriation of the Roswell extraterrestrial spacecraft by the Army. Now, identifying all those involved, Colonel Corso reveals how a deep-cover council officially discounted all UFO reports to the American public, and cleared the path for his R&D team at the Pentagon to analyze and integrate the Roswell

artifacts into the military arsenal and the private business sector.

John Alexander of the National Institute for Discovery Science (NIDS) told me that Corso is "a conundrum" (Alexander also told me in February 1997 that he was not sure when Corso was promoted from a lieutenant colonel to a full colonel). Yet Alexander supported Corso's claims in a letter to *Saucer Smear,* published in April 1997. Alexander reminded the UFO community that Corso has testified before Congress twice before with "remarkable tales" that were true:

> His testimony in both 1993 and 1996 was covered by major media (network TV, *U.S. News & World Report, Newsweek,* etc.). Face it—in round one he exposed a war that had gone on for decades, but almost no one knew about it. The second was an extensive [Korean] POW exploitation effort conducted by the KGB for almost 50 years. Also note that it was Corso who provided the outside world with information about "Project Horizon."
>
> It seems that NASA used a classified U.S. Army plan that already existed to put men on the moon. Phil Corso got that declassified and released.

Karl Pflock issued a rebuttal in *Saucer Smear* the next month:

> As for Corso's alleged heroic exposure of sordid and secret Cold War activities concerning POWs and decades of U.S. incursions into Soviet airspace with significant losses of aircraft and aircrews—baloney! Most of what Corso had to say to Congress was *old* news, and much of the rest was highly questionable. And Project Horizon, the Army's moon-base plan? Anyone who has paid any serious attention to U.S. space programs since the 50s has known about it for decades. I think I

first heard of it from the late science-fiction great Robert Heinlein in the mid-60s, and somewhere in a box in my garage, I have a fairly lengthy, unclassified summary of the Army plan.

Corso claims to have followed Lt. General Arthur Trudeau's orders to give American R&D a "giant leap" by feeding selected projects with bits of alien technology. This idea is a modern-day version of the premise of Erich von Daniken's *Chariots of the Gods?* (1968), which attributed ancient monuments and innovations to alien influence. For example, Corso explains how he seeded the idea behind the night-vision image intensifier project under way at Fort Belvoir by passing on "an innocuous-looking eye shield an unknown GI had picked up out of the sand near a UFO crashed into a rock in the lonely desert outside of Roswell in a lightning storm fourteen years ago." Corso also claims the first "junction transistor" made of a microscopically thin silicon sandwich was developed in 1948 thanks to Roswell debris that had been made available to physicist William Shockley at the Bell Telephone Laboratories.

Among the other R&D developments that were nudged along by alien technology, according to Corso, are irradiated food, fiber optics, supertenacity fibers, and a particle-beam accelerator for use as a directed-energy weapon. Corso also contends that the Strategic Defense Initiative (SDI), or "Star Wars," was developed to target UFOs, not Soviet warheads. "These creatures weren't benevolent alien beings who had come to enlighten human beings. They were genetically altered humanoid automatons, cloned biological entities, actually, who were harvesting biological specimens on Earth for their own experimentation."

In a lecture for Las Vegas MUFON in March 1997, George Knapp claims to have interviewed Philip Corso "5 or 6 years ago." He noted one of the "coincidences" of Corso's story would be fuel for the critics—Corso told him he had two encounters with aliens while he was at White Sands Missile Range in the 1950s. According to Knapp, when Corso asked, "Friend or Foe?" the alien replied, telepathically, "Neither."

There's also controversy over the sequence of events in the development of these technologies. Pflock reported on a March 24 phone conversation with John Alexander of NIDS, published in the May 1997 *Saucer Smear:* "John told me his investigations confirmed what he (and I) thought to be true: (1) The historical record of these technologies is clear, complete, and unambiguous, establishing without a doubt that they are products of good ol' homo sap skull sweat, with no help of any sort from alien know-how. . . ."

It doesn't help Corso's credibility that Senator Strom Thurmond, who wrote the foreword to Corso's book, told the Associated Press on June 5 that he had not been properly informed of the content of the book. According to the press statement, Thurmond believed the book was a memoir entitled *I Walked with Giants: My Career in Military Intelligence.* When Thurmond learned about the UFO content, the senator insisted, "I did not, and would not, pen the foreword to a book about, or containing, a suggestion that the success of the United States in the Cold War is attributable to the technology found on a crashed UFO."

In a *CNI News* interview with Corso's coauthor, William J. Birnes countered, "Senator Thurmond agreed to write the new foreword—which he did—and sent it to Corso. I have copies of both forewords as well as Thurmond's signed release to use his new foreword in *The Day After Roswell.*"

Despite Birnes's claims, his publisher, Simon & Schuster, has agreed to remove Senator Thurmond's foreword and cover blurb from all future editions of the book. *The Day After Roswell* has been reprinted without a foreword.

There's another problem with Corso's story, which can be found in the discussion on laser R&D. Corso lets drop an oblique reference to MJ-12 when he states that "most high-ranking officers at the Pentagon" knew about Roswell technology being inserted into R&D projects under development, and "They were also vaguely, if not specifically, aware of what had happened at Roswell itself and of the current version of the Hillenkoeter/Bush/Twining working group, which had personnel stationed at the Pentagon to keep tabs on what the military was doing."

In a message to UFO UpDates on March 27, 1997, Kevin Randle notes that Corso made references to his involvement in MJ-12 in his original book proposal:

> In that proposal Corso claims to be a member of MJ-12. He worked on the staff. Now I'm told that all references to Corso being a member of MJ-12 have been eliminated from the book. To me, this suggests that Corso, credentials and all, is not a solid source. It seems to me that he is another of those who is jumping on the Roswell bandwagon at this late date.

Randle has good reason to be wary. He cowrote *UFO Crash at Roswell* with Donald R. Schmitt, former director of special investigations for Center for UFO Studies (CUFOS). Up until he resigned in April 1995, Schmitt was listed by ParaNet right after Richard Hall as one of the "Ten Most Credible Ufologists."

Then Schmitt's claims of being in law enforcement and working on a doctorate in criminology were revealed as fraudulent by Gillian Sender, a reporter for a Milwaukee magazine. Schmitt was actually a U.S. postal worker with a high school diploma. Randle complained about Schmitt's duplicity in the *San Francisco Examiner* in March 1997, adding that the scientific community ignores UFOs "because they don't want to be associated with a field full of kooks and nuts. And the fact is, it is full of kooks and nuts."

Roswell Autopsy Film

Any evidence that appears to support the theory that an alien aircraft crashed at Roswell is a hot-ticket item. The Roswell evidence that arguably had the biggest impact on the public was the alleged military recording of an autopsy of alien bodies recovered from the 1947 crash. Over ten million Americans watched the first broadcast of the Fox documentary "Alien Autopsy: Fact or Fiction" in August 1995.

Kent Jeffrey of the Roswell Initiative pointed out in the *IRI Bulletin* that a number of tactics were used to manipulate the facts: "Through a selective presentation of the facts and selective editing, programs like Fox network's 'Alien Autopsy: Fact or Fiction' have misled the public by giving the impression that a number of interdisciplinary experts, including pathologists and film-makers, feel that the . . . footage might be genuine."

Trey Stokes polled fifteen of his movie industry colleagues about the Roswell alien autopsy footage and posted the results on his webpage as "How to Build an Alien." All fifteen special-effects experts agreed the film was a fake. Among the group were several Academy and Emmy award winners, including Stan Winston (*Jurassic Park*), who was interviewed in the Fox documentary. After the broadcast, Winston clarified his position about the footage in a *Time* magazine interview: "Do I think it's a hoax? Absolutely."

The Fox documentary featured Ray Santilli, owner of Merlin Productions, a small London video distribution company that acquired and marketed the film footage. Santilli released a "detailed statement" entitled "The Cameraman's Story," which claimed the cameraman had been stationed in Washington, D.C., and was flown by way of Wright-Patterson AFB in Ohio to Roswell (after having been told that he was going to film the crash of a Russian spy plane). Santilli eventually released the name of the cameraman as "Jack Barnett."

For the researchers trying to pin down the truth about the alleged autopsy film, it didn't take long to discover that the most important facts about the film's origin were unverifiable. In the *IRI Bulletin* "SCAM" article, Jeffrey explains, "The real Jack Barnett was born of Russian parents on January 1, 1906, and died in 1967. Although he was a newsreel cameraman on the Italian front during WWII, he was never in the U.S. military."

Santilli was confronted with this discrepancy during a live interview on TFl's French "Jacques Pradel" special in October 1995. Santilli changed his story, saying it wasn't Jack Barnett but a different military cameraman who had sold him the footage in 1992—instead of 1993, as he had previously stated. Along the way, Santilli also changed his claim that he obtained "15 10-minute reels" of film from the cameraman to make it "22 3-minute reels."

Santilli's autopsy film gained a measure of credibility because of an error in a Kodak chart that was used to identify edge codes on film. The edge code, a solid square and a triangle, was used on film from 1927, 1947, and 1967. But on the Kodak chart, the square and triangle code for 1967 is misrepresented as outlines rather than a solid form. According to Bob Shell, as posted on UFO UpDates on April 16, 1997, "When Ray first saw the film in Florida, he says he phoned Kodak while he had the film in his hands, talked to them about edge codes, and was told that the film was absolutely from 1947. That's why he agreed to buy it. Later, in a letter on Kodak stationery, an official of Kodak Denmark stated that the film was definitely from 1947."

The Roswell Initiative continues to maintain that there are important offers of verification that could settle the film's authenticity. Jeffrey points out,

Eastman Kodak in Rochester, New York, has been standing by since July 1995 with an open offer to authenticate the film's date of manufacture. I confirmed this fact in a recent telephone conversation with Tony Amato, the Kodak motion-picture product specialist who would oversee the authentication process. Amato told me that Kodak has received repeated promises during the last six months from Santilli through an intermediary in the United States that film meeting the required criteria was "on its way."

Verification of the 1947 date of the "alien autopsy" footage would make the film worth its weight in gold. Yet during the live TFl interview, Santilli reiterated that the film belonged to a private collector and that he had done all he could to get a sample for testing.

The London *Sunday Times* proclaimed, "Film that 'proves' aliens visited earth is a hoax," as early as July 30, 1995. Journalist Maurice Chittenden focused on the unusual security markings on the footage of the "tent autopsy" scene, and noted that "restricted access" is not a recognized U.S. military code. Chittenden dismissed the A01 classification as "pure Hollywood."

In Italy, the TV producer who bought the Italian rights for $400,000 was quoted in *UFO Magazine* in September 1996 as saying, "We knew it was a hoax when we bought it, but it was good show biz."

Area 51 Alien Interview Film

The "alien autopsy" quickly became an indelible motif in UFO folklore. Footage of the Santilli alien model appeared in the Access CD-ROM game "The Pandora Directive." The popular TV series "The X-Files" claims to possess the "authentic" footage of the alien autopsies as compared to the "fake footage."

It was only a matter of time before Area 51 was linked to the Santilli alien autopsy. On April 14, 1997, the syndicated television newsmagazine "Strange Universe" broadcast an exclusive sneak preview of an alien interview that allegedly took place at Area 51.

Attempting to place this alien interview in context, the "Strange Universe" program repeatedly claimed that the alien autopsy film was also filmed at Area 51. But Santilli has consistently tried to establish a date of 1947 for his film—and that's at least eight years before the Groom Lake facility was begun.

The distributor for "Strange Universe," Rysher Entertainment, announced in its press release, "This 'Strange

Universe' exclusive will feature video from a six minute piece of footage smuggled out of Area 51 by a mysterious person known only as 'Victor.' Victor claims that he had 'occasion to be there' and took this while the entire contents of a massive series of interviews with a number of alien creatures was being downloaded from video to analog."

"Victor" was interviewed in a backlit silhouette, with his voice modified electronically. He refused to say whether he was employed by a contractor at Area 51, but he claimed he smuggled the tape out of Area 51 by wrapping it around his hand.

On the Area 51 mailing list Archives, James R. Graham posted his opinion on April 15, 1997: "What I think the bigger mystery is why would a guy who risked his life stealing USG property sell it to a rinky-dink (no offense) production company rather than give it to Peter Jennings or one of the other reputable news guys. I mean if the guy is in a position to observe a live alien at Area 51, don't you think he would at least be making a decent salary?"

"Strange Universe" showed less than ten seconds of the "six-minute interview" of an alien who is being questioned by a U.S. general and a telepathic aide. Briefly, the image of the alien appears on a TV screen, apparently being recorded through a one-way mirror, while a nearby heart monitor can be seen with a light moving up and down. The frame rate seems to be slowed, meaning there are fewer frames than it appears. The lighting is poor and the image of the alien is so vague that the shape of the head isn't even clear. But with only a brief glimpse, it could be interpreted as a typical "gray."

"Strange Universe" offered no technical analysis of the footage. Instead, it showed the entire interview to a panel of experts consisting of Whitley Strieber, Robert Dean, Steve Neill, Jesse Long, and Alice Leavy. The best endorsement Rysher Entertainment could find for its official PR was a quote from Whitley Strieber, author of *Communion* (which detailed his repeated abductions by aliens): "There are things about this footage that are particularly striking. Some of the least known features reported by witnesses are presented here. If this tape is not authentic, then it must have been made by people with very special inside knowledge." Yet these so-called experts are actually a few abduction researchers, a special effects designer, and a former NATO officer. Where was the video analyst or image processing expert?

The one panelist who wasn't mentioned in the official PR was Robert O. Dean. Dean is a former NATO officer, retired from the Army after twenty-seven years as a command sergeant major who served in combat as an infantry unit commander in Korea and Vietnam, and in intelligence field operations in Laos, Cambodia, and North Vietnam.

Dean appeared full-force in the UFO community in the late 1980s when he sued the Pima, Arizona, Country Sheriff's Department for passing him over for the position of emergency services manager. Dean had served fourteen years with FEMA as an emergency services coordinator, and in the complaint filed in the Superior Court of the State of Arizona, Dean's attorney alleges:

> Defendant Dupnik told Defendant Serna that he did not want to hire Plaintiff because of Plaintiff's interest in and/or beliefs about unidentified flying objects (UFOs) and/or his association with people who have an interest in and/or beliefs about UFOs; on that basis, and contrary to the findings and recommendations of the EEO Office, Defendant Serna denied Plaintiff's grievance on October 24, 1990.

An out-of-court settlement was reached, though the details were not included in the stipulation and order for dismissal filed in April 1993. Dean got his promotion, but he immediately quit Emergency Services, and began talking about UFO-related material he claimed to have seen not long after he was commissioned to serve as a NATO intelligence analyst at the Supreme Headquarters Allied Powers Europe (SHAPE) in June 1964.

The NATO study Dean saw was "at least eight inches thick" and entitled "An Assessment: An Evaluation of a Possible Military Threat to Allied Forces Europe." Dean says his "Cosmic Top Secret" security clearance allowed him access to the selectively distributed NATO study while working with the inner command staff with the Supreme Allied Commander Europe.

Dean currently sells a video of a one-hour lecture and slide presentation on the NATO assessment entitled *UFOs: The History, the Reality and the Future.* Dean also coproduced *Interdimensional ETs* with his wife, Cecilia Dean, which proposes that ETs are not only from our own solar system, galaxy, and universe, but from other dimensions. Dean states on his Stargate International website that he is a "dear and good friend" of Richard Boylan, the disbarred psychologist who supports the "Aviary" and "Jesus was an ET" conspiracy theories.

In an interview with Randy Koppang, "Resolving History and the Rights of Man," in 1995, Dean said "Roswell was the tip of an iceberg." "I know of at least a dozen crash retrievals involving bodies and survivors; besides Roswell— our government knew in 1949 essentially the same thing the SHAPE 'Assessment' published in 1964."

Dean claims he's just part of the gentle "trickle" of classified information either being leaked or allowed to be talked about despite the violation of his oath. Dean told Dennis Stacy in a 1994 *Omni* article, "I wanted so badly to copy this thing. I did take a photograph of the cover sheet, which wasn't in and of itself classified. But I didn't want to wind up in Fort Leavenworth. So instead I would go to the bathroom and take notes—surreptitiously, very carefully."

I sent repeated e-mails to Dean's website, Stargate International, asking about his opinion of the Area 51 alien interview, and whether he still believed, as he told Koppang, that "Having been on the inside—not only for 27 years in the Army, but for 14 years working with FEMA—I saw it first hand! We've given away some of our most precious rights: and those are the rights to know and to participate; as enlightened individuals of our Government. They've taken that from us!" I really wanted to hear from Dean since it was yet another link between FEMA and UFOs. But I never got a response.

Capitalizing on Roswell

For some people, money is clearly the motivating factor for becoming involved in UFOs. *The Philadelphia Inquirer* had an item on publisher Bob Guccione, who is said to have paid as much as $200,000 to print photographs of "real aliens" in his September 1996 issue of *Penthouse*. Guccione compared his acquisition to locating "an actual photograph of Jesus Christ hanging on the cross."

Yet on a talk show, Guccione denied that he had paid anything for the photos, which had already been published and debunked in *Fortean Times* in December 1995. Guccione should have known better—his first foray into UFO research was with *Omni* to finance Project Open Book, but it never quite got off the ground.

As for the "alien" photos, they continue to occasionally pop up around the world as "proof" of ETs. But the body has been identified as the model constructed for Paul Davids's made-for-TV film *Roswell* in 1994, now on display in the International UFO Museum in Roswell, New Mexico.

At the celebration of the anniversary of the Roswell crash, people were offered the chance to "sleep at the site where some believe an alien spacecraft crashed 50 years ago." For this privilege, Roswell rancher Hub Corn asked ninety dollars a night. With the number of campers "limited" to two thousand, and the event spread over six nights, the Corns stood to make over a million dollars—if there are people interested in paying for all twelve thousand camping spots.

Estimates are that over one hundred thousand visited Roswell over the Fourth of July weekend, proving there's no end to what people will do to get their "alien fix." If you can't do without one, there's even a four-foot replica of the Roswell alien available in the Sharper Image Christmas catalog for $1,695, which includes the glass chamber.

Unfortunately, too much attention goes to the Roswell case, weakening the efforts to legitimize UFO research because ufologists get caught up in the pro-and-con debate. But people make good money off the Roswell crash, so in the interests of capitalism, maybe it's better that the truth is never known. With the number of "explanations" growing every year, Roswell will inevitably go down in history as a big mythical question mark—right next to the death of Marilyn Monroe and the shooting of JFK.

CHAPTER 7

Sightings at Area 51

.

M ARK FARMER is a pilot and photojournalist, formerly
for the U.S. Coast Guard, so he's seen plenty of
research and development aircraft. But in January 1994
while on a visit to Area 51, Farmer saw something that he
couldn't explain.

It was a Wednesday night—rumored to be the fly night
for black-project aircraft at Area 51. Parked about a mile
and a half off Highway 375 in the Tikaboo Valley behind
Hancock Summit, Farmer relates, "I'm sitting there, and
this light pops up beyond the jumbled hills, south of Freedom Ridge, south of Area 51. It's shimmering, about
twelve to sixteen miles away and the size of my little fin-
gertip held out, one-fourth to one-half degree of angular
distance. I took photographs with 1,250-millimeter, high-
speed film."

The resulting photographs revealed little more than a
light streak in the sky. Even through his Celestron telescope, Farmer says,

I couldn't see the object, only the shell of an electrostatic
discharge. It almost had aspects of St. Elmo's fire, the

static electric discharge you see in a storm. I've seen it
clinging to the mast of a ship, glowing green. But this
was three distinct colors—bright crimson on the bottom,
gold in the center, and greenish-blue on top.

Farmer watched the light for the next hour and forty-five
minutes. "It would hover for ten minutes, drop, then wobble
away—wallowing around, is the best way to put it. Then
it would move instantaneously." A record of Farmer's
sighting is posted on Tom Mahood's Bluefire website,
along with Mahood's statement that he has a lot of respect
for Farmer's "knowledge of aircraft and various forms of
cutting edge technology."

Farmer has been flying since he won a writing contest
at fifteen years old on "Why I Want to Fly." He remembers
that when he was four or five years old, his father, who
worked for NASA, brought home a deep space image of
Earth, and Farmer says, "Somehow I was able to put it
together that we live on that planet."

Farmer has shot an archive of photographs of Area 51
and the Nellis Range, both from the ground and on aerial
fly-bys. His work has graced national magazines such as
Aviation Week and Space Technology, Popular Science,
and *Popular Mechanics.* His image of the near-flooded
Groom Lake revealed that the thirty-thousand-foot Runway
14R-32L is actually built up higher than the lake bed.

As a comparison to his UFO sighting, Farmer also re-
counted his sighting of the infamous "Senior Citizen" flying
near Area 51. "I was in the Pahranagat Valley filling my
car up with gas—of course you never have your camera in
your hand when you need it! I looked up and saw a black
wedge flying to the east—three of them, one after another.
They passed so low that everyone around me was looking
up and pointing."

Once I started looking, I found reports of all kinds of
sightings near the Nellis Range. Glenn Campbell posts the
most reliable reports on the Area 51 section of the Ufomind
website. Other sightings are maintained in the Area 51

Mailing List Archives, where you can find anything from the truly mysterious to anonymous reports and rumors.

Kiefer and Kathie Scott posted their sighting on the Area 51 Mailing List. On the night of Tuesday, January 7, 1997, the Scotts were in the vicinity of Area 51, parked on "some kind of mound that held a huge tank of some sorts." It wasn't long before

> we saw something moving above the north horizon. It was twinkling like a star but had moved enough for both of us to recognize that it wasn't a star. It didn't have a specific flash, just random twinkling. We noticed that it went straight up and down, and back and forth. We also observed a hovering ability on the craft. I know that this is a military installation and that we were probably being watched and or listened to. So I ruled out extraterrestrial activity.

The Scotts describe the aircraft as hovering approximately two thousand feet above the top of the mountain range. Among the maneuvers that were seen were "series of loops and what looked like rolls."

The couple headed in that direction and after driving a few miles on one of the bigger dirt roads, "sure enough we ended right in front of the gate to Area 51." When Kathie Scott took a photograph of the signs warning against taking photographs, a security vehicle lit up and chased them back down the road. The post concludes:

> We then drove off the Extraterrestrial Highway and stopped at a Texaco where a man who had just been interviewed by the Discovery channel, told us about what we may have seen. He said that the military is testing a new stealth fighter that supposedly has hover capabilities. If this is true, I think the military has some sort of craft to steal technology from. I've worked around aircraft for many years and this craft handled like no other I'd seen.

A common sighting at Area 51 has a prosaic explanation. Magnesium flares, which are used in military exercises, are often misidentified. As Campbell explains in the *"Area 51" Viewer's Guide*, "The most important alternate explanation is orange magnesium flares, which are extremely bright and can hover for several minutes. They will wink on, burn a while (suspended on parachute), then go out fairly rapidly. These flares are often launched in groups of 1–4 to illuminate ground exercises."

Thomas Fischer posted a sighting he and his wife had in Rhyolite, Nevada, on November 9, 1994:

> To the north, just beyond a jagged mountain were two or three lights suspended in a horizontal pattern just above the mountain. They were separated by a distance of about a mile or two. They were a brilliant, steady orange-yellow, somewhat like automotive headlights, only more orange and certainly brighter. They appeared to be no more than 3 to 5 miles from us, relative to the mountain. The sight of these lights hovering above and to either side of a mountain maybe 2 miles distant, the surrounding hills bathed in the half moonlight and depicting clear definition to the mountainous terrain, was at once astonishing and frightening.

Campbell noted at the bottom of this report that it sounded very much like orange magnesium flares, yet Fischer adds an unusual twist:

> . . . and as I turned the lights winked and now there were 3 or 4 lights (my wife thought she saw 4; I thought I saw 3), still in the same horizontal line but in different positions and spanning a larger width than before. This phenomenon occurred almost literally in the blink of an eye. There was no flash or burst of energy prior to the split; only the wink. The multiple objects all retained the same apparent size and characteristics.

During my visit to the southern Nevada desert in February, I saw numerous magnesium flares dropped over Tikaboo Valley as well as, surprisingly, east of U.S. Highway 375, well outside the Nellis Range. The orange flares that I observed seemed to wink as they appeared in formation, then gave off a steady glow.

One of the early sightings on Ufomind is in Campbell's post "UFO Sightings in Lincoln County in 70s & 80s," including one from an acquaintance, a longtime driver for UPS. Campbell claims he has been driving up and down U.S. 93 for years, and he is a private pilot who is very familiar with operations on the Nellis Range.

Campbell's "knowledgeable witness" had several sightings. One night in 1975, about 2:00 or 3:00 A.M., he was driving on U.S. 93 approximately forty-five miles southeast of Groom Lake. Campbell recorded that the driver watched as

a bright golden orange ball descended slowly in front of him. It appeared to him to be about 100 yards away and to be the size of "the front end of a car." He and a couple of other cars pulled over to watch it. Although it was originally descending, it stopped, hovered, and then took off upward at great speed. He couldn't see any details in the object, except that it was spinning. It almost seemed like the object was reacting to his presence.

Nellis UFO on Film

The same year Farmer saw the UFO over the jumbled hills south of Area 51, another UFO was recorded over the Nellis Range by a camera at Area S-30. This remote tracking location helps monitor the 7,700 square miles above the range, recording jet-fighter training and tactical exercises. Usually the cameras at the tracking stations are deactivated when black-project exercises are under way.

On film, the UFO is a white light that seems to jump around erratically, probably due to the automated tracking of the camera trying to follow its abrupt movements. Images of the Nellis UFO were posted at the OVNI Chapterhouse website, which explained, "The videotape was smuggled out by base employees at considerable risk and presented to the TV show 'Sightings.' All of the video and audio clips are from captures of the 'Sightings' episode."

The "Sightings" episode aired in April 1996, over a year before the "Strange Universe" broadcast of the alien interview, so perhaps it was this story that inspired "Victor's" claims that he smuggled the tape out of the base "wrapped around his hand."

The Nellis film shows the same sort of electrostatic discharge as Farmer described in his UFO. According to OVNI Chapterhouse, "The object was photographed by a very good remote controlled fixed mounted camera, but still has that fuzzy sort of gassy cloud cotton-ball look about it which seems to be common among some UFOs."

The shape of the object appears to shift and change almost from frame to frame. At one point, the UFO appears to be four white glowing spheres separated by a dark X in the middle.

This part of the Nellis image is remarkably similar both in shape and the surrounding glow to a Brazilian UFO videotaped in 1991. As John Velez of Intruders Foundation Online posted on UFO UpDates in April 1997:

The Brazil video was obtained from a local television news broadcast. (A Brazilian researcher sent it to Budd [Hopkins] 5 years ago, and I blew the dust bunnies off of it and reviewed it.) I guess the Brazilian media aren't as "paranoid" as our homegrown version. The Brazilian "sky show" lasted over an hour (as per the anchorman reporting), and according to him, the event was witnessed by thousands.

I'm sure there are alternate explanations for these sightings—there always are!—but I wasn't able to find any. Then again, NORAD hasn't offered (yet) an explanation

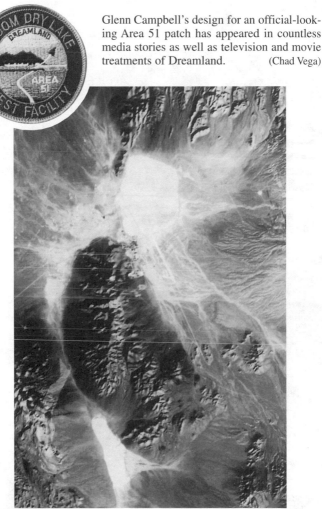

Glenn Campbell's design for an official-looking Area 51 patch has appeared in countless media stories as well as television and movie treatments of Dreamland. (Chad Vega)

This image from a U.S. satellite taken in December 1991 of Groom dry lake north of Papoose dry lake was never authorized to be released to the public. You can clearly see the runways crossing the southwestern edge of Groom Lake, and the structures of the air base. On Papoose Lake, you can see the "spur" of the mountain ridge on the eastern side, with no clear roads or structures on the dry lake.

(Courtesy of Center for UFO Stories [CUFOS])

Glenn Campbell with Sensor.   (Mark Farmer/Agent X Enterprises)

Robot Security Camera. These sophisticated electronic devices secure the borders of Area 51. No need for a bulky "Berlin Wall" in the Nevada desert in the twenty-first century. Some people who have crossed the border unawares have been held at gunpoint for hours by unidentified "cammo dudes" until the Lincoln County Sheriffs deputies can arrive to arrest them for trespassing.   (Mark Farmer/Agent X Enterprises)

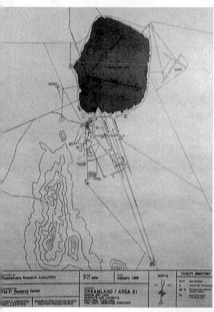

Groom Dry Lake Runways and Taxiways. (Chad Vega)

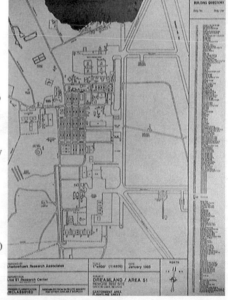

Remote Test Site: Cantonment Area and Flightline Areas. When the 1991 satellite image was anonymously given to Glenn Campbell, he ordered blueprints to be made by Shadowhawk Research Associates. Now the Area 51 Research Center offers these detailed blueprints of the secret base to the rest of the world out of Rachel, Nevada 89001.

(Chad Vega)

Looking due west, this perfectly graded dirt highway points straight toward Groom Lake inside Area 51. In the distance, just beyond the jog in the road, lies a gully where the border signs warn that trespassers may be shot, while a Jeep Cherokee usually waits nearby out of sight.

(Kelly Beaton)

The blinding white Groom Lake Road is far more distinctive than the so-called Extraterrestrial Highway that runs north–south along the border of Nellis Range.

(Kelly Beaton)

The *Popular Science* cover story by Stuart F. Brown, "Searching for the Secrets of Groom Lake," was one of the media stories that publicized the secret base to the world. According to official Federal Aviation Administration pilots' charts and U.S. Geological Survey topographic maps, the air base doesn't exist. (Chad Vega)

The Interceptors are an ad hoc pack of plane spotters who seek out research and development aircraft. This photograph was taken on Freedom Ridge before the Air Force completed its land grab. Jim Goodall is in the center in camouflage, with Glenn Campbell to his left, and Bill Sweetman, to Campbell's left, wearing binoculars.

(Mark Farmer/Agent X Enterprises)

The day after the *Roswell Daily Record* publicized the army press release that a flying saucer had been found, the official retraction from General Ramey hit the headlines of papers across the country.

(Fortean Picture Library

This shows the difficulty in capturing a good image of a UFO. Farmer photographed this UFO at approximately 11:00 P.M. on January 11, 1994, over the jumbled hills south of Groom Lake using a tripod-mounted Olympus OM.4F with a Celestron C-5t 1250 mm F10 lens with Fuji HR 1600 film @ 3200. The color shades from a brilliant green at the top to golden yellow in the middle and red at the bottom.
(Mark Farmer/Agent X Enterprises)

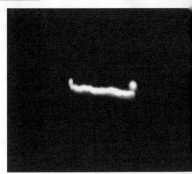

Mark Farmer edged into restricted airspace to capture this breathtaki view of a temporarily wet Groom Lake with the base beyond, taken fro the east at 10,000 feet.

(Mark Farmer/Agent X Enterprise

Large black and silver globes were seen over Basel on August 7, 1566, and were immortalized forever by the proto-media in a small printed pamphlet. Five years earlier, Hans Glaser carved a similar woodcut of the "very frightful spectacle" seen in the sky over Nuremberg, Germany, on April 4, 1561.

(Fortean Picture Library)

This triangular UFO was spotted by radar and visual sightings on March 30–31, 1990. The Belgian military announced that two F-16s gave chase, yet they were unable to close with the UFO for a positive identification. The mystery continues today with these distinctive triangular UFOs most recently seen over Phoenix in March 1997.

(CUFOS)

This is a rare photograph of a tunnel entering Rainier Mesa complete with narrow-gauge railroad, ventilation system and plenty of power. Bob Lazar claims he worked in an underground complex built into the mountain next to Papoose Lake where he claims the U.S. military is back-engineering alien flying saucers. Researchers such as Tom Mahood say that Lazar's story is an elaboration on the vast network of tunnels in the neighboring Nevada Test Site.

(CUFOS)

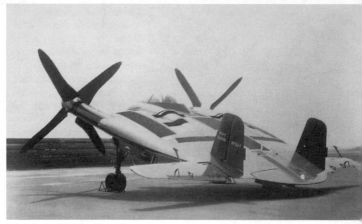

Vought XF5U-1. The Navy designed a number of "Flying Pancake" aircraft beginning in the 1940s. This version never got off the ground. You can see on the far right-hand horizon the distinctive desert landscape where these secret aircraft were tested.

(National Air and Space Museum)

Vought V-173. This version of the "Flying Pancake" did make it off the ground. It's easy to see how these secret aircraft could be mistaken for UFOs if seen from the air or the ground. These Flying Pancakes may also be the basis for rumors that the American government is engineering flying saucers based on alien technology.

(National Air and Space Museum)

for the UFOs that appeared over sensitive military and missile installations in North America in the winter of 1975.

We know that as of December 1952, the CIA still hadn't identified the UFOs that appeared over military installations. CAUS was given a declassified memo dated December 1952 from the assistant director of scientific intelligence for the CIA to then CIA Director Walter Bedell Smith, stating, "Sightings of unidentified objects at great altitudes and traveling at high speeds in the vicinity of major U.S. defense installations are of such nature that they are not attributable to natural phenomena or known types of aerial vehicles."

Research and Development Aircraft

Based on records released by projects Sign and Grudge to CAUS in late 1996, Barry Greenwood believes that in 1948, the military's best guess was that a "vast majority of the objects" were "similar to flying wing-type aircraft of low aspect ratio (i.e. thin or flat)." The documents Greenwood received were

> recommending reference should be made to past experiments by the Air Force's Engineering Division and to present experiments by the Navy. In other words many of the UFO reports could have been caused by the sighting of experimental vehicles by the military. We can relate this to modern reports of strange aircraft near Area 51.

One example of an early R&D craft is the Chance-Vought "Flying Flapjack" or "Navy Flounder" shown in *Jane's All the World's Aircraft*. This pre–jet age aircraft took off vertically, and could fly from 35 mph up to 400 mph.

Some ufologists claim that our government R&D projects would be smart to disguise their surveillance aircraft in "flying saucer" shapes since sightings would then be discounted or ridiculed—if they were reported at all. Indeed, many aircraft tend to have a saucerlike shape from certain angles—including, notably, the stealth fighter. NASA's X-36 is also disclike when seen from head on.

But what about the Belgian UFOs—those black triangles that are alleged to be R&D aircraft? Mark Farmer says, "Those were perfect triangles. There's no R&D craft that I know of that are perfect triangles, except bad rumors of the Sentinel aircraft."

Stealth technology was first developed after World War II, when aircraft designers looked for ways that bombers could avoid radar detection. According to most accounts, this was the beginning of Area 51—when Lockheed arrived to develop the U-2 spy plane. Lockheed's famed "Skunk Works" also developed the early stealth aircraft, the SR-71 Blackbird.

It wasn't until the 1960s and 1970s that materials able to absorb radar energy were developed that were strong enough to be used on combat aircraft. These early carbon-fiber composites and high-strength plastics reduced radar signature reflection, making the craft essentially transparent.

The shape of the aircraft also needed to be designed to direct radar energy in the least revealing directions. This meant avoiding right angles, sharp curves, and large surfaces. The ordnance was carried internally, and engine intakes and exhausts were set flush with the external surface of the aircraft.

Stealth aircraft can't use radar for navigation because the emissions can be intercepted. Instead the craft relies on inertial guidance or nonemitting navigational systems such as laser radar, which scans the ground ahead of the craft with a thin, almost undetectable laser beam.

Steve Douglass wrote in "Project Black: Monitoring the Airwaves for Secret Aircraft," posted on the Intercept website, "In 1974, the Defense Advanced Research Projects Agency (DARPA) asked five major military aircraft manufacturers to submit designs for developing a low observable (stealth) fighter aircraft. The team studied and evaluated at least 10 separate 'black' aircraft programs."

Farmer agrees that President Carter is the one who deserves credit for the development of the Stealth, though Reagan is the one known for his arms buildup. "It was in the 1980s that Area 51 took off and the large runways were created," he notes.

The existence of the stealth program was first announced by the U.S. government in 1980, and the first operational aircraft designed with stealth technology was Lockheed's single-seat F-117A (1983). Six years later, Northrop's B-2 strategic bomber was in the air.

Both aircraft have unconventional shapes to reduce radar reflection. The design of the B-2 is a series of complex, large-radius, curved surfaces, while the F-117A is chiseled into numerous small, flat planes. The F-117A has a short, pyramid-shaped fuselage and sharply swept wings, while the B-2 was a "flying-wing design" only slightly longer than a fighter yet with the enormous wingspan of the B-52.

When the Air Force retired the SR-71 Blackbird, they claimed it was because they could now rely on satellite surveillance. But spy satellites have a limited fuel supply for shifting orbits and they can be thwarted by something as simple as heavy cloud cover—so reconnaissance aircraft will probably never go out of style.

The Federation of American Scientists (FAS) released a 1992 report entitled "Mystery Aircraft" that concluded black-project aircraft probably existed but couldn't be proven until the government declassified them. The problem was due to "a signal to noise ratio" when dealing with secret aircraft: "It is useful to consider mystery aircraft not simply as an engineering product, but also as a sociological and epistemological phenomenon."

Black-project craft are *intended* to be stealthy and difficult to spot. They fly very fast and usually very high. Often the only indication is the sonic boom, and then it's too late—the aircraft has already passed by.

But military monitors have a better way of finding

stealth aircraft than by watching through binoculars. Just as the radio frequencies revealed to me that security at Area 51 is using FEMA frequencies, the airways can signal a patient scanner that a stealth approaches.

Steve Douglass says that's how he was alerted to a black-project craft at an annual military exercise, "Operation Roving Sands." Douglass was monitoring the airwaves with his Radio Shack Pro-2006 digital scanner while filming the activity over the White Sands Missile Range, when he heard something different. This wasn't the usual stealth F-117s he had tracked—it was a slower sound.

Douglass describes what happened in his article "TR-3A Project Black":

> I had been taking some video of some B-1Bs taking off for a night strike on the range when a triangular-flying wing-type aircraft was spotted reconnoitering the area. Although it was after dusk, I was able to shoot some video of it. It doesn't reproduce well in print and is a fuzzy image on video. But with the help of computer enhancement we can make out the general shape of the craft. I would estimate that it was a flying wing-type aircraft about half the size of the B-2, with a slightly different planform. . . . The aircraft moved slowly and silently as it observed the B-1s hitting targets on the White Sands Missile Range.

Douglass only had seven seconds of tape left in his video camera, but he managed to get an image of the secret TR-3A or "Black Manta." Military monitors believe the Black Manta was used in the Gulf War, but the Air Force won't admit that it exists.

The Black Manta is believed to be a triangular-shaped aircraft about forty-five feet long and fifteen feet high, with a sixty-five-foot wingspan. The aircraft is described as a "span-loaded-flying-wing design" or "bat-wing stealth." According to Douglass's sources, Northrop signed a contract with the Air Force in 1982 to build one hundred tactical stealth aircraft, which could be the Black Manta that he filmed. As Douglass later said, "Seven seconds. You live for those moments. You listen all those hours for that kind of gold nugget."

Douglass and his wife Teresa are avid military monitors, publishing *Intercepts*, a newsletter for monitors. Their loose network of military monitors refers to themselves as the Groom Lake Interceptors, and includes Glenn Campbell, Mark Farmer, Bill Sweetman, Paul McGinnis, Jim Goodall, Stuart Brown, Phil Patton, and Tom Mahood, with Jeri Mahood as an honorary member. A well-known Interceptor, David Darlington, a staff writer for *The New Yorker,* wrote *The Dreamland Chronicles: The Legend of America's Most Secret Military Base*, 1997.

Steve Douglass offers the Groom Lake Interceptors space on his website, Project Black: The Intercepts Files, to post their articles. He also runs a BBS and operates the Above Top Secret forum (under Aviation, Military) on America Online. He is a stringer for CBS, and monitors fire and police channels for the *Amarillo Globe Times*, where he spent six years as a news photographer. He is also the author of *The Comprehensive Guide to Military Monitoring,* with everything the astute listener needs to know.

Military monitors are often confused with UFO devotees. Even Phil Patton remarked on how Douglass's framegrabbed print of the bat-wing stealth looked like a flying saucer. Douglass says the word *UFO* doesn't necessarily mean flying saucer: "Yes, these are objects, they fly, and they are unidentified."

Aurora

It was also by monitoring with scanners that Douglass was able to capture the first pictures of the "donut on a rope" contrail associated with the rumored Aurora reconnaissance plane. Phil Patton describes the event in an article in *Wired,* "Stealth Watchers":

In 1989 Douglass picked up communications between "Joshua control" and an aircraft calling itself "Gaspipe." He realized it was flying close by. He ran out of his house, slapping film into his Canon AE-1. He could hear the rumbling sound of the engine, even feel it in his chest, but all he saw of the craft itself was "a silver glint of light, a metallic shape." Even with a 400-mm telephoto lens he managed to photograph only the plane's contrail with the Aurora's purportedly characteristic "donut on a rope" shape, suggesting an advanced pulse-jet engine. *Aviation Week* ran the photographs.

Three years earlier, in 1986, a censor forgot to black out a line in the public version of the Pentagon budget—a hefty billion-dollar budget item billed to "Aurora." Others, like Mark Farmer, insist that this new spy plane is known by a different Pentagon designation, "Senior Citizen."

Regardless of the name, military monitors were already alerted and looking around to see if a new secret aircraft would appear. That's when Chris Gibson, an expert aircraft observer having served for twelve years with the Royal Observer Corps' international aircraft recognition team, saw a strange wedge-shaped aircraft over the North Sea.

It was in August 1989, and at the time, Gibson was on the oil rig *Galveston Key* where he was working as a drilling engineer. In a recent posting to a military aircraft mailing list, Gibson described the wedge-aircraft, which was refueling with a KC-135 and escorted by two F-111s:

I am trained in instant recognition, but this triangle had me stopped dead. My first thought was that it was another F-111, but there was no "gaps," it was too long and it didn't look like one. . . . My next thought was that it was an F-117, as the highly swept planform of the F-117 had just been made public. Again the triangle was too long and had no gaps. After considering and rejecting a Mirage IV, I was totally out of ideas. Here was an aircraft, flying overhead, not too high and not particularly fast. A recognition gift and I was clueless. This was a new experience.

At the time, Gibson was writing an aircraft recognition manual and he had in his briefcase a Danish Luftmelder-korpset "Flykendingsbog," one of the most comprehensive aircraft recognition manuals available. But the wedge didn't match anything in that book either.

Gibson had signed the Official Secrets Act, so he didn't tell anyone about the aircraft except for Peter Edwards, a group officer in the ROC, and other members of the recognition team "in the hope that they could shed some light on the subject." Then Gibson saw an illustration from *Jane's Defense Weekly* that matched what he had seen, and he contacted Bill Sweetman. "Bill reckons it was Aurora, Agent X [Mark Farmer] reckons it was the FB-119. I don't know what it was. It is the only aircraft I have ever seen that I could not identify. Pete Edwards told Bill Sweetman that if I didn't know what this aircraft was, it isn't in any book."

Sonic booms from the testing of an unknown hypersonic aircraft were first heard in 1990 in California. They were so loud, they were recorded on earthquake detection equipment, leaving unique seismic signatures. As Douglass points out in "Project Black," another essay on the Intercept website: "The seismic sensors indicated the approximate direction of travel of the aircraft was over California and into Nevada, again pointing to the super-secret test base at Groom Lake as being the possible base of operations."

This hypersonic aircraft is estimated to reach extreme speeds of Mach 8, which means it must fly beyond the testing airspace over Nevada and California. That's probably why Gibson saw the aircraft in the North Sea, and why there have been sightings in other countries. According to the February 1992 issue of the *Scotsman Sunday Post,* high-altitude tests of an American hypersonic aircraft have been spotted on radar over the North Atlantic and are believed to be landing at the U.S. Special Forces base at

Machrihanish, Scotland. Glenn Campbell says in the *"Area 51" Viewer's Guide,* "The safest bet for an unacknowledged aircraft operating around Groom would be a batwing Stealth, a cross between the F-117A and B-2."

Yet it was the Aurora that Chuck Clark, a local resident in Rachel, Nevada, claims to have seen at Area 51. Clark has also seen a UFO while observing near the "black mailbox," on the turnoff to Medlin Ranch. Clark saw a bright yellow-white pulsating light that rose up from the mountains south of Area 51. It hovered and began to sink, much like a flare, but as it neared the ground on Clark's side of the ridge, it suddenly took off at a right angle at rapid speed, traversing 4.8 miles of the desert in one and a half seconds—he estimates from 9,000 to 14,000 miles per hour.

Unlike the UFO, the Aurora that Clark saw wasn't in the air—it was in a hangar at Groom Lake. Clark's sighting was subsequently questioned by British aviation observer Chris Gibson, as reported in the *Desert Rat,* July 1995:

> Chuck Clark, "Astronomer," has turned up in a British scientific magazine called *Focus.* He claims he got a look into one of the hangars at Groom, having walked to a viewpoint "undetected." He says he saw a black, delta-shaped craft, about 130ft long, all in the space of 20 seconds.

As Gibson points out, the hangars are twelve miles away, and even through a telescope, Clark doesn't explain "how he could come up with the length of 130ft AND see that the vehicle was a delta." Clark's reported aircraft was also twice the length of the one Gibson saw.

Chuck Clark was laughing like a kid the first time I saw him. He and a buddy, Bill, had been up on some nearby buttes photographing B-52s when one flew right over them, "not twenty feet above the top of the ridge" where they stood. As the craft passed over, the pilot dropped a load of chaff packs—radar-deflecting material that is usually dropped to confuse enemy missiles. This time it had been dropped to delight the photographers.

Jim Wilson cited Clark (along with Bob Lazar) in the *Popular Mechanics* article in June 1997 as providing additional proof that Area 51 had been abandoned: "Chuck Clark, author of the *Area 51 & S4 Handbook*, tells me he thinks the airfield's last secret plane, the Aurora, left a year ago." Of course, Area 51 didn't go anywhere—Wilson simply got lost and made a big jump in logic to reach his conclusion.

Later the same year that Chuck Clark says he saw the Aurora, a "holiday-maker," David Morris, took a photograph that appeared on the cover of the British UFO magazine *Encounters*. The photograph was of an Air Force KC-135 strato-tanker refueling a black flying triangle. *Encounters* explained, "David had gone out to photograph the sunset but due to a double cloud layer had no chance. His attention was caught by the loud noise of planes out at sea. They appeared to be in a pack formation, heading north. He took quick aim and captured an image."

Aviation journalist Bill Sweetman, author of many books on stealth technology, contacted Chris Gibson, who investigated the story, quickly proving that it was a hoax. Sweetman said, "The pic was produced by Bill Rose, an astronomer and photographer, for *Astronomy Now*, a UK magazine. It illustrated an article by Rose on UFO photos and how easily they could be faked."

What's in a Name?

One of the first things Mark Farmer insisted when I spoke to him was that everyone should stop misidentifying these secret aircraft. His opinion is also posted on the Area 51 Archives in March 1997:

There has never been and will never be an "aurora" or TR-3A. The Aurora budget line item request for "a hypersonic air-breathing follow-on to the SR-71" was nothing more than a cloak over Lockheed's nonwinning stealth bomber design. The TR-3A designation makes no sense since the TR or tactical reconnaissance moniker is no longer used (the U-2 was briefly designated TR-1 then back to ·U-2R/S). The stumpy bat-wing craft that Douglass and myself have spotted is out there, but who knows what it is, who built it and what it does (strike/recon and Northrop-Grumman is a good guess).

Paul McGinnis agreed, after looking through a list of secret defense research and development programs taken from the National Defense Authorization Act for Fiscal Year 1993 (House of Representatives Report 102–527). McGinnis posted his opinion on June 8, 1993, on the Area 51 Mailing List and sci.skeptic newsgroup:

Reading the budget documents shows me that the aerospace press may be mistaken in identifying "Aurora" as "Senior Citizen." According to the '93 budget, "Senior Citizen" is listed as a tactical aircraft (presumably the TR-3A) while another project (under intelligence funding) describes "Senior Year" operations. So, "Aurora" may actually be "Senior Year."

Some aviation experts say the XB-70, not the Aurora, leaves the strange contrails that are caused by a new propulsion technology called "PDWE" or Pulsed Detonation Wave Engine. There have been multiple sightings of a large delta-shaped aircraft, approximately two hundred feet long. This XB-70 type craft could be used to launch a transatmospheric reconnaissance vehicle that enters low earth orbit at high speeds, streaking across enemy nations above the range of defensive weapons.

Others say that Aurora flies without a pilot. There have been numerous remote-controlled development projects in recent years, including, notably, a 1997 announcement in *Popular Science* that NASA is currently testing the Hyper-X, a twelve-foot-long unpiloted prototype aircraft. The

Hyper-X is designed to fly hypersonic speeds of Mach 5, or 3,600 mph plus, and four are said to be contracted at $150 million each.

The largest unmanned aircraft being built is Global Hawk, unveiled at Teledyne Ryan Aeronautical in San Diego in early 1997. This craft has a wingspan of 116 feet and a range of 14,000 miles and will be used for reconnaissance.

Another interesting unpiloted aircraft comes from NASA and the U.S. Army. According to an April 1997 release from NASA News, their new "Free Flight Rotorcraft Research Vehicle" (FFRRV) is a miracle of modern surveillance, carrying a movie camera, still camera, video downlinks, and infrared cameras. The FFRRV is basically a remote-controlled helicopter that reportedly could be used for "a wide range of tasks" including emergency services often performed by FEMA, such as hazardous spill inspection, fire surveillance, crowd security, border patrol, and emergency medical delivery.

Aviation Week in February 1994 confirmed that prototypes of various stealth helicopters have been tested at the Groom Lake base. In the *"Area 51" Viewer's Guide,* Campbell adds, "Groom Lake has been used in the past to test ultralight aerial reconnaissance platforms. In theory, these stealthy flying wings might loiter over a target for days."

All this speculation finally got to the Secretary of the Air Force, Donald Rice, who issued a denial in an attempt to discredit the existence of the Aurora. In a letter to the editor of *The Washington Post,* Rice stated:

Let me reiterate what I have said publicly for months. The Air Force has no such program either known as "Aurora" or by any other name. And if such a program existed elsewhere, I'd know about it—and I don't. Furthermore, the Air Force has neither created nor released cover stories to protect any program like "Aurora." I can't be more unambiguous than that.

Rice went on to explain that when the "latest spate" of "Aurora" stories appeared, he asked his staff to look into each alleged "sighting" to see what could be "fueling the fire." Along with the sightings that didn't have enough information to investigate,

> Other accounts, such as of sonic booms over California, the near collision with a commercial airliner and strange shapes loaded into Air Force aircraft are easily explained and we have done so numerous times on the record. I have never hedged a denial over any issue related to the so-called "Aurora." the Air Force has no aircraft or aircraft program remotely similar to the capabilities being attributed to the "Aurora." While I know this letter will not stop the speculation, I feel that I must set the record straight.

Contrary to what Rice insists, however, military monitors point out that the sonic booms and near collision with the commercial airliner have not yet been explained.

Obviously it's not the "enemy" the Pentagon is trying to hide secret craft from. It's the American taxpayers who are being kept in the dark about how much money is being funneled into these military aircraft. Congress may also be complicit in allowing huge budgets to pass, and inevitable rumors of kickbacks and wasteful expenditures cling to government spending. As Paul McGinnis posted on June 8, 1993:

> To get more of a feel for how "black" programs operate, I read several reports prepared by the House Armed Services Committee about defense procurement, the Navy's canceled A-12 Stealth fighter (the drawing of it looks like a two-man flying pizza slice), and the B-2 Stealth fighter (which indicated that key members of Congress knew a good deal and appear to have supported it because subcontracts were given in 46 states and affected 383 Congressional districts).

Observation

Mark Farmer sums up the frustration of trying to determine what UFOs are this way: "When it comes down to it, what do we really have? We have anecdotal evidence from qualified observers—beyond that there's nothing. Oh, there's a few radiation burns or marks, but the case rests on what we've seen."

When you're asking questions about observation, who better to study the UFO phenomenon than a perceptual psychologist? Dr. Richard F. Haines, Ph.D., has been a scientist for NASA since 1967, working for two decades at the Ames Research Center on "Human Factors in Space" research studies. Haines has also made an extensive study of aircraft pilots and how they perceive objects and/or atmospheric phenomena under various sorts of stress, such as g-forces or the effects of carbon monoxide. While doing so, Haines amassed over three thousand reports of UFO sightings by pilots.

When Dennis Stacy interviewed Dr. Haines in 1988 for *Air and Space Magazine* Haines agreed "that normal perception isn't infallible. Very bright objects, for example, can appear to be much nearer than they actually are. Autokinetic or self-generated, movement of the eyeball can make distant objects like stars and planets appear to move."

Glenn Campbell's current rule of thumb is that objects that appear to "jump" less than the width of the moon can usually be explained by autokinetic illusions. It helps if you can establish reference points in the distant mountains or nearby structures (or the stars if you have sufficient astronomical knowledge). Be aware that aircraft strobes are also mistaken for UFOs at great distances, because the eye can see two or three "ghost" objects at the same time when light is being strobed.

Campbell points out that even cameras aren't 100 percent reliable. Saucerlike spots can appear on pictures because of a defect in the film emulsion or on the final print.

If the saucer shape is bright, it could be a case of lens flare, a light leak in the camera, or a reflection from outside. Yet in the *"Area 51" Viewer's Guide,* Campbell concedes, "Nonetheless, we should not entirely discount the possibility that the camera might see something that the eye does not. For one thing, the camera has a wider field of view, at least for detailed objects, than the eye does at any one instance."

Cameras also can capture events that happen very fast, faster than your visual centers can register. And film is sensitive to a slightly different spectrum from that of the human eye, and could distinguish a spot that we would be unable to see.

The Mutual UFO Network has established ten handy ground rules for what to do when you sight a UFO. MUFON has investigators in all fifty states and around the world standing by to check into people's sightings.

If you have a camcorder or camera handy, then definitely record the event. Prop the camera on a stable surface—your car or a fence—to steady the frame. MUFON recommends, "Try to keep reference points in the field of view, as this will aid researchers in analyzing the film. If you do not have a camera or camcorder then draw pictures of what you saw and the area around it."

Many people stake out hot areas and watch for UFOs, and they carry tape recorders so they can describe the event as it happens. Again, this includes reference points so that someone can return to the spot and listen to the tape, reconstructing the events as they happened. Or you can jot down notes of your position relative to the UFO and its movements.

Count the seconds between movements—e.g., it took three seconds for the object to move from the pine tree by the fence to just left of the chimney. You can hold your hand out to judge how many fingers above the horizon the object is.

MUFON suggests using the same technique to get a visual reference for the size of the UFO. Reach out your hand at arm's length and estimate what sort of object you would have to hold to just cover the UFO: a quarter? a penny? a dime? an aspirin? Or would it take something bigger? a golf ball? a baseball? or a tennis ball?

If there are multiple witnesses, MUFON believes it's best not to discuss the sighting until everyone has written down or recorded what they saw. Since only an estimated one in ten people reports their sighting, MUFON urges everyone to contact a UFO research organization for further investigation. UFO sightings appear in waves, so each one is more important than you might think in establishing a pattern of appearance or occurrence.

CHAPTER 8

Sightings by Pilots and Astronauts

SINCE THE best evidence of the UFO phenomenon is eyewitness testimony, who qualifies as the best observers? Obviously, it's people who are in the air, flying alongside the unidentified objects, attempting to intercept them and interacting with their evasive movements.

Even the term "flying saucer" came from an early pilot sighting of a UFO—when Kenneth Arnold reported seeing nine crescent-shaped objects skimming at high speed over Washington's Cascade Mountains in June 1947. Arnold was also probably the first pilot to regret the publicity that came with his sighting, later commenting, "If I ever see again a phenomenon of that sort, even if it's a 10-story building, I won't say a word about it."

Pilots have been known to die while involved in UFO sightings. Perhaps the most famous case is Captain Thomas F. Mantell's crash in his F-51 Mustang in 1948. Mantell was investigating an unidentified object near Godman Field at Fort Knox, Kentucky. Project Blue Book proposed that Mantell succumbed to hypoxia, or oxygen starvation, and crashed while chasing the planet Venus.

Later evidence indicated Mantell was pursuing a top-secret, high-atmosphere Skyhook balloon. The balloons, designed for upper-atmosphere research, were later used by the CIA for surveillance.

Tony Dodd interviewed a contemporary of Mantell, James F. Duesler, for "The Fatal Flight of Thomas Mantell" in Great Britain's *UFO Magazine*. Duesler was a former captain in the U.S. Army Air Corps, stationed at Godman Field (Fort Knox) in 1948, serving as an investigator of air crashes. Duesler claimed that he never issued an official statement concerning the Mantell crash, though one by the Department of Defense has his name on it. Instead, Duesler insists, "The damage pattern was not consistent with an aircraft of this type crashing into the ground. The official report said that Mantell had blacked out due to lack of oxygen. This may well have been the case, but the aircraft came down in a strange way."

Dr. Richard F. Haines, perceptual psychologist with the NASA Ames Research Center, is also interested in pilot fatalities connected with UFOs. Haines published a book in 1987 called *The Melbourne Episode: Case Study of a Missing Pilot*. The pilot, Frederick Valentich, was a flight instructor with the Air Training Corps in Melbourne, Australia, when he was killed in the crash of his rented Cessna 182 while pursuing, or being pursued by, an alleged UFO.

Haines's collection of UFO sightings grew out of his work with pilots while performing focused-vision research, a necessary part of designing cockpits of the future. Naturally, while discussing the strange things pilots saw while they were flying, they ended up reporting UFOs. From 1986 to 1988, while Haines was chief of the Space Human Factors Office for NASA/Ames, he compiled AIRCAT, a computerized catalog that listed more than three thousand UFO sightings by aviators for the previous forty years. He is currently still gathering reports and is looking for help in computerizing the data.

Haines has also written *Observing UFOs* (1980), a handbook of methodology for accurate observation, and he was the editor of *UFO Phenomena and the Behavioral Scientist* (1979), a collection of psychologically oriented essays on UFOs. More recently, Haines, a Fund for UFO Research board member, wrote a scientific report for FUFOR entitled *Project Delta: A Study of Multiple UFO Sightings* containing more than four hundred reports by two or more witnesses of UFO sightings. According to Haines, most sightings that involve at least two witnesses and last at least five minutes are good enough to eliminate a number of explanations, such as meteors and balloons.

In an interview for *Air and Space Magazine* in early 1988, Haines told Dennis Stacy that pilots make the most reliable witnesses: "They have a unique vantage point simply by being in the air, if for no other reason than if the phenomenon is between your eyes and the ground, you can calculate the slant range, and you're establishing an absolute maximum distance the object could be away. You can't do that with the object against the sky background."

The way we see external events depends on the body's perception of itself in space, so acceleration and inertial forces can sometimes disrupt the inner ear's sense of balance and lead to optical illusions. Yet Haines contends that many induced illusions are short-lived and cannot account for the majority of AIRCAT's cases:

> If a pilot describes a disk-shaped airform with no visible means of propulsion pacing his right wing for 30 minutes, doing everything he's doing—and I have plenty of cases like that—then that's not an optical illusion, it's not a bird or balloon or meteor, it's not any of those prosaic explanations. We don't know what it is necessarily but we know quite clearly what it isn't.

Haines has gathered evidence of the phenomenon from the readings made by various electromagnetic sensors onboard the aircrafts. The cases in AIRCAT include events that were detected by ground or airborne radar, and sometimes they are accompanied by recordings of radio static or brief engine interruption.

In the Computer UFO Network CUFON interview posted in September 1995, Haines says that the "chief goal" of ufology today should be to "stay focused on the current phenomena and disregard mythology." As for the future of UFO research, he maintains, "Unless we can recruit fresh, creative, new talent from many different areas (science, social science, theology, etc.) there won't be a future as we now know it. It will drift into entertainment media."

Other UFO researchers agree with Dr. Haines and are currently gathering pilot reports and UFO-aircraft encounter cases, including Marco Orlandi, Victor Kean, Dominique Weinstein, and others. Weinstein's "Aircraft/UFO Encounters Catalogue" contains 920 cases from 1916 to present, contributed by over a dozen researchers. The catalogue is available from Project 1947.

Pilots who report UFOs often take a risk with their flying career. There was a time when a pilot was grounded if he claimed to have seen a UFO. Yet when the best witnesses are afraid to step forward for fear of persecution, that only buries the problem deeper.

Jacques Vallée talks about a man he interviewed who was a "very-high ranking naval officer" and at one time a test pilot. When Vallee asked why the officer hadn't reported his three UFO sightings when according to regulations he was supposed to, the officer replied: "Maybe I was, but if they have the slightest doubt about what you are seeing up there, you are [considered to be] crazy—they won't let you near the cockpit of an experimental plane."

Actually, that's why I got interested in exploring the UFO phenomenon in the first place—when I heard about a pilot who refused to speculate on something right in front of his eyes because of the stigma against UFOs.

It started when my parents saw a light remarkably similar to the one Mark Farmer saw over the Nellis Range. Ann and Bob Wright were in their former home south of the Superstition Mountains in Arizona (east of Phoenix) when they saw a glowing object hanging directly over the mountain. It had three vibrant colors—ruby red on the bottom, white in the middle, and green on top. It was about three-quarters the size of a thumbnail held out at arm's length. They watched it for more than two hours through the spotting scope that sat in their front window. The globe continued to hover over the mountain while the stars moved behind it. After a while, two smaller lights rose up and hovered near the larger one.

They lived in a fairly deserted area, with only about five neighbors on their dirt road, but one of them happened to be a commercial airline pilot. When my parents called him, the pilot went outside along with everyone else—seven or eight people in all. He only took one look before turning away. All he would say is, "We don't talk about things like that."

NASA Video and Audio Recordings

If pilots make good observers, how much better are astronauts? They go into space, where there are fewer distortion effects from the atmosphere and ionosphere. More important, astronauts are up there for hours and days at a time, with elaborate cameras and observation setups that can be instantly focused on any anomaly.

NASA is an odd and amazing entity—a civilian agency funded by the defense budget and run by scientists. Most of the astronauts are subject to military security regulations, and missions regularly go up with Pentagon payloads that are classified "Secret."

Yet NASA gives out free pictures to anyone who asks, and they broadcast the recordings made by the space shuttles in real time on NASA Select TV. The recordings made during the STS-48 Mission, launched in September 1991, are still being debated by ufologists.

The video made a splash when Don Ecker of *UFO Magazine* appeared on "Hard Copy," and later, "Larry King Live," with a copy of what is called Event 2. The film shows a night view of Earth with city lights on the surface, and above, the halo of atmosphere with a lighting storm in progress.

First there's a flash of light that brightens and fades, then two odd streaks come in from the left of the screen. Suddenly the light streaks make sharp, right-angle turns, shooting off in different directions into space. Throughout Event 2, other lights move across the field of view at varying speeds and trajectories.

James Oberg says it's all explainable. Oberg is an aerospace writer and a "skeptic" as an active member of CSICOP, the Committee for the Scientific Investigation of Claims of the Paranormal. The UFO subcommittee of CSICOP is led by Oberg; Robert Sheaffer, author of *The UFO Verdict;* and Philip J. Klass, contributing avionics editor of *Aviation Week and Space Technology.*

Oberg, author of *UFOs and Outer Space Mysteries,* is a manned space operations specialist. As he told Karel Bagchus, "I've spent 22 years in Mission Control work on the space shuttle, as a contractor to NASA, but never exactly a NASA employee."

Not exactly, huh?

Karel Bagchus conducted an extended e-mail interview with James Oberg, released in May 1997 under the title "Conversations with James Oberg." Oberg supports NASA's claim that the flash in Event 2 was from an adjuster rocket correcting the course of the shuttle. Donald Ratsch points out that the earth doesn't appear to move in the frame, but Oberg contends, "He's been told again and again but he just doesn't learn: the jet which fired was a fine tuning engine with a resulting angular rate of about 0.05 degrees per second, much too small to be visually detectable. That's exactly what the telemetry records—which Ratsch never asked NASA for—show." Oberg claims the streaks came from amorphous or "shapeless" ice that had been frozen around the rim of the valve of the waste water dump, then broken loose during the adjustment.

Physicist Jack Kasher, Ph.D., disagrees with Oberg's assessment. Kasher performed a rigorous technical analysis of the videotape and presented the results in "A Scientific Analysis of the Videotape Taken by Space Shuttle *Discovery* on Shuttle Flight STS-48 Showing Sharply Accelerating Objects," funded and made available by the Fund for UFO Research.

Kasher's basic arguments are presented mathematically, proving that the fast-moving lighted objects do not conform to the ice particle explanation. "Instead, the trajectories and motions of the objects, after factoring out the motions of the shuttle itself, indicate true UFOs and extraordinary performance."

Bagchus pointed out to Oberg that the lighted objects move differently in the STS-48 video from the ice particles he had viewed in the video of the launch of the Apollo 11. "When the first stage is disconnected, a lot of ice particles are breaking off too. The difference with the way the ice particles are moving away is that in this video, the particles are tumbling and rotating in circular waves. I don't see that kind of movement in the STS-48 video, where the supposed particles are moving in straight lines and making sharp turns."

Bagchus says he sent two e-mails reiterating his questions, to which Oberg briefly replied, "Well, I'm really out of time for now, but I hope you find your answers somewhere out there on the 'net."

Some people believe that NASA is now censoring its broadcasts—when the National Security Agency isn't doing it for them. Yet on a more recent space shuttle mission, STS-82, a strange conversation was recorded on NASA TV by John Locker on February 18, 1997. Locker, a satellite and communications consultant, transcribed the conversation, which was printed in the *AUFORA News Update* in April:

Crew member A: "What was that flash?"
Crew Member B: "I don't know"

A: "That light flashed possibly just here.. . . .and again" *(Laughs)*

B: ". . . I see it"

A: "I just thought it was my imagination"

B: "I saw it too . . . so it's not . . . there was two of THEM"

A: "There's another one . . . WHAT *ARE* THEY?" *(11 sec silence)*

A: "I just saw the lights flickering in here"

B: "I wonder if they're taking pictures?"

A: "WHAT IS THAT?" *(excitedly)*

B: "This thing passed in front of us"

A: "Where are the lights?"

B: "Which ones?"

A: "I dipped surveillance for a second, but I had that one the whole time"

B: "Yeah, I got that one too!"

The two crew members sound justifiably concerned and surprised. Most objects they encounter are space debris which could cause serious damage to the tiles on the shuttle. Usually NORAD spots the debris on its radar and warns the crew of their approach and whether they need to shift orbit in order to avoid a hazardous situation.

Astronauts

Some astronauts have been irrevocably changed by their experiences in space. The so-called rookies of Apollo 12, Apollo 15, Apollo 16 are good examples: Alan Bean became a painter of haunting lunar seas; Jim Irwin became an evangelical Christian missionary; Charlie Duke became a minister.

Barely two years after astronaut Edgar Mitchell walked on the moon, he left NASA in order to scientifically study paranormal phenomena. His experiments into ESP while he was on the Apollo 14 mission—with dramatic results, Mitchell believes—were headline news at the time.

In 1971, Mitchell worked with Andrija Puharich, a scientist whose interests included psychedelics, ELF (extremely low frequency) electromagnetic waves, and UFOs. Together they helped bring the Israeli psychic Uri Geller, famous for bending spoons with his mind, to Stanford Research Institute in California. Two physicists, Dr. Russel Targ and Dr. Harold Puthoff, were less interested in spoon bending than in the potential to use telepathy to transmit images and information. This, of course, led to the CIA development program in "remote viewing" (for more information, see Chapter 10).

Mitchell wrote an autobiography in 1996, *The Way of the Explorer*. During an interview on "Dateline NBC" on April 19, 1996, Dennis Murphy asked him to elaborate about his research into "close encounters of the third kind." Mitchell admitted, "I have no firsthand experience, but I have had the opportunity to meet with people from three countries who in the course of their official duties claim to have had personal firsthand encounter experiences." Mitchell also insists that if extraterrestrials have been to this planet, then the "governments" are definitely covering up the evidence: "From what I now understand and have experienced and seen the evidence for, I think the evidence is very strong, and large portions of it are classified."

Some astronauts are clearly on record about their opinions and the sightings they've had in space. Commander Eugene Cernan, commander of Apollo 17, said in a *Los Angeles Times* article in 1973, ". . . I've been asked (about UFOs) and I've said publicly I thought they (UFOs) were somebody else, some other civilization."

Other astronauts protest that they are the focus of false claims and/or are misquoted out of context. Timothy Good in *Above Top Secret* (1988) claimed that the "hitherto unconfirmed reports" that Neil Armstrong and Edwin "Buzz" Aldrin saw UFOs on the moon on July 21, 1969, have now been corroborated by Maurice Chatelain, former chief of NASA communications specialists, who, according to Good, "confirmed that Armstrong had indeed reported seeing two UFOs on the rim of a crater. 'The encounter was common knowledge in NASA,' he revealed, 'but nobody has talked about it until now.' "

Good also mentioned what he recalled about the Apollo 11 moon landing: "I remember hearing one of the astronauts refer to a 'light' in or on a crater during the television transmission, followed by a request from mission control for further information. Nothing more was heard."

Yet a fairly recent quote from Buzz Aldrin himself is actually much more revealing than secondhand reports. On an August 1996 episode of "Politically Incorrect," Buzz Aldrin was discussing the *Penthouse* Roswell-alien photos. Aldrin said that there was absolutely no truth to UFOs and that it is all hype "created by con men" whose only motive is to make money off "people living in a fantasy world."

When Bill Maher replied that the government, "God bless them, they try, but they don't have what it takes to keep a big secret like this, do they?" Aldrin agreed, "Not for forty years, not about alien bodies and Roswell, but I certainly hope that the government can keep a secret at Area 51, because we're, they're protecting us against individual terrorists, they're developing countermeasures out there, and they're developing the security of this nation. . . ."

Now, Maher never said a word about Area 51—it was Aldrin who suddenly switched from talk of aliens to the secret base and the "security of this nation." You also have to wonder which stealth aircraft—the NASA automated surveillance and control helicopter?—is being developed to use against terrorists.

Maybe Aldrin confused "we're, they're" because NASA astronauts are used to thinking of Area 51 as their own. NASA has more astronauts than it needs for the shuttle missions; a few of the shuttle pilots used to be test pilots and may have flown some black-project aircraft out of Groom earlier. Astronauts have even been known to be assigned to "Pittman Station," the cover location for the Groom Lake facility.

Gordon Cooper

Gordon L. Cooper was one of the original seven Mercury astronauts with NASA. He was an Air Force lieutenant and a jet pilot at the age of twenty-two. After obtaining an aeronautical engineering degree, he became a test pilot, and then joined NASA in the American space program.

On May 15, 1963, Gordon Cooper was our last astronaut to go into space alone, setting a record for the longest flight by an American. Cooper orbited the earth twenty-two times for thirty-four hours in the spacecraft *Faith 7*.

In a recent interview by Yolanda Gaskins, broadcast on the television show "Paranormal Borderline" in May 1996, Cooper stated:

> To my knowledge the only thing that was ever seen, on any of our space flights, and believe me all of us would like to have seen something, was on Jim McDivitt's Gemini 7 mission where they saw this glint of something metallic off in the distance, and he reported it and nobody had it listed on the ground so he tried getting a picture of it. But sun unfortunately was glinting off of it so bright all he got was just glint, there was no detail on what it was, but never any uh, any further sighting at all on it.

Cooper confuses Gemini 7 with Gemini 4, which was the mission that McDivitt and E. H. White were on. Nevertheless, when asked directly, Cooper didn't claim that *he* had personally had a sighting in space. Yet there are persistent accounts in popular UFO books that describe a UFO encounter with Cooper's Mercury 9 space capsule in 1963. The UFO was reportedly a glowing greenish object that was allegedly picked up by Muchea Tracking Station near Perth Australia on Cooper's final orbit of Earth.

When Frank Edwards described this incident in his 1967 book, *Flying Saucers: Here and Now,* he claimed that "the object which approached him was also seen by the two hundred persons at the tracking station. It was reported twice on the NBC radio network before Cooper had been picked up by the rescue craft. He was not permitted to comment on it."

In fact, Cooper has been quite outspoken about UFOs from the beginning, seeking to bring a level of credibility to the phenomenon. He states over and over again the need for well-qualified people to help with research. In an interview on the "Merv Griffin Show," aired April 10, 1978, Cooper said, "I would like to see the time when all qualified people not trying to make a dollar selling some weird and way-out stories could really work together, to really properly investigate these types of stories and either refute them or prove them. . . . I'm rather interested in maybe eventually in the near future putting together a few people of science and engineering, and so on, to properly investigate this type of thing."

In early 1985, Cooper addressed a UN panel discussion on UFOs and ETs, chaired by then UN Secretary-General Kurt Waldheim. According to a transcript as copied by *UFO Universe* magazine in November 1988, Cooper stated his opinion for the record:

> I believe that these extraterrestrial vehicles and their crews are visiting this planet from other planets, which are a little more technically advanced than we are on Earth. I feel that we need to have a top level, coordinated program to scientifically collect and analyze data from all over the Earth concerning any type of encounter, and to determine how best to interfere with these visitors in a friendly fashion.

Though Cooper points out that "I am not an experienced UFO professional researcher—I have not as yet had the privilege of flying a UFO nor of meeting the crew of one," he did discuss his own sighting over Neubiberg air base in Germany: "Also, I did have occasion in 1951 to have two days of observation of many flights of them, of different sizes flying in fighter formation, generally from west to east over Europe. They were at a higher altitude than we could reach with our jet fighters. . . ."

In a 1977 interview with Lee Spiegel for *Omni Magazine,* Cooper described what he had seen over twenty-five years earlier:

> They were large groups of metallic saucer-shaped vehicles at great altitudes coming over in flier [sic] formation in various sized numbers and for the greater part of two days these kept coming by. They were in fingertip formation, flights would cross under, back and forth, just the same kind of formations we used in fighter groups. They had the capability of changing directions a little faster than a typical fighter would, stopping, rapid starting, changing directions. . . .

On the "Paranormal Borderline" show, Cooper described how "we sent a report forward on it," and the answer that came back that "they were probably high flying seed pods, which didn't sound very logical." Yet Cooper had mentioned in an earlier interview with Lee Spiegel for the "Credibility Factor" record that "I'm not sure we really ever realized the impact of it, at that point in time, really."

A skeptical James Oberg agrees that the other witnesses didn't think it was a memorable event either. When Oberg contacted contemporaries of Cooper in the 525th Fighter Squadron of the 86th Fighter Wing, people who had been listed in the December 1950 base phone book, he got back more than a dozen responses from commanding officers and weather officers, and "their opinions were unanimous that no such event had occurred at Neubiberg."

The other Cooper/UFO incident took place in 1957, while Cooper was supervising flight testing at Edwards Air Force Base in California. His military camera crew filmed an unidentified saucer-shaped object landing nearby. In the

1996 "Paranormal Borderline" interview, Cooper described the encounter:

> As they were sitting there filming a little saucer came from, I say a little saucer, it was *a* saucer, came flying over their heads, put down three little landing gear and landed right out on the dry lake bed. Then they picked up their cameras and started over toward it filming as they went, and when they got in fairly close it lifted up—put the gear back in the wheel-wells—tipped up and took off at a great rate of speed. And so they brought, came into my office and told me what had happened and I sent them over to develop the film, and then had to go through all the proper regulations of reporting this, and we wound up having to send the film forward to Washington in the base jet airplane, and uh, I don't know whether anyone's ever seen it since.

Cooper wasn't at the site when it landed, but he did view the film before he sent it to Washington. When Yolanda Gaskins asked "how similar was it to the very first sighting you had back in 1951?" Cooper replied,

> Quite similar. It was about basically the same planform vehicle. They were a double saucer, lenticular. If you're going to go in and out of atmospheres like Earth or other places might have, you certainly need a little more aerodynamic type of vehicle, and the saucer has the capability of going through the air at tremendous rates of speed and handling the bow and trailing wave without making a shock wave. So it can be very silent while traveling big rates of speed through the atmosphere.

Though Cooper has been quite clear about the fact that the film mysteriously disappeared, making it impossible to corroborate his story, in the past he used to downplay any suggestion that there was a government cover-up of an alien presence, as in the *Omni* interview: "If any UFO information is being suppressed, it's certainly not by the U.S. Air Force, because I was at a high enough level to know about it."

Twenty years later, he is being more forceful in his opinion that the classified information he knows is being withheld should be released. In 1996 Cooper told Gaskins:

I think we'll see our government having a totally different approach really to the UFO situation, or extraterrestrial or whatever you want to call it. I think the pressure that comes to bear on the government from whatever reason they withhold information is certainly getting more and more and more so I would like to think that they're going to really release all the information.

Intellectual Property

As James Oberg researched Gordon Cooper's history of support for UFO investigation, he came to the conclusion that Cooper has repeatedly been on the receiving end of frauds and fabrications. In "In Search of Gordon Cooper's UFOs," a three-part series posted on UFO UpDates in May 1996, Oberg points out that during a publicity blitz for Columbia Pictures' *Close Encounters of the Third Kind*, a plastic model called "Authentic Bendable Extra Terrestrial Figure" was marketed:

On the back of the cardboard wrapper originally containing the "authentic" (whatever that meant!) alien was a sensational quotation from two-time space veteran Gordon Cooper: "Intelligent beings from other planets regularly visit our world in an effort to enter into contact with us. NASA and the American government know this and possess a great deal of evidence. Nevertheless, they remain silent in order not to alarm people. I am dedicated to forcing the authorities to end their silence."

Although Cooper reportedly denied making that statement, the quote sounds remarkably like him when he spoke on the 1996 "Paranormal Borderline" show.

Oberg sums up Cooper's role in the UFO phenomenon this way:

> His usefulness to UFO proponents is based on his honest advocacy of serious UFO research (a desire shared by many serious researchers in the field, including myself) and on the UFO stories associated, not always accurately as we have seen, with his name. . . . People who have used Cooper's stories to "prove" the reality of UFOs . . . seem to have neither known nor really cared about the real truth behind the stories.

Both Edgar Mitchell and Gordon Cooper have been most recently associated with the Center for the Study of Extraterrestrial Intelligence (CSETI). Among the other key supporters is Richard Boylan, the disbarred clinical psychologist who worked with abduction victims. Boylan wrote an essay called "Recent Astronaut Statements on UFO Reality," posted on the Internet in September 1996, which claimed:

> NATO Command Sergeant-Major Robert O. Dean, U.S. Army (Ret.) is working with CSETI's Dr. Steven Greer, in concert with former astronaut Gordon Cooper, other astronauts, another high-ranking military officer, and a General, to plan the release of UFO information to which they are privy. Dr. Greer and Sgt. Major Dean are part of a Starlight Coalition which has been putting together the best evidence of UFO/ET reality.

Also a member of the Starlight Coalition is Dr. Brian O'Leary, a former astronaut and professor of physics at Princeton University. Dr. O'Leary gave his views in an essay, "Taking Off the Blinders That Suppress New Science," originally published in the *New Science News* in 1994, a newsletter for the International Association for New Science, which O'Leary helped cofound.

O'Leary contends that technological advances in free energy research have been "100 percent repressed" by government, the press, and the lack of support from the technical community. "Could it be that such airtight suppression comes from a higher intelligence, whether it be from a group mind, collective unconscious, or alien control that somehow doesn't want free energy to happen? Perhaps the veil of denial has been placed over all of us, but it is now lifting."

The founder of CSETI is Dr. Steven M. Greer, an M.D. from North Carolina in emergency medicine. Dr. Greer conducted the "CSETI DC Briefings" from April 7 to April 11, 1997, in which he told reporters and congressional officials in separate closed-door briefings that CSETI's assessment of extraterrestrial activities required urgent federal attention for the good of humankind.

CSETI is trying to obtain a government disclosure of the existence of UFO-related technology that "would be of immense benefit to humanity, IF used for peaceful purposes." The *CSETI DC Briefing Report* (1997) by Greer summarizes: "The goal of the CSETI Project Starlight initiative is to present the best available evidence and witness testimony in a manner which would constitute a definitive disclosure regarding the reality of the UFO/ET subject. This is to be done in a scientific, non-sensational and hopeful manner, assiduously avoiding an alarmist tone or emphasis."

At the conference on September 8, 1996, in the UFO Forum, Greer stated, "we know that over 90% of the information out there is disinformation, designed to psychologically prepare us for conflict with the ETs, and this is extremely dangerous, and a very dangerous game is being played out here."

Ironically, the tables were turned when the CUFOS-FUFOR-MUFON (CFM) UFO Research Coalition accused Greer of "pirating" a copy of *The Best Available Evidence*.

This book was written by FUFOR's Don Berliner, with Marie Galbraith and Antonio Huneeus, and was financed by multimillionaire Laurance Rockefeller. The Fund for UFO Research placed the following statement on its website on June 6, 1997: "Dr. Steven Greer, M.D., leader of CSETI (the Center for the Study of Extraterrestrial Intelligence) has improperly published and distributed scores of copies of a preliminary draft of the BEST AVAILABLE EVIDENCE briefing document. He knew it was original material of the UFO Research Coalition which was protected by copyright law against unauthorized reproduction."

Just three days earlier, on June 3, Greer responded to Michael Lindemann's accusation in a CNI article. Greer claimed the allegations were "falsehoods, poorly researched information and egregious and libelous statements":

> After beginning the CSETI Project Starlight UFO/ETI disclosure effort in the summer of 1993, I was invited to a meeting at Mr. Laurance Rockefeller's JY Ranch near Jackson Hole WY, where I met Mrs. Marie (Bootsie) Galbraith. I shared with Ms. Galbraith and the others gathered there our plans regarding collecting the Best Available Evidence regarding UFOs and our plans to provide briefings for world leaders and the public on the subject.

Greer admits that CSETI removed the original cover of the document and substituted one of its own that assigned to him and the CSETI Starlight Team the responsibility for the "concept, title, strategy and case selection."

On behalf of FUFOR, part of the UFO Research Coalition, Rob Swiatek emphatically stated that neither Greer nor CSETI had any involvement at any stage in the preparation of the genuine document:

> Greer's pirated version of the document retained the name of the true author—Don Berliner—to avoid accusations of plagiarism. Berliner states emphatically that

he received no input from Greer or any of his associates at any stage of the planning and writing of the document. In particular, Greer's claim that his "Starlight Team" (whatever that is!) selected the cases summarized in the document is completely empty, as Berliner insists he, alone, chose the cases for the document. And he finds the implication that he worked with Greer and CSETI to be highly insulting, and damaging to his reputation as a professional writer.

FUFOR is concerned that Greer publicly "tries to give the impression that he is a moderate, logical spokesman for the UFO field," yet a list of CSETI's positions makes it clear that Greer "actually represents the most extreme faction of the private UFO community."

The CSETI report on the DC Briefings and other documentation written by Greer and his coalition members is located on the CSETI website. Unfortunately the text lacks references and bibliographies, making it impossible to verify statements that are presented as if they are the result of research and evidence.

Some of these assertions include "more than one extraterrestrial civilization is represented in the current activities involving earth," and that these "beings have bases within this solar system," as well as "a plan is in place to allow for gradually broader and deeper contact with human society." Where did CSETI get this information?

One example of Dr. Greer's scientific methods was revealed on "48 Hours," when he described leading a Rapid Mobilization Investigative Team (RMIT) to Mexico in 1993 to study the ongoing wave of UFO sightings. This team set up an observation post and an array of cameras and signaling equipment near the small town of Metepec, which happens to be about fifty miles from the busy Mexico City airport. Yet Greer stated that one UFO: "interacted beautifully, though, in terms of the off and on. I mean, that was incredibly good CE-5. In no way could a conventional craft move in a way where it could signal back and forth like that with the lights on and off."

Jan Aldrich of Project 1947 commented on June 10, 1997, on the electronic mailing list that Greer's conference in Washington, D.C., was simply a copy of the "long and quiet campaign" of the CFM Coalition to contact a number of congressional staffers and congressmen. Aldrich wryly adds, "If Greer got to Congress, what would congressmen think of signaling aliens with high powered flash lights?"

As a result of a warning letter from a Washington, D.C., law firm on behalf of the UFO Research Coalition, Steven Greer for CSETI has agreed to stop offering the Coalition Briefing Document for sale and misrepresenting it as a CSETI product.

I decided to check the facts on some other document related to CSETI researchers. I turned to something I could verify among the documents written by Starlight Coalition members. Presumably, they are the ones who supplied the evidence supporting the CSETI documents (I have to presume because of the lack of bibliography).

I came across a "Report On the Star Knowledge Conference" in South Dakota, June 12–16, 1996, written by Richard Boylan, Ph.D. This conference was attended by members of Native American nations, as well as former NATO and FEMA officer Robert Dean, Harvard professor John Mack, author Whitley Strieber, Professor Courtney Brown, assorted abductees, and others.

After everything I had read about these participants—particularly about Boylan, with his claims that his license was taken because he was being persecuted by the government—I had to check it out. Boylan's report concerned the Star Knowledge Conference and Sun Dance that was "convoked by Lakota (Sioux) spiritual leader Standing Elk in response to a vision." Standing Elk is identified as the Lakota Keeper of the Six-Pointed Star Nation Altar.

I called Chub Black Bear, one of the spiritual leaders of the Lakota nation, whom my parents had met when they were in South Dakota in 1996. They went to the reservation to support a close friend who underwent the deeply spiritual rite of the Sun Dance for the first time.

After being passed along a chain of Lakota, I finally reached Sinte Gleska University, where Stanley Red Bird remembered the conference that had been held in June 1996. Boylan quoted Standing Elk to make it sound like there had been a serious decision to unveil the Lakota's "sacred knowledge": "The Lakota/Dakota Medicine Men are now being instructed to share the spiritual knowledge of the Star Nations, because of the contamination of Mother Earth and the pollution of the air."

But Red Bird brushed off the idea that Sinte Gleska University was involved: "Too New Age for us. It was boycotted by Lakota grassroots people. They couldn't agree with what these New Age groups were saying." Red Bird became concerned when I mentioned Boylan's report was entitled "Star Knowledge Conference." Red Bird's father had been involved in the scholarly study *Lakota Star Knowledge: Studies in Lakota Stellar Theology,* by Ronald Goodman.

To settle his concerns about issues of intellectual property rights, I sent him a copy of Boylan's conference report, while he referred me to the university to get a copy of Goodman's fascinating book. *Lakota Star Knowledge* is based on the research of coworkers, including the late Stanley Red Bird, the founding chairman of the Board of Regents of Sinte Gleska University.

The Lakota stellar theology reflects "a vivid relationship between the macrocosm, the star world, and their microcosmic world on the plains." This is a temporal spatial theology, in which the movements of the stars instruct the Lakota how they should move across the land.

Nowhere in the book was there any mention of entities actually living in the heavens. In fact, it's a radically different sort of cosmology, more like Plato's version of an abstract, perfect world reflected in the physical manifestations here on earth.

Basically, the "Star Knowledge Conference and Sun

Dance" had nothing to do with Lakota religious beliefs. The conference didn't even take place on the reservation—it was held somewhere else in South Dakota. "Standing Elk" is reportedly a pseudonym of Lauren Zephier, a Yankton, who doesn't speak the language and apparently doesn't understand the true Lakota star knowledge. The term "Star Nations" is never mentioned among the numerous star knowledge legends.

Stanley Red Bird had only one response when I asked about aliens: "The last time we recognized aliens, they took our lands, attacked our religion and violated our women. *After* we saved them from starvation."

CHAPTER 9

Engineering UFOs at Area 51

THE PROBLEM with the lack of scientific criteria in the UFO field means that anyone can claim anything, and it will be put forth in the public domain with as much seriousness as the results of Richard Haines's decades-long work with visual perception. In particular, the Las Vegas area has turned into a UFO mecca, where a number of UFO experts, witnesses, media personalities, and investigators ply their trade in UFOs around the world.

Art Bell is the talk-radio host of "Coast to Coast AM," the most popular overnight radio show in America, carried by more than 320 stations and reaching as many as fifteen million listeners. Bell has been doing his show for over ten years, broadcasting nightly from a studio in his home in Pahrump, Nevada. On Sundays, from 7:00 to 10:00 P.M., he broadcasts "Dreamtime."

Anyone with persistence and a story to tell can go on the air, though Bell usually limits the calls to three minutes or less. He also interviews special guests who discuss paranormal topics, UFOs, and/or aliens, mingled with political discussions and current events.

Bell's official website provides transcripts of caller interviews. People can retain their anonymity or give a fictional name—unlike journalists, Bell doesn't check his sources. When Chuck Shramek sent his image of the Hale-Bopp companion to Bell, he was the first to publicize the anomaly. Bell was also one of the first to publicize expert opinions debunking the "alien companion." Bell not only initiated the wave of rumors, he actively engaged in the speculation, even sponsoring an inane contest on what to call the comet's alien companion—"Hale Mary" captured a whopping 35 percent.

Bell says his show is "entertainment" and therefore *caveat emptor,* let the buyer beware. But people still generally believe what they hear on the radio. Isn't the 1938 Orson Welles production of H. G. Wells's "War of the Worlds" enough to prove that?

Check out, for example, a message posted on UFO UpDates asking if anyone had heard Bell speaking to a pilot who had landed somewhere near Area 51:

Art Bell had the man LIVE on his show, I guess by CB or something, don't know how he could maintain phone contact out there. Well anyway, I heard something about him seeing an F-16 or other military aircraft flying overhead, or he was being warned about being pursued by military aircraft. About 10 minutes after his alleged warning, Art totally lost radio contact with the man.

This woman wasn't sure if it was a real incident or not, but at least she checked. A few days later, she got hold of Bell on America Online and found out that it was an April Fool's joke. How many *millions* of people heard the story going on in the background while they were busy with other things and believed that something like that did indeed happen? But it's good fun if you remember, as Glenn Campbell says, "On Art Bell, it is April first all year long!"

Bell is not the only one to give his guests anonymity if they wish. Many ufologists quote unnamed sources in the government, and UFO documentaries regularly feature testimony of witnesses who conceal their identity, eliminating any chance of corroborating their testimony.

These include stories about sightings and landings of UFOs near Area 51, as well as former government employees who insist that alien saucers are being concealed out at the Nellis Range. They know because they say they've worked on the engineering programs that are trying to develop a human version of the alien technology.

George Knapp recited a long list of these mostly named sources at a 1994 Triad UFO-research conference. Knapp, the evening news anchor on KLAS-TV, Las Vegas, is also the producer of a commercial video series, "UFOs: The Best Evidence." The series is a review of selected topics in the UFO field, including government cover-up, cattle mutilations, abduction, and UFOs through history. It is based in part on Knapp's 1989–90 series "Best Evidence," consisting of local news stories aired on KLAS and the Bob Lazar interviews.

Unlike Bob Lazar, Knapp says some of his sources still work for government contractors, so going public would mean losing their jobs. Knapp claims his sources have been threatened after he talked with them, and he himself has been "bugged and followed" by government agents.

There is no doubt that there is technological information being kept secret by the government at Area 51. There is also no doubt that there are bound to be leaks of various bits of information. Usually these leaks are fairly general, as in the case of tips given to *Aviation Week and Space Technology,* describing the Air Force's costly stealth fleet, exhibiting "exotic propulsion and aerodynamic schemes not fully understood at this time."

However, George Knapp claims he's gotten information from "more than two dozen current or former employees" that alien technology is being researched at Area 51. In the September 1996 issue of *UFO Magazine,* Knapp reiterated that "Saucer-shaped craft have been witnessed at or near the facility since the 1950s."

Knapp notes that his best source is a member of a prominent Nevada family who insists on remaining anonymous. But this witness has supposedly agreed to give Knapp a videotaped deposition to be released upon his death. Knapp drops tantalizing clues that his source occupied a position of senior management at Groom Lake during the late fifties and early sixties, and that this source knew of an extraordinary craft that had been test-flown and taken apart.

Bob Lazar

George Knapp introduced Bob Lazar to the world in late 1989 on KLAS-TV. In his first appearance, Lazar's identity was concealed and he used the pseudonym of "Dennis." In these reports, Lazar spoke of things he claims to have witnessed at S-4, a secret facility south of Area 51, on the edge of Papoose dry lake.

Lazar's identity was quickly discovered, and a month later, Knapp interviewed Lazar under his real name for KLAS-TV's "On the Record," which aired on December 9, 1989. Lazar said he was coming forward in spite of the secrecy agreements he signed and the pressure that was put on him: "Everything up to death threats. I mean *constant* reminders of it, signing away my constitutional rights for fair trial and that sort of thing."

Lazar doesn't speak much for himself anymore, except in the occasional documentary interview. He did release his own video in the early nineties, and is said to be making a new version. He even has his own website, TriDot, a fairly new endeavor.

Missing from the website is the "Lazar Synopsis," written by Lazar's friend and fellow flying saucer watcher, Gene Huff. Huff told their story in the "Lazar Synopsis" and in March 1995 posted it on the World Wide Web on alt.conspiracy.area51.

Gene Huff claims to have witnessed the flight of a flying saucer when he was with Lazar. I e-mailed Huff and we went back and forth as I tried to set up some kind of an interview with Bob Lazar. Huff answered a few of my questions, but kept forgetting who I was, saying "we get so many thousands of calls from people who want to talk to Bob."

Huff was a real estate appraiser in Las Vegas when he met Lazar in 1985. Lazar had recently moved from Los Alamos, New Mexico, where he worked for a short time at the Los Alamos Meson Physics Facility, either for the lab or for a contractor there.

Lazar claims that in 1988 he wrote to physicist Edward Teller, whom he had met briefly in 1982 in New Mexico. Teller, the physicist who helped develop the H-bomb and was part of the Star Wars program, was also cited in faked documents as a member of MJ-12. Lazar says that Teller put him in touch with someone (he lost the paper with the name on it), and that man hired Lazar to work at S-4 on a propulsion project "for what I was told anyway was the United States Navy."

Lazar says he reported to the EG&G building at Mc-Carran Airport and flew out to Area 51 with his "personal security guard" Dennis Mariani, before being bused down to S-4. As Huff narrates in the "Lazar Synopsis":

S4 was a combination of buildings and hangars built into the side of a mountain. Armed guards were everywhere, and security was oppressive. Bob even got an armed escort when he went to the bathroom. They arranged Bob's I.D. and gave him a physical which included a test for allergic reactions to substances which were not identified for Bob. After this he was placed in a briefing room by himself to read some briefings as part of his indoctrination. As Mariani closed the door to leave Bob alone, Bob saw a poster on the back of the door. It was a "flying saucer" hovering over a dry lake bed and it was captioned, "They're Here." Bob opened the top folder on the desk and it contained 8 × 10 glossy photos of 9 different flying saucers, including the one on the poster.

In a tape-recorded "informal" press conference held at the 1993 UFO convention at the Little A'Le'Inn (about twenty miles away from the boundary of Area 51), Lazar complained about "the lack of equipment" at S-4 and that "that high level of security does not go well with scientific research."

Lazar says he was hired to be part of a "back engineering" team taking apart the nine alien flying saucers. According to Huff, Lazar eventually witnessed "a brief, low altitude test flight" of one of the discs. He was also briefed on the discs' ability to distort space-time to achieve interstellar travel.

The technology behind the S-4 flying saucers involved "warping the field between points" using gravitational forces—not magnetics, as many popular theories hold. Lazar also told Knapp that he had "HANDS-on experience with the anti-matter reactor."

Yet according to the transcript of the press conference at the Little A'Le'Inn in the 1993 *MUFON UFO Journal,* when a questioner asked Lazar about Townsend Brown's respected theories of harnessing electromagnetic energy, Lazar replied, "I've seen all kinds of crazy claims about how they operate . . . and I mean most of them are ridiculous."

Lazar says he only went out to S-4 six or seven days, total, between December 1988 and April 1989. Yet he claims that his main contribution was identifying the chemical element that was the source of power for the spacecraft. In an interview with Michael Lindemann in "UFOs and Alien Presence," Lazar said, "I was the one who identified 115. That was my only contribution to the project. And I don't stand on the fact that it's 115, but if it's not, it's 114. It's right in there."

When Lindemann, apparently unable to believe what he's heard, asks Lazar again if he discovered a new element, Lazar replies, "Yes, and there again, this confirms what I said, that this project was apparently just being worked on for some time, several years I would imagine, and they had no idea what the fuel was. We're talking about a very basic thing, certainly a reasonable starting point."

Tom Mahood, an Interceptor who maintains the Bluefire website, did extensive research on Bob Lazar's claims of what went on at Papoose Lake, entitled "The Robert Lazar Timeline," 1995. Mahood responds to Lazar's claim that he "identified 115": "First off, he's on the job for the equivalent of about a week, and on top of all the other things he's claimed to have seen or done (getting up to speed, the medical exam, security briefing, reading the various reports, watching the test flight, etc.) he discovers just what the magic material is that does all this. If true, it would seem Lazar had one of the better first work weeks in the history of mankind!"

Lazar claimed that "Los Alamos was apparently involved in some of the analysis of the 115," but he didn't know "if they knew what they were doing." Huff tried to explain Lazar's identification of the element:

> He didn't "discover" the 115, he helped correlate others' research and was the first one to come to a conclusion. . . . He did not state that even the people at S4 had been working everyday trying to identify this fuel, with no success. There were many facets to the project at S4 and who knows what their priorities were.

It's usually big news when a new element is discovered. In early 1997 a team of international scientists at a German research institute detected a single atom of a new metal, number 112, a heavier, still unnamed relative of zinc, cadmium, and mercury. The story was carried by the Reuters newswire on February 22. It was an important news story, with the German science minister Juergen Ruettgers commenting, "Proving the existence of element 112 provides important confirmation for theoretic nucleus structure models."

The institute spokesman stated, "According to theory, element 114 should be especially stable," so apparently the element Lazar discovered was *not* 114. Conspiracy theorists would say the reason the world has never heard about Lazar's amazing discovery is because of the secrecy that shrouds the activities at places like S-4.

But heavy elements are nothing when there's real spacecraft flying around. Huff says the first night Lazar took him out to see the flying saucer was on Wednesday, March 22, 1989. Along with Lazar's former wife, they went out the Groom Lake road "about 5 miles" and soon they saw "a bright light rise above the mountains which were between us and S4." Huff doesn't mention the fact that John Lear was with them, but Lazar described at the 1993 UFO conference how Lear pulled out a huge Celestron telescope the first night they went to look at saucers in order to focus in on the object.

The group went saucer-watching for three Wednesdays before they were chased off BLM land. Huff says, "A short time later a Lincoln County cop named LaMoreaux pulled us over and hassled us. He took our I.D.s and radioed our identities into the security base station."

That was when Lazar's career at S-4 ended. His security clearance was revoked, then they tried to convince Lazar to go out to the Nevada Test Site for some kind of "final debriefing," but he refused. He believes they had no intention of letting him leave again. His security guard, Dennis Mariani, reportedly called and threatened him, but Lazar stood firm.

Shortly after this, Lazar revealed his story to George Knapp, who won a UPI individual achievement award because of the 1989 interviews. While making the documentary, Knapp checked Lazar's credentials, but there were no records of his schooling, and Los Alamos denied that Lazar ever worked there.

Lazar claims that his records were destroyed by the government, in an effort to discredit him. He was prompted to do the first Knapp interview because "What had happened was, I sent in a request for my birth certificate, and as it turned out it wasn't there anymore, that I wasn't born at the hospital!"

His claim is backed up by a reference in a June 27, 1982 article in the Los Alamos *Monitor* about Lazar and his Honda jet car. The article appeared on the front page, and it identifies Lazar as "a physicist at the Los Alamos Meson Physics Facility." In this article, Terry England describes the Honda with a real jet engine Lazar had built into it that propelled the car up to 200 mph: "It's something he's been working on for years. It started 'awhile ago' when working with another researcher in NASA on the technology. Lazar modified the original design 'and put out more power.' "

It's a confusing quote, but it sounds like Lazar worked with NASA, since he says he collaborated with "another researcher in NASA." This claim and the attribution of being a physicist at Los Alamos were not disputed at the time. More important, Lazar claims he has master's degrees in physics and electronics technology from MIT and Cal Tech, stating that he left MIT in "probably eighty-two because I think I left there and went to Los Alamos."

Both George Knapp and UFO researcher Stanton Friedman checked with the administration of Cal Tech, but there were no records of Lazar's attendance. Glenn Campbell checked the Institute Archives at MIT but was unable to find a listing for Lazar in the 1978 to 1990 student directories, or in the 1989 MIT *Alumni Register*. Friedman checked with the MIT registrar's office and the alumni office and found no record of Lazar's attendance.

Tom Mahood posted "The Robert Lazar Timeline" (1995) on the Blue Fire website, a summation of statements, interviews, and records taken from documents and reels of microfilm containing public records. On Lazar's marriage certificate to his first wife, Carol Nadine Strong, in 1981, in Woodland Hills, California, Lazar's occupation is stated as "electronics engineer" and his highest school grade completed is listed as twelve. He moved to Los Alamos about a year later.

In an article about Lazar's credibility published in the

MUFON UFO Journal in February 1994, Glenn Campbell pointed out:

> At a conference in May, Lazar willingly provided the names of two of his professors—one at MIT and one at Cal-Tech—with the same apparent sincerity as his description of anti-matter reactors. Didn't check out. Prof. Hohsfield or his ghost never haunted MIT, while Prof. Duxler was never at Cal-Tech, only at the junior college where Lazar did once take classes.

George Knapp seems to gloss over Lazar's credentials problems on the "AREA 51: Discovery Channel UFO Series," aired in January 1997. Knapp actually suggests that MIT has a lot of government contracts, so they could be pressured to wipe out Lazar's records.

Another wrinkle emerged in one of Lazar's interviews with George Knapp, when Lazar admitted he had installed a computer system for a local brothel. According to Huff, the local vice cops charged Lazar with six felonies. Lazar plead guilty to pandering, and was sentenced to three years probation and community service. As Huff said, "Naturally, most following Bob's story thought this was a setup by the federal government to discredit him, and they may have been involved, but that is unknown to this day." But in an *Omni* interview with Lazar in April 1994, his involvement is more thoroughly described: ". . . while on vacation in Nevada, he wound up buying into a legal Reno brothel; the investment proved so profitable that he didn't have to return to full time employment for a while."

Both pandering and prostitution are fairly common in Nevada, and even Glenn Campbell, one of Lazar's toughest critics, says that "Lazar is, by all accounts, an eccentric and creative guy, and people like this who do not fit any social mold do tend to get themselves in embarrassing messes. Questions about 'character' do not change the facts of what did or did not happen at Area S-4 and do not provide a 'smoking gun' to prove or disprove the saucer claims."

The polygraph examiner who tested Lazar for the "Discovery Channel UFO Series" in 1997 sounded as if he didn't know whether to believe Lazar or not. When Lazar answered questions about Area 51, he seemed deceptive, but when he described the craft themselves, the examiner saw no signs of deception.

Campbell has spent numerous hours trying to find some trace of Lazar's records, and he posted this assessment of the broadcast of the Discovery series: "Lazar gives his usual fine performance describing the flying saucers, projecting a sincerity that is hard to fake. How does he do that? In spite of all the evidence to the contrary, I find it almost impossible not to believe the guy when he talks about being in the hangars with the craft."

Lazar's official website, TriDot, is rather defensive in tone. It claims to give the real Lazar story with the "full knowledge and input of Bob Lazar" and it begins with "A Word to the Wise," acknowledging, "just because it's written down doesn't make it so." The website also points fingers: "Two prime examples of 'ufologists' that have consistently lied and spread disinformation about Bob Lazar are Stanton Friedman and Glenn Campbell, both of whom make their living selling UFO related merchandise."

Yet Bob Lazar is also making a living off his tales of saucers at S-4—at the very least, selling his videos and receiving speaking fees. According to John Lear, Lazar bought his Corvette with part of the money he got from the sale of his story to a film company. Lazar's "Zeta Reticuli Corporation" was funded for a short time by millionaire Robert Bigelow, and his "Sport Model" disc was produced as a plastic model by the Testor Corporation.

Lazar said it was a "dream job" out at S-4, and it was the most exciting thing he ever worked on, but he left because he was being "pressured." Huff says that Lazar is absentminded, but in one of his first UFO conference appearances in 1993, when Lazar was asked if he stopped working at S-4 in 1989, his best guess was "Something like that."

Lazar also doesn't like to talk about the government reports he read out at S-4, because they "could be disinformation." Yet he did tell Knapp in the second interview that he read an "autopsy report":

> The reason I call it an autopsy report is I saw the carcass—it was obviously a dead alien—carcass cut up and it was all dark inside like it had an iron base. The reason I say iron is because it was very dark blood or whatever. I'm not a doctor, but it seemed to be one large organ in the body as opposed to identifiable heart and lungs and that sort of thing, but just one gooey mess in it.

Campbell's article in the 1994 *MUFON UFO Journal* describes Lazar's story as the sort that appeals to engineers, computer programmers, and other technical types—like himself. Most of the information Lazar gives involves plausible technical details rather than an emotional base of reference: "I could believe because it is subtle, detailed and restrained, involves only a very limited government conspiracy and does not digress into any kind of speculation."

Yet UFO researchers agree that Lazar's lack of credentials can't be factored out of the picture. If he could only turn up one document from his schooling, one professor who could confirm that Lazar attended his class, then there would be some sort of proof of a government cover-up.

Despite reading everything that Lazar saw and read (including government reports that these craft are coming from Reticulum 4), as a questioner at a UFO conference pointed out, "It seems as if even knowing that we possess alien technology hasn't made you a believer."

"That's probably true," Lazar replied.

Papoose Lake

The site that Bob Lazar identifies as S-4 is better known as Papoose Lake. The northern tip of the dry lake bed is about four miles south of the Area 51 boundary, and ac-

cording to maps of Nellis Range, the lake bed is under Air
Force jurisdiction.

There is a real identified S-4 southwest of Papoose Lake,
within the Nevada Test Site, extending for miles across a
desert plain. At this S-4, there are a number of towers with
antenna, microwave dishes, and series of earthen covered
bunkers as if storage for explosives. There's no airstrip, but
according to Tom Mahood's Bluefire website, there are
maps that list a heliport. Best guesses claim that Site 4 is
a testing location for "purloined" Soviet radar equipment,
which would explain the presence of towers.

Lazar says the real S-4 is at Papoose Lake, where there
isn't a large complex. On the contrary, when Mahood took
one of many trips up Mount Stirling on January 29, 1997,
as he headed down to the "mining site," he says "It turns
out a good hunk of Papoose Lake is visible even from that
lower location, and it was well lit. I could clearly see two
structures of some sort that seem to be in the lakebed, about
the size of a guardhouse or wellhouse."

The only listing for Papoose in the *Area 51 Security
Manual* is on Papoose Peak: five microwave buildings, a
power shed, and a latrine. These small buildings can be
seen in satellite photographs. There is no mention of anything being on Papoose Lake.

Lazar described the facility to Timothy Good as being
built into the base of the Papoose Range, with nine hangar
doors sloped at about a 60-degree angle. He said the doors
had a sandlike texture coating to them, and Gene Huff later
said they were roll-up type doors. There were nine hangar
bays, one for each of the nine saucers.

Mahood summarizes what has been revealed by "Lazar
and company" in his 1996 "Papoose Lake Primer," which
includes maps, photos, and lore of the area. The claims
include:

That S-4 is on the east side of a dry lake (most probably
Papoose Lake), about a 30 minute bus ride from Groom
via a good dirt road. The facility seems to be either built

into a ridge spine, or disguised as a ridge spine, with portions of the facility being on either side. The hangar side must be at least 600' long, perhaps longer. There is a chain link fence with a gate surrounding the personnel entrance, but it's possible to walk around to the other side of the ridge to access the hangar area directly.

Underground facilities are rife in UFO lore. The "Dulce Complex" under Los Alamos is just one example. Dulce consists of approximately sixty buildings, and the underground part is estimated to be over one hundred feet below the mountain.

There were also rumors of black helicopters over Napa County, California, which carried supplies to a secret underground facility located on BLM land "without the knowledge or permission of the Bureau," as reported by Harry V. Martin. Martin says the *Napa Sentinel* obtained numerous fly-by photographs and over two hundred pages of unclassified and secret documents which outlined three purposes for this secret base:

- Direct satellite communication.
- Continuity of the U.S. Government in case of nuclear attack or other disasters.
- Secure communication links with the outside world in the event of a disaster.

But at Papoose Lake, there has been no disturbance on the dry desert floor recorded in the series of excellent-resolution Soviet satellite photos taken in the late 1980s and early 1990s. As Mahood points out, looking at the 1988 satellite photo:

Even assuming the facility is hidden in the hills, there is no sign of an access road (which Lazar described as good), no sign of a fenced area (and the accompanying marking of terrain it would leave), no sign of terrain scuffing from people walking around or even from hauling discs out of the hangars onto the lake. It's not as if these things won't show up on the photo, as they do in other areas near Groom. Guard vehicle turnaround spots on the dirt roads are clearly seen.

There's also the fact that Lazar has repeatedly complained about the lack of equipment at S-4, yet the facility itself would have to be fairly sophisticated to be built inside a mountain with all traces of its existence carefully scoured from the lake bed. During Mahood's trip up Mount Stirling, he reported, "Papoose Lake just sat there, looking uninteresting, as it always does. Not a saucer to be seen anywhere. But they never are when *I'm* around! They always know when I'm in the Spring Mountains and keep the hangar doors down. These guys are sharp!"

When Knapp asked, in the second interview in 1989, How long have they had this technology up at Nellis? Lazar replied, "It seems like quite a while, but I really don't know."

When Lazar was discussing element 115, he said the scientists had been working on it for "several years, I imagine." So I wrote to Gene Huff, trying to pin down exactly when Lazar's S-4 complex was built—for example, how did it compare to the facilities at Los Alamos? Did it have ultramodern equipment such as built-in electronics or sophisticated surveillance devices? Huff replied on behalf of Lazar in April 1997:

He has no idea how old it was. It was a generic building made of concrete, concrete block, etc. with generic, dull, boring paint jobs so there was little to give him any hints. Quite frankly, he was only there less than a dozen times and there were many more interesting things for him to address than how old the installation was. I'm sure you can understand that.

Actually, I think I would have been a little more curious about something as remarkable as a huge research facility with nine bays holding nine saucers built completely inside a mountain. When I pressed Huff, he added, "The only way for him to know this was via those briefings he read and they didn't contain anything on the facility. They did say that the discs had been in our possession since at least 1979 but they didn't specify where."

Since Lazar didn't have a guess, I tracked down who had jurisdiction over Papoose Lake. Tri-party and even five-party agreements are common in the area, say Department of Interior representatives. Aside from the U.S. Fish and Wildlife Service, BLM and the Air Force are also involved in whatever happens on the range.

There are Air Force targets located east of Papoose Lake, in Fallout Hills, listed on the Nellis Range chart as Range 64A. However, only Area 51 is placed in the center of a "box" of highly restricted airspace that was created on January 15, 1962. As Mahood points out, half of the airspace over Papoose Lake is not even restricted, which means that any of the Nellis flights could pass right over where supposedly highly secret saucers are being test-flown. Mark Farmer has overflown Papoose Lake many times, and he says he's never seen anything—in photos or through binoculars—that supports the existence of a facility.

Not only is Papoose Lake on the Nellis Range, but it's also within the boundaries of the Desert National Wildlife Range. This creates a conflict of interests, to say the least, between the Air Force, which uses the Nellis Range as a mock battlefield, and the wildlife people in the Department of Interior who try to protect the natural state of the desert.

Since the Air Force wasn't forthcoming with any information on Papoose Lake, I contacted the Desert National Wildlife Range people, who sent me a copy of a memo from January 11, 1971, proposing Papoose Lake as a "Research Natural Area."

Research Natural Areas are defined as areas where natural processes are allowed to predominate, and they are preserved for the primary purpose of research and education. According to the Papoose Lake RNA proposal, "This is one of the few dry lake beds (playas) in the area that has not been badly disturbed by man's activities. It should be set aside as an example of a primary area and as a demonstration area of primitive ecological succession." Roger D. Johnson, refuge manager, wrote the proposal for the Papoose Lake area in 1971, which is defined as

> located within the Las Vegas Bombing and Gunnery Range and is proximate to the Nevada Test Site of the Atomic Energy Commission. Because of its relatively small size and location near A.E.C. installations it has not been subjected to bombing and gunnery use. The military has indicated no interest in the lake bed; however this attitude could change. Designation and use as a research area would in no way conflict with current military requirements and it would serve as justification for restricting future military expansion.

The Papoose Lake RNA was approved on January 19, 1973, signed by John D. Findlay and officially initialed by four department heads. A map is included with the RNA designation, showing the exact tract of land that makes up the 23,680 acres of Papoose Lake Research Natural Area. This includes not only the lake bed but the alluvial fan that juts far into the Nellis Range, within Lincoln County.

In return, I sent the Desert National Wildlife Range copies of DoE documents that recorded higher levels than usual of radiation in the Papoose waterhole. They knew nothing about these recently declassified tests.

Some people may say that the "Research Natural Area" is a cover for the secret S-4 base that was built at Papoose Lake—but why on earth was such a good cover story allowed to stay buried for eight years after Lazar started talking? Beside, there was no need to plant such an elaborate cover story way back in 1971—not when the Air Force was just beginning to see the advantages of having a secret base at Area 51 and began seriously diverting more money into developing those facilities.

The Desert National Wildlife Range officials said that no other UFO researcher has ever asked them about Papoose Lake. When I started calling, they were courteous and helpful. They didn't consider the Papoose RNA to be a big deal—just another part of an enormous range of desert that it's their job to protect and maintain. As far as I can tell, if there's any conspiracy going on, it's not in this corner of the Department of Interior.

Even George Knapp, the one who had introduced Lazar to the public, surmised in the September 1996 issue of *UFO Magazine*, "There are no vast underground facilities at the base, nor are there any hangars built into the hills of Papoose Lake; three witnesses who've been to the base in the past three years for inspections have confirmed this."

John Lear

At the 1993 UFO conference at the Little A'Le'Inn in Rachel, Nevada, Lazar was asked, "Why did you tell John Lear?" Lazar replied, "I haven't the slightest idea why I told John. I really didn't know him that well then."

John Lear was the first to tell sensational stories about UFOs out at the Nevada Test Site. As Lazar told Knapp in the second 1989 interview:

Well, there was a very brief time there I had sent out resumes to several places, and I wanted to get back into the scientific field again. Almost simultaneously, I met John Lear and read some of his material. And initially, I thought he was just absolutely crazy. But apparently, he did have a good source of information because, as it turns out, some of the information that he had I actually had hands-on experience with.

As Campbell points out in his article in the *MUFON UFO Journal* in 1994, Lazar's association with Lear "raises the suggestion that Lazar's own UFOs-at-the-Test-Site story was a hoax generated initially for Lear's benefit that evolved from there into a media event."

Then again, others claim that if the government wanted to leak UFO information, it couldn't have found a better candidate than a physicist in Las Vegas who was friendly with John Lear. Or it's possible that it is exactly as Lazar claims—that his clandestine trips to see the government saucer with Lear and Huff got him into trouble, and without Lear to prompt him to go to George Knapp, we would never have known about S-4 at Papoose Lake.

John Lear was listed in the Las Vegas phone book, so I called and found he was extremely accessible, despite his assurances that he is getting out of the UFO field. I interviewed Lear at his home on Sunrise Mountain in February 1997, and ended up listening to his stories for hours.

Lear's enormous study is crammed full of books, photographs, six video screens, a pull-down movie screen, world globe, telescopes, and piles of papers on the various tables. At one end, in a huge stone fireplace, a fire crackled briskly as Lear showed me NASA pictures of "artificial structures" on the moon, and computer DEM images that revealed a square hole on the northeastern tip of Papoose. But then he informed me that, because of some sort of high-altitude electromagnetic interference when he was flying with his laptop, the hole appears only on the copy of the program he made, not the original.

Lear insisted that the government is actively using mind control on American citizens. "Lazar stopped working at Papoose Lake because he realized he was losing time, and he knew he had better quit before they took over his mind," he claimed.

When I asked Gene Huff if it was true that Lazar had stopped working because he was afraid the government was performing some kind of mind control on him, Huff replied,

Actually the act of using fear to control people is a form of mind control and mind control, generally speaking, comes in many forms that are not what people envision it to be. So, that being said, I don't know that Bob Lazar would deny anything like that. If Lear implied that he was a zombie in a trance, then yes Bob Lazar would deny that.

It isn't easy to figure out John Lear. When Jeff Papineau reposted Lear's article on the newsgroup alt.alien.visitors in October 1992, he repeated the rumors that ran through the UFO community that Lear might be a source of CIA disinformation.

Lear's situation is ironically the reverse of Bob Lazar's. Lazar can't prove his background, while Lear has impeccable credits as a test pilot. A "Statement" released by John Lear on December 29, 1987, lists his credentials:

John Lear, a captain for a major US Airline has flown over 160 different types of aircraft in over 50 different countries. He holds 17 world speed records in the Lear Jet and is the only pilot ever to hold every airline certificate issued by the Federal Aviation Administration. Mr. Lear has flown missions worldwide for the CIA and other government agencies.

Photographs cover every inch of Lear's study, along with framed newspaper clippings documenting his amazing successes and death-defying crashes. I counted thirteen National Aeronautic Association awards for around-the-world speed records, with Lear as a member of the Learjet crews. Currently, he tells me, he's flying for a cargo airline—he had to leave the passenger business in part because of the controversy over his interest in UFOs.

Lear's father, William P. Lear, was the designer of the Learjet executive airplane, the eight-track stereo, and founder of Lear Siegler Corporation. William Lear also had an interest in UFOs, and in February 1956, while visiting Bogotá, Colombia, Lear told a news conference that flying saucers were real. The AP picked up the story and carried it in America.

In Donald Keyhoe's *The Flying Saucer Conspiracy,* the author discusses William Lear's assertions: "Within twenty-four hours Lear amplified his first statement: 'I feel the flying saucers are real', he said, 'because of four points.' " According to Keyhoe, Lear's four points were "numerous manifestations over long periods of time," simultaneous observations, "great possibilities linked with the theory of gravitational fields," and progress in efforts to "prove the existence of anti-gravitational forces and to convert atomic energy directly to electricity."

Yet John Lear publicly stated that he became interested in UFOs in 1986, after "talking with United States Air Force Personnel who had witnessed a UFO landing at Bentwaters AFB, near London, England, and three small aliens walking up to the Wing Commander."

Lear says he was a pilot for the CIA, and he told me about missions he flew in the Middle East, "Israel to Egypt, four times a week," in Air Sinai planes according to a "Camp David Accords agreement." He says he gets his inside information about UFOs from his sources in the U.S. intelligence community.

Many researchers claim Lear is effectively a government disinformation agent who undermines the credibility of UFO research by making the entire subject sound as ludicrous as possible. I know my head was spinning as I jotted down names and book titles as fast as I could, hearing about dozens of conspiracies Lear was able to weave together, seemingly creating the fabric of some far-reaching government plot.

Jarod-2

Bob Lazar's story is supported by an anonymous man who goes by the alias "Jarod-2" (pronounced JAY-rod), after the alien he said he saw at Area 51. Jarod-2 claims he worked as a consultant for thirty years on a secret government project designing flight simulators for human reproductions of alien flying saucers.

Jarod is now seventy years old and his real name has been withheld "to avoid unwanted attention from UFO believers." Glenn Campbell confirmed that Jarod worked on NASA's NERVA ("Nuclear Engine for Rocket Vehicle Application") nuclear rocket assembly program:

> Jarod-2 says that although his main employment was in the disc simulator program, there were many periods when his work there was held up for months at a time due to various technical hang-ups outside his group (presumably glitches in the development of the operational craft). At these times, Jarod was reassigned to other defense or space projects, like NERVA, where his skills would not be idle.

Jarod-2 says the government is covering up the fact that they've been working with aliens for years, ever since a UFO crash near Kingman, Arizona, first reported by Raymond Fowler in the late 1970s.

Skeptics say that Jarod-2 built his own UFO story out of Bob Lazar's claims. Jarod-2 does have sufficient technical knowledge to discuss the flight simulator aspects of his work, since he claims to have designed only the boxes and shells of various assemblies.

Jarod-2 also knows a surprising amount of information about aliens. He says that the aliens keep clean by taking a "bug bath," which Campbell interprets as a "microbe shower." Jarod-2 also claims the aliens speak "a higher form of Hungarian" and that they are mainly trading with the U.S. government for boron, a relatively scarce element. Though Jarod-2 says he worked with them for over thirty years, he never communicated directly with any aliens.

Jarod-2 says the project started in the mid-fifties, when all of the U.S. government's UFO information was isolated in the "satellite government." The aliens are allegedly giving us their old technology (in Jarod-2's words "their old

B-52s") so we can reproduce the alien craft within our own technical and social framework.

Jarod-2 says this satellite government has been separated from the rest of the government for over forty years. In May 1995, Jarod-2 said the man in charge of this satellite government was an "astrophysicist," not a general: "At the time it was thought it would be a general that was put in charge. But [the aliens] were smart enough to put in charge someone who was technically competent. You get too many politicians and they don't know the technical aspects of many of the things that we're following today."

Thus, this satellite government evolved in its own way, adapting to the unique requirements of the subject matter. It is very compartmentalized, which keeps sensitive information within small units. Jarod-2 says the satellite government was founded by Nixon, and that he was allowed to tell people because "Nixon is dead."

Jarod-2 says he is speaking with the permission of his superiors, and there is certain information he can give and other things he can't. "I was shot at the other day," he told me in April 1997.

"Are you saying someone tried to kill you?" I asked, startled.

"They're warning me," Jarod-2 said.

So . . . maybe he's leaking too much information. There are plenty of people who know who Jarod-2 is, though he won't let himself be publicly identified. But I told him that if people are shooting at him, maybe his best bet is to come forward and tell everyone what he knows.

I communicated with Jarod-2 several times by phone and e-mail, and he was a very pleasant and friendly man, but when we were supposed to get together in Las Vegas for the interview, there must have been some sort of mix-up because he left me sitting at Boomtown for over two hours. During that time, I read a book I had handy, occasionally mulling over the Watergate investigation, when Bob Woodward dealt with his anonymous informant, "Deep Throat."

What many of these anonymous UFO informants don't

consider is the fact that Deep Throat was actively pushing Woodward toward *evidence*. He wasn't just supplying rumors and theories—he insisted that Woodward track down the money. That led to Watergate, and another money trail later led to the Iran-Contra arms-for-hostages deal.

But the only way to track the money of secret government investigations into UFOs is for the Congress or the Government Accounting Office to get in there and start digging around. With that thought in mind, I packed up my stuff and went back to my hotel, without having gotten the evidence, the "concrete" Jarod-2 had promised to supply, that would confirm which agency was actually the "satellite government" in control of Area 51.

CHAPTER 10

Scientific Analysis

Twenty years ago, the American Astronomical Society allowed Stanford University physicist Peter. A. Sturrock to survey their members on the existence of UFOs. Of the 1,365 members who responded to a survey, 53 percent thought UFOs "certainly" or "probably" should be investigated further. In addition, 62 astronomers said that they had seen or recorded a UFO but less than one third, only 18, ever reported their experience to anyone.

Surveys published by *Industrial Research* magazine show similar support for UFO research among engineers and scientists. Dozens of professional scientists are involved in some way in UFO research, and many more would likely join in the effort if federal funding were available.

The problem is, you can't get government grants when you're investigating a phenomenon that has been declared nonexistent. Without proper investigation, using the equipment available to scientists, skeptics can continue to claim that the UFO phenomenon defies the laws of physics as we understand them.

But one scientist who spent decades studying UFOs concluded that they "obey, not defy, the laws of physics." Paul Hill, a NASA scientist, was able to look beyond the incomprehensible because of his achievements on the cutting edge of research and development in mechanical engineering and aeronautics. Among other things, Hill designed two unique wind tunnels during his long employment with Langley Research Center, NASA, from 1939 to 1970.

Not only was Hill a well-respected NASA scientist, but he had his own UFO sighting five days before the Washington Wave of 1952. Hill applied his extensive aeronautic expertise to the problem, explaining, "Some degree of technological sense has to be made of the unconventional object, even to make 'seeing believing.' Otherwise, we are still apt to be in mythology, or dealing with the occult."

For nearly twenty years, Hill says he served as the "unofficial" clearinghouse for UFO reports at NASA, collecting and analyzing sightings purely for their physical properties and propulsion possibilities. He gleaned UFO information from various reports that were "passing through" NASA.

Hill didn't finish his decades-long analysis until after his retirement in 1970. He incorporated many sighting reports from the 1950s through the mid-1970s, and the results were published posthumously much later, in 1995, in *Unconventional Flying Objects: A Scientific Analysis*. In his introduction, Hill says,

I was prevented from making any pronouncements about this application of my work by official National Advisory Committee for Aeronautics (NACA) policy. That policy was that flying saucers are nonexistent. The NACA Director, Dr. Hugh L. Dryden, made a public pronouncement to that effect about that time [1952] and I had been instructed by my superior in official channels that my name could not be used in connection with my sighting or in any way that would implicate the NACA with these objects.

Hill explains that when the name of the organization was changed from NACA to NASA, the National Aeronautics and Space Administration, "the same officials remained in charge, and one could notice no change in the policy."

Robert M. Wood, for thirty years the research and development manager of the McDonnell Douglas Corporation, wrote the foreword to Hill's book. Wood emphasized the fact that Hill "peripherally mentions his role at NASA, noting an attitude of tolerance for his interest in the UFO phenomenon," but then he adds that NASA denies having any interest in UFOs.

However, Wood says that, at NASA, Hill had access to "a wide variety of direct reports, which provided him with ample data to begin his analysis." Hill also studied investigations done by the civilian UFO organizations, the Aerial Phenomena Research Organization (APRO) and the National Investigations Committee on Aerial Phenomena (NICAP).

Since Wood retired from McDonnell Douglas in 1993, he too has begun to focus his attention on the "very important" UFO phenomenon. Wood rightly recommends Hill's *Unconventional Flying Objects* as "a model for the case investigator" that follows the fundamental principles of physics:

> Hill's approach was 20 years ahead of its time. He never became trapped in the endless speculation about the reality of UFOs; he accepted the reports at face value and let his analysis of the observed phenomenon speak for itself. And his methodology was impeccable. He took the reported observations and then directly evaluated alternative hypotheses, exploring all relevant avenues of inquiry.

Hill's straightforward scientific prose can be dense and technically daunting at times—as are the numerous mathematical equations—but it's fascinating to see the solid research on observed shapes, spectral shifts, maneuvers, acceleration, and trajectories come together in meaningful patterns.

Hill's analysis includes recognition of one of the most consistently observed characteristics of UFO flight—the tilt-to-maneuver movements. Reports of UFOs tend to describe the objects sitting level to hover, tilting forward to move forward, tilting backward to stop, banking to turn, and descending by a "falling-leaf" motion, rocking back and forth. Though these motions are not aerodynamic, detailed analysis by Hill reveals that they are totally consistent with some form of repulsive force-field propulsion.

Hill even arranged to have various types of jet-supported and rotor-supported circular flying platforms built and tested. Acting as the test pilot in early classified projects, Hill discovered that the motions that had been observed were indeed the most economical for control purposes.

As Hill points out, "exploratory research is usually done with a modicum of good data," and the first step of analysis is to accept the data that fit a consistent pattern. Hill called for more measurements of gravitational and magnetic fields near sightings of UFOs, and measuring electromagnetic wave characteristics from the lower gamma wave frequency through X-ray, ultraviolet, visible, and even radio frequencies.

Dr. Bernhard Haisch agrees. Haisch has been an astrophysicist at Lockheed Martin's Solar and Astrophysics Laboratory since 1983, and associate editor of a leading journal in astrophysics. Haisch is also the editor in chief of the *Journal of Scientific Exploration,* a peer-reviewed research journal which reviews scholarly investigations on phenomena not part of the currently accepted scientific paradigms. *JSE* is published out of Stanford University.

Haisch has authored more than one hundred scholarly papers, and in an essay reprinted in the *American Reporter* in 1996, he acknowledged that there appear to have been events that were recorded on film and in view of qualified observers such as law enforcement officials, astronauts, pilots, and military aviation experts and that deserve objective study. Haisch does not attempt to reach conclusions, yet he maintains that "something is going on" in our skies, and that ufologists should try to agree on a scientific agenda for researching UFOs.

In an article in the *MUFON UFO Journal* in March 1996, Haisch urged everyone who is concerned about the state of ufology to take action:

> How would one bring about government-sponsored research analogous to that of astronomy or the other sciences? As Goldin urged us to do on behalf of NASA's research: write, call, visit your representatives and senators. Constituencies count. No doubt about it. NASA funds astronomical research because the American people want this; even if most of it is too esoteric for public consumption, the highlights such as Hubble images and first extra-solar planets do make the newspapers and people read with interest about what their tax dollars are paying for.

As Dr. Haisch points out, the public climate is increasingly receptive to new ideas and is open to the possibility of other intelligent life in the universe. Haisch believes that a "public mandate for government-sponsored UFO research" could be called:

> Evidence needs to be properly analyzed and then properly presented using techniques and venues as close as possible to those of mainstream science. The disparity of the evidence appears to be confusing enough without layers of unproven theory and conspiracy. Somehow out of organization of evidence there could arise not the truth—that is too much—but there could arise a consensus on simply what to do next, who would plan it, who would execute it, how would money be spent in a responsible, accountable way if made available.

Technological Leaps

In the 1960s, physicist William Markowitz categorized the study of UFOs as "metaphysics" rather than "physics." When Markowitz calculated the energy released during the takeoff of a spacecraft, he theorized it was impossible for UFOs to be physical entities. In "The Physics and Metaphysics of Unidentified Flying Objects," in *Science,* September 1967, he noted that "To lift a spacecraft of mass 5000 kilograms with an acceleration of 1g from the Earth would require a power of about 3×10^3 watts. (This is about 30 times the electrical generating capacity of the entire world)."

Other scientists, such as nuclear physicist Enrico Fermi, agreed that interstellar travel would require incredible resources, more than our civilization was capable of at our current technology. Yet leaps in technology have historically made production and transportation suddenly much easier and cheaper—such as the development of the internal combustion engine, and more recently, the computer microchip.

Paul Hill offers excellent arguments for UFOs to be powered by gravity field propulsion. This theory is supported by a 1994 paper by Dr. Bernhard Haisch and Dr. Harold Puthoff showing that the control of gravity and inertia are now technically feasible. Puthoff, a theoretical physicist in quantum electrodynamics at the Institute for Advanced Studies in Texas, was also a former director of the CIA's remote viewing programs. In a 1986 paper, "Something for Nothing," Puthoff states, "In fact, according to quantum theory, the vacuum, the space between particles of matter as well as between the stars, is not empty, it is filled with vast amounts of fluctuating energy."

Many scientists claim that Einstein's barrier must first be overcome to make interstellar flight cheap and practical. But most breakthroughs aren't that revolutionary—such as the recent announcement from Nijmegen High Field Magnet Laboratory in the Netherlands. Nijmegen released startling photographs of a live frog and a water ball levitating inside a solenoid in a magnetic field of about 16 tesla. A. K. Geim described the technological development in *Physics World*, April 1997: "It has become common knowledge that superconductors are ideal diamagnetics and magnetic fields must expel them. On the other hand, the enclosed photographs of water and a frog hovering inside a magnet (not on board a spacecraft) are somewhat counterintuitive and will probably take many people (even physicists) by surprise."

Everything on earth has a weak molecular magnetism, therefore everything on earth—people, stone blocks, even cars—can be levitated. Geim claims that there are no adverse effects of strong static magnetic fields on living organisms. In fact, the Nijmegen frog floated in a magnetic field of the strength comparable to ordinary in-vivo imaging systems.

These technologies are not as far away as you might imagine. A recent essay by Paul A. LaViolette, Ph.D., claims that electrogravitic (antigravity) technology has been under development in U.S. Air Force black R&D programs since late 1954 and "may now have been put to practical use in the B-2 Advanced Technology Bomber to provide an exotic auxiliary mode of propulsion." This inference is made due to a March 9, 1992 *Aviation Week and Space Technology* article that disclosed that the B-2 electrostatically charges its exhaust stream and the leading edges of its winglike body.

According to electrogravitic research carried out by physicist T. Townsend Brown, such a differential space charge would set up an artificial gravity field on the aircraft. Townsend Brown (one of the founders of the early civilian UFO research organization NICAP) discovered that it is possible to create an artificial gravity field by charging an electrical capacitor to a high voltage. Then he created an electrostatically induced gravity field acting between the capacitor's oppositely charged plates. By 1958, Brown had developed a fifteen-inch-diameter model saucer that could lift over 110 percent of its weight.

Brown's experiments launched a new field of investigation which came to be known as electrogravitics, the technology of controlling gravity through the use of high-voltage electric charge. This is a scientifically valid area of research, as can be seen in the 1956 paper "The Gravitics Situation," prepared by Gravity Rand Ltd., a division of Aviation Studies Ltd., which included text from Brown's 1928 gravitor patent.

A number of people have reproduced the Townsend Brown experiments. R. L. Talley of Veritay Technology Inc., under the sponsorship of Edwards Air Force Base, did a two-year study published as two reports: AFAL-TR-88-031 (April 1988) and PL-TR-91-3009 (May 1991) entitled "21st Century Propulsion Concept."

Further testimony to NASA's interest in the research and development side of the UFO phenomenon was mentioned by Fawcett and Greenwood in *The UFO Cover-up*. A January 26, 1976 document, entitled "International Congress of Space Medicine," summarizes information presented at the International Congress in September 1975. The bulk of the document is censored except for a brief paragraph:

> U.S. scientists believe that low magnetic fields do not have a serious effect on astronauts, but high magnetic fields, oscillating magnetic fields, and electromagnetic fields can or do have considerable effect. There is a theory that such fields are closely associated with superconductivity at very low temperatures, such as in space. This in turn is related to the possible propulsion system of UFOs. There is a rumor that fragments of a possible UFO found in Brazil bore a relationship to superconductors and magnetohydrodynamics.

Where are these "rumors" of "fragments of a possible UFO" coming from that they would be important enough to discuss at a serious scientific conference? Fawcett and Greenwood figure it probably refers to "pieces of an exploded UFO over Ubatuba, Brazil, in 1957." These fragments consisted of 100 percent pure magnesium that were researched by Paul Hill, who called it one of the "most believable" of the UFO artifact stories:

> The believability stems from the supporting facts developed by Brazilian government laboratory tests showing the sample tested to be nearly 100 percent pure magnesium and entirely without the metallic trace elements characteristic of Earth manufacture. Another strange result that simply baffled the laboratory scientists was the finding that, although pure, the magnesium was 6.7 percent heavier than ordinary pure magnesium.

Among a series of heavily censored follow-up memos and cables regarding the "International Congress of Space Medicine," reprinted in *The UFO Coverup,* is a more personal note sent from an unidentified individual at the CIA, dated July 14, 1976:

> At a recent meeting to evaluate material from . . . [deleted] mentioned a personal interest in the UFO phenomenon. As you may recall, I mentioned my own interest in the subject as well as the fact that [CIA's] Domestic Collections Division had been receiving UFO related material from many of our S&T [Science and Technology] sources who are presently conducting related research. These scientists include some who have been associated with the Agency for years and whose credentials remove them from the "nut" variety.

What sort of "UFO related material" was arriving at the CIA's DCD? Statistics? Sightings reports? Or actual material that was suspected to be from UFOs? Whatever it was, it appears there was active R&D research being done on UFOs in the 1970s.

In current research and development, we have the work of Leik Myrabo, an associate professor of mechanical engineering at Rensselaer Polytechnic Institute in Troy, New York. Myrabo is working on an aircraft that will fly on a beam of microwaves. The driving force of the lightcraft will be a shaft of pulsed microwave energy from an overhead satellite that converts sunlight into microwaves. According to *Popular Mechanics* (September 1995), Gregory T. Pope, science/technology editor, says that if the magnetohydrodynamic (MHD) fanjet engine performs according to Myrabo's calculations, then it could deliver unheard-of performance, going from Mach 1 to Mach 25 in ten seconds.

In 1991, at the Naval Research Laboratory, Myrabo added a magnetic field to his laser-induced propulsion apparatus to preview the MHD fanjet, successfully doubling the thrust. NASA and the Air Force were impressed by Myrabo's air-spike experiments conducted in a shock tunnel.

As Pope pointed out, "glowing, highly energetic" aircraft that are shaped like discs have long been associated with the secret side of the aerospace establishment: "Myrabo's concept may offer a terrestrial explanation for the nightsky sightings that rational people tend to dismiss or ignore. Perhaps. Or perhaps it's just a concept that looks good on paper, or is ahead of its time. You never know with visionaries."

SETI

The Search for Extraterrestrial Intelligence (SETI) and the scientific establishment are as committed to their version of the extraterrestrial hypothesis as the most strident ET believer. The first formal SETI searches began in 1960 at the National Radio Astronomy Observatory at Greenbank, West Virginia, and even today, teams of observers search the heavens with their radio telescopes, hoping to hear a signal that would indicate the presence of alien intelligence.

The SETI Institute has received over $58 million in government funding and has a long history of cooperation with NASA. SETI searches have been conducted by NASA, the Planetary Society, universities, private astronomers, and astronomical organizations.

The current goal of SETI's Project Phoenix is to find evidence of intelligence elsewhere in the universe using radio telescopes. From December 1, 1993, through June 30, 1995, their research required a total of $7.5 million to double the bandwidth of the NASA Targeted Search System. Project Phoenix also conducted sixteen weeks of dedicated SETI observations at the Parkes Radio Observatory in Australia.

Right up front on its website, SETI makes it clear that it does not conduct investigations of UFO sightings or alien abductions. SETI gives a "practical reason" for this—the closest star to Earth is over four light years away, or in human terms, twenty-four trillion (24,000,000,000,000) miles away. With our current rocket technology, SETI speculates that it would take around 300,000 years to travel there, posing "a daunting engineering problem even for a more advanced civilization."

Yet Paul Hill says that's faulty reasoning. Hill claims that if a UFO starship left Zeta 1 Reticuli bound for Earth *thirty-seven light years* away, at a velocity $v=0.9999c$, it would only take about seven months to reach Earth. Hill says people are confused about the idea that nothing goes faster than the speed of light, pointing to the tricky relativity factor: "Nothing goes faster than light, but spaceships can go more quickly as reckoned by their own time."

SETI says it also conducts no UFO research because "there is no scientific evidence to prove it. Personal accounts are not physical or verifiable evidence. These reasons are sufficient to exclude UFO's from the research objectives of the SETI Institute."

Yet as Hill points out, there is quite a backlog of data that hasn't been analyzed. And that's not taking into account new events occurring every day that *could* be scientifically investigated. As Brian Zeiler points out in "The Formulation and Predictions of the Extraterrestrial Hypothesis," inductive reasoning is a valid scientific approach. It is the same process that lent validity to the Big Bang hypothesis, which is also supported by no physical proof. "Both induce a hypothesis to explain a set of observations without violating known laws of physics according to our existing body of knowledge. Both also make predictions that have been corroborated, and both explain the observations superior to any alternatives."

Brian Zeiler and Jean van Gemert produce the "Science, Logic, and the UFO Debate" website on the Internet, which lists over seventy articles on UFOs in scientific journals such as *Aeronautics and Astronautics, American Journal of Physics, Bulletin of the Atomic Scientist, Industrial Research and Development, Nature, Technology Review,* and *Journal of Scientific Exploration.* But the scientists who have written articles favoring the ET theory for UFOs have risked ridicule from their peers. John Alexander at the National Institute for Discovery Science (NIDS) claims that many of their scientists write their papers anonymously because of the lack of respect for those who examine the UFO phenomenon.

The SETI website does cite sociological studies that indicate the discovery of a signal from extraterrestrials would "lead to confusion and excitement," with the prevailing desire on the part of individuals to "know more." SETI believes that such knowledge would precipitate a gradual change in worldview rather than dramatically upset the day-to-day conduct of society.

SETI merely listens; it is not in the position of attempting to communicate with extraterrestrial life, so any decision to return a signal would rest on "world leaders." Several official attempts at sending a message from planet earth have been notable. The Arecibo Interstellar Message was transmitted as a radio signal in binary code on November 16, 1974, from Arecibo Observatory in Puerto Rico to the globular cluster M13, about 25,000 light-years away.

The signal contained 1,679 bits of information about Earth. The Arecibo Message was prepared by the staff of the National Astronomy and Ionosphere Center, operated by Cornell University under contract with the National Science Foundation.

Also, on the off-chance that another civilization might encounter our interstellar craft, the Pioneer 10 and 11 spacecraft each bear an engraved plaque with a message from Earth. Voyagers 1 and 2 carry an elaborate recorded message of words and music. All four of these spacecraft are currently heading out of our solar system.

Most skeptics argue, why would NASA go to the trouble of funding SETI if they already had evidence of extraterrestrials? There would be no need to listen to the stars if the aliens were already "among us." But in the brisk debate on the electronic message boards, other possibilities are raised: that our government knows little more about the phenomenon than that it exists and represents unconventional technology. Or that NASA listens to the stars looking for corroborating evidence of alien existence before announcing its findings.

Extraterrestrial Life

They found life on Mars! Or did they? Scientists have been debating the evidence detected in a Martian meteorite ever since the August 1996 announcement was made by the scientific team led by David McKay at the Johnson Space Center near Houston.

The debates were heated at NASA's 1997 Lunar and Planetary Science Conference held at Johnson Space Center. Using electron microscopes and other state-of-the-art instruments, researchers in a wide range of planetary and biological specialties analyzed chips the size of rice grains. Plenty of skeptical reports were issued indicating that the carbonate is inorganic, and that the tiny globules of carbonate were formed from a boiling vapor much too hot to support life.

Yet other reports refuted the charges that the sample was contaminated by Antarctic meltwater, and supported the existence of fossil nanobacteria with comparable rock samples from deep within the earth's crust. A member of McKay's team, Everett Gibson, asserted at a press conference during the conference, "We feel stronger about our position now than we did last August."

The question of whether there were bacteria living on ancient Mars is very important—it would prove the existence of extraterrestrial life. But the scientific jury is still out, and not likely to reach a conclusion any time soon. The surface landings of the Viking space probes in 1976 were an unsuccessful attempt to find evidence of life on Mars. The summer 1997 Pathfinder missions can perform extensive soil tests, but the evidence of life will not be confirmed until an unmanned sample-return mission.

Now that the debate about life on Mars has been revived, the White House added a total of one billion dollars to the NASA budget proposal for the years 1998 through 2002. This should ensure that a sample-return mission can be launched as early as 2005 with samples returned in 2008.

Even while the debate continues, most exobiologists do agree that the carbon cycle of life is at work elsewhere in the universe. According to computer simulations, life should appear in a suitable environment after about three billion years. Our own sun is reckoned to be six billion years old, while the galaxy is around twelve billion years old. According to the concise *Columbia Electronic Encyclopedia,* scientists estimate that as many as fifty thousand planets in our galaxy have earthlike conditions. And a substantial fraction of these are likely to have cultures as technologically advanced as our own.

The Green Bank equation, more commonly known as the Drake equation, was devised by U.S. astrophysicist F. D. Drake as a way to estimate the number of technically advanced civilizations in the Milky Way galaxy. The equation is a mathematical formula of probabilities assigned to the following variables:

1. the rate of star formation each year in Earth's galaxy
2. the fraction of such stars that would have planets similar to Earth
3. the number of planets on which life could actually develop
4. the evolution of intelligence on such a planet
5. the attempt by intelligent life to communicate with other intelligent life, and
6. the average lifespan of technical civilizations.

Depending on the estimate for each variable, the number of advanced civilizations in the Milky Way has been estimated in figures ranging from one (ours) to one million.

Metaphysical Research

The metaphysical approach to UFOs was formulated by the French astronomer Jacques Vallée, who believes that UFOs "must be something more" than the ET hypothesis. In his autobiographical book *Forbidden Science,* Vallée summed up his views on UFOs after decades of research:

The UFO Phenomenon exists. It has been with us throughout history. It is physical in nature and it remains unexplained in terms of contemporary science. It represents a level of consciousness that we have not yet recognized, and which is able to manipulate dimensions beyond time and space as we understand them.

Vallée's hypothesis postulates that UFOs are a manifestation of our perception of reality. After writing nearly a dozen books on the subject, Vallée's research into mythology and folklore shows a remarkable likeness between our modern concept of UFOs and historical ideas of demons, fairies, and other supernatural tricksters. As Vallée once said, "It no longer matters whether UFOs are real or not, because people *behave* as if they were, anyway."

He considers the UFO phenomenon to be one of the

most exciting challenges ever presented to science and human reason. As Vallée pointed out in *Dimensions: A Casebook of Alien Contact* (1988), the scientific establishment sneered at UFO reports while the American public was snatching up Whitley Strieber's *Communion,* sending it to the top of the *New York Times* best-seller list. "This coincidence between scientific arrogance and a new socirend illustrates an important fact in our society: while science consistently refuses to consider phenomena that lie outside the safe regions of its current understanding, the public is eagerly reaching for explanations that fit its experience."

On the "social" level, Vallée's theory is similar to Carl Jung's ideas on a collective unconscious. In Jung's book *Flying Saucers,* he comments, "They behave not like bodies but like weightless thoughts."

Yet Vallée also believes there are physical effects taking place. He has gathered a great deal of relevant data on the small amount of space that appears to be affected by UFOs, which is characterized by the pulsed light and electromagnetic radiation from a large source of energy.

In the USAF Academy textbook "Space Sciences" chapter, the Vallée case for physicality is summed up as of 1968:

Jacques and Janine Vallée have taken a particular type of UFO—namely those that are lower than tree-top level when sighted—and plotted the UFO's estimated diameter versus the estimated distance from the observer. The result yields an average diameter of 5 meters with a very characteristic drop for short viewing distances, and rise for long viewing distances. This behavior at the extremes of the curve is well known to astronomers and psychologists as the 'moon illusion'. The illusion only occurs when the object being viewed is a real, physical object. Because this implies that the observers have viewed a real object, it permits us to accept also their statement that these particular UFO's had a rotational axis of symmetry.

These physical manifestations often have a biological effect on UFO witnesses. Reports often include incidents of paralysis, hallucinations, space and time disorientation, and personality changes from the contact.

Vallée refuses to speculate that UFOs are interplanetary visitors, a conclusion that "is not only premature but is contradicted by several basic facts" when one considers the historical perspective of UFOs. Yet other metaphysical theories include the potential for entities that exist within the electromagnetic spectrum, such as John Keel's *The Mothman Prophecies* (1975), and Gregory Little's 1994 book *Grand Illusions.*

For those who think that metaphysics isn't a scientifically viable area of research—think again. Concepts like telepathy and out-of-body experiences were the subject of a twenty-four-year government-sponsored ESP program at the Stanford Research Institute (SRI) and Science Applications International Corporation (SAIC).

When the remote viewing project ended, less than three hundred pages of SRI reports were declassified and released in July 1995 by the CIA. Along with the National Security Agency, the CIA has yet to release the thousands more documents that surely were generated during the decades-long study.

Former director Dr. Harold E. Puthoff has discussed the SRI efforts to psychically view top-secret facilities in the former USSR. Puthoff, currently with the Institute of Advanced Studies in Austin, Texas, has a background as a naval intelligence officer and as a civilian employee at the National Security Agency, which made him a natural to head up the program for thirteen years, from 1972 to 1985.

In a 1995 article, "CIA-Initiated Remote Viewing at Stanford Research Institute," Puthoff stated that twenty years earlier,

As a result of the material being generated by both SRI and CIA remote viewers, interest in the program in government circles, especially within the intelligence community, intensified considerably and led to an ever-increasing briefing schedule. This in turn led to an ever-increasing number of clients, contracts and tasking, and therefore expansion of the program to a multi-client base, and eventually to an integrated joint-services program under single-agency (DIA) 6 leadership.

These contracts included an "ESP teaching machine" for NASA. This device was a random number generator, with the subject trying to predict which one of four pictures would appear.

Another former director, Dr. Edwin May, assessed his program's results as approximately 15 percent successful in obtaining photographic reconnaissance quality data. And after hundreds of remote viewing experiments were carried out at Stanford Research Institute (SRI) from 1972 to 1986, Russell Targ of the Bay Research Institute stated in *The Journal of Scientific Exploration,* "We learned that the accuracy and reliability of remote viewing was not in any way affected by distance, size, or electromagnetic shielding, and we discovered that the more exciting or demanding the task, the more likely we were to be successful. Above all, we became utterly convinced of the reality of psi abilities."

Jessica Utts, a professor of statistics at the University of California, Davis, and a fellow of the American Association for the Advancement of Science, claims that "using the standards applied to any other area of science," she has concluded that "psychic functioning has been well established."

A dissenting report was issued by psychologist Ray Hyman, a professor at the University of Oregon. Yet despite his doubts, Hyman agrees with Utts that further investigations are warranted and should be funded. CIA and NSA chose to end the remote-viewing study because a 15 percent success rate—while it is scientifically notable—is not reliable enough for military applications.

National Institute of Discovery Science

Hal Puthoff, along with Dean Radin, another former remote viewing researcher and currently a professor at the University of Nevada–Las Vegas, has been affiliated with paranormal philanthropist Robert Bigelow and his National Institute of Discovery Science (NIDS). Dr. Puthoff posted the NIDS mission statement on USENET in March 1996.

That same month, Bigelow, a Las Vegas real estate mogul, advertised in *Science Magazine* for specifically trained Ph.D.s to fill positions at NIDS. Bigelow eventually gathered a group of "blue ribbon" scientists that includes astronaut Edgar Mitchell, airplane designer Burt Rutan, conspiracy theorist Gordon Novel, and the director of NIDS, John Alexander. Dean Radin has since left NIDS.

As it turns out, Bigelow has a history of funding paranormal projects, though not always to their conclusion. Reportedly Bigelow's attempt in the mid-1990s to fund a joint research project (some say for as much as a million dollars!) for the CUFOS-FUFOR-MUFON coalition fell apart over issues of control and academic freedom.

In the past, Bigelow has provided funding to Budd Hopkins and Linda Moulton Howe, and also to Bob Lazar as the "Zeta Reticuli Corporation." Zeta Reticuli is on Nevada state records as a corporation, but its mission wasn't defined. Glenn Campbell recounts that missions he's heard included: "(a) Space weapons research, (b) finding a cure for AIDS, and (c) experiments on samples of Element 115, which Lazar once had in his possession but that somehow got 'taken back.' "

Nothing ever came of the Zeta Reticuli Corporation, or of Bigelow's reported interest in Jarod-2. As Campbell described in the *Desert Rat*, a meeting was convened between Jarod-2 and members of NIDS, including Dean Radin:

Recently, several of Bigelow's latest flock of associates talked saucers with Jarod-2. It seems Burt Rutan and

Gordon Novel are interested in building one, but J-2 thinks their anti-gravity capacitor system is ridiculous. J-2 invited me to attend a luncheon meeting with three other Bigelow aviary members, but Alexander reacted strongly when he heard this: Glenn Campbell was not to be involved because he would write about it in the *Desert Rat.*

NIDS has been active for a few years now, based in Las Vegas. Bigelow has also purchased the Sherman ranch in eastern Utah's Uintah Basin near Fort Duchesne. The reason for this purchase was reported in the *Las Vegas Sun* in December 1996: "[Terry] Sherman said he and other members of his family had seen lights emerging from circular doorways that seemed to appear in mid-air, had three cows strangely mutilated and several others disappear. The rancher also reported unusual impressions in the soil and circles of flattened grass in a pasture."

This remarkable amount of activity led Bigelow to buy the ranch for $200,000 so that the phenomena could be researched by his newly formed National Institute for Discovery Science. Some people maintain that certain areas are gateways or windows into other dimensions—Sedona, Arizona, is often considered to be one such place. Bigelow is hoping the Sherman ranch will be another, and that scientific research can be conducted on the matter.

The results of NIDS research are posted on their website on the Internet. In spring of 1997, Puthoff contributed an informative book review of Paul Hill's *Unconventional Flying Objects,* which was originally published in the *Journal of Scientific Exploration* in 1996. Puthoff describes Hill's book as the "most reliable, concise summary of engineering-type data available."

Another member of NIDS is Dr. Bruce Maccabee, a Ph.D. in physics and a research physicist at the Naval Surface Weapons Center in Silver Spring, Maryland, since 1972. Maccabee has a long history of UFO research as a member of NICAP (National Investigations Committee on

Aerial Phenomena), a state director for the Mutual UFO Network (MUFON), and one of the founders and current board members of the Fund for UFO Research (FUFOR). Maccabee was also one of the UFO researchers who submitted FOIA requests in the late 1970s along with CAUS and Ground Saucer Watch, as part of the effort that unearthed so many damning documents implicating the FBI, CIA, and other agencies of involvement in UFO research.

Maccabee's essay posted on the NIDS website in June 1997 claims that recent verified videos, what he calls "hard evidence," show UFOs accelerating and even disappearing. "These videos provide, for the first time, quantitative evidence that UFOs are capable of extreme acceleration and speed."

Maccabee asserts that such extreme acceleration is achieved in the "absence of any apparent means of propulsion" such as rocket blasts, explosions, electric or magnetic phenomena. His discussion concerns the apparent lack of "action-reaction" mechanisms in UFOs.

One of the key areas of NIDS research and investigation at the Sherman ranch focuses on animal mutilations. George E. Onet, D.V.M., Ph.D., cites the fact that animal mutilation cases have been reported worldwide since the early 1960s. On the NIDS website, Onet's essay adds,

> They have been accompanied by all kinds of speculations regarding their nature. Journalists focused on these cases with a great deal of sensationalism that sometimes distorted realities. Their circumstantial association with unusual lights, unidentified helicopters, and other sightings conferred such events with an aura of mystery, which had a negative impact on further scientific study by veterinary diagnostic specialists.

In 1975, there was a rash of cattle mutilations in the northern states, coinciding with the reports of UFOs over nuclear missile sites, and at Malmstrom AFB Montana and Wurtsmith AFB Michigan. The FBI investigated these reports in its 1979 investigation, noting that "mutila-tion accounts are often accompanied by sightings of strange helicopters or UFOs." The report adds that this allegation is further supported by the discovery of carcasses with "broken legs and visible clamp marks, indicating to some investigators that the animals are being airlifted to another place where they are mutilated, then returned to the spot they are found."

Glenn Campbell discusses cattle mutilations near Area 51 in his *"Area 51" Viewer's Guide:* "Cattle mutilations *have* been reported nearby. Reputable ranchers in Lincoln County claim to have lost a number of animals to this mysterious 'disease'—that is, all blood drained from the body without a drop on the ground, laser-like "zipper" incisions in the corpse and parts of the body surgically removed—but most such incidents happened in the 70s and 80s."

From field offices based in New Mexico, the report estimated that by 1979 approximately ten thousand head of cattle had been "mysteriously mutilated." Yet the FBI investigation concluded that animal predators were responsible for all of the mutilations.

In addition to mutilation investigations, NIDS also performs laboratory analysis of "alien implants," small devices allegedly placed inside of humans by aliens. In a report on "implants" that were removed from abductees by podiatrist John Leir, the language of the letter of opinion is very technical and there is no explanatory text to summarize the results in real human terms: "Interspersed with the metal grains are other minerals rich in iron and/or nickel such as troilite, FeS, and schreibersite, (Fe, Ni) . . . Elemental analysis done by X-ray Energy Dispersive Spectroscopy (EDS) indicated iron and phosphorus as major constituents of the cladding material surrounding the iron core."

Two thirds of the way through the "Letter of Opinion (Samples T1, 2 and T3)," it reads: "This may not be a problem after all, since the specimens could be just a small fragment of a larger meteorite body."

So it's a meteorite fragment! No . . . because immedi-

ately after that, an "altogether different hypothesis" is formulated based on the fact that these objects came from a
human body. Yet there was no overarching conclusion, and
I was left to wonder—what does this mean?

The head of NIDS, John Alexander, isn't known to be
a UFO researcher—his pioneering work is in the area of
nonlethal weapons, beginning back in 1980 when he published an article in the U.S. Army's journal, *Military Review.* In "The New Mental Battlefield," Alexander proposed
that telepathy could be used to interfere with the brain's
electrical activity.

I tried to see Alexander, but he preferred to have a brief
phone interview in February 1997. Alexander claims his
aim with NIDS is to "get information into the hands of the
public and making sure that information is correct." Ufology today, he says, needs peer research group standards
rather than "poor—if any—research. They're well-
intentioned folk, but the political infighting in the UFO
community destroys any efforts they make." Alexander also
repeated two or three times that he was busy with work
other than NIDS right now, saying, "Nonlethal is now
pretty high on the list."

After retiring from the Army in 1988, Alexander began
working at Los Alamos National Laboratories in nonlethal
projects. He chaired the second major nonlethal weapons
conference in March 1996, as well as the first one in November 1993. According to a letter to *Saucer Smear* in May
1996, Alexander also does work for NATO.

A *Nexus Magazine* article in 1993, "Psychic Warfare
and Non-Lethal Weapons," described the type of psycho-
tronic weapons Alexander worked on, including high-
power, very low frequency acoustic beam weapons which
can cause nausea, vomiting, and abdominal pains. Nonlethal weapons are described as being most useful in regional
and low-intensity conflict such as terrorism, drug traffick-
ing, domestic crime, ethnic violence, and situations such as
the Los Angeles riots.

Alexander published *The Warrior's Edge* in 1990

(coauthored by Janet Morris and Major Richard Groller), describing various ways individuals can achieve "optimum performance." This rose out of Alexander's work with the Jedi Project, focusing on human willpower and concentration with the aim of constructing "teachable models of behavioral/physical excellence using unconventional means."

"Unconventional" is the one trait all of these scientists interested in UFO research have in common. The goal is best put by the international Society for Scientific Exploration (SSE), founded in 1981, which offers the peer-reviewed *Journal for Scientific Exploration:*

> The primary goal of SSE is to provide a professional forum for presentations, criticism, and debate concerning topics which are for various reasons ignored or studied inadequately within mainstream science. A secondary goal is to promote improved understanding of those factors that unnecessarily limit the scope of scientific inquiry, such as sociological constraints, restrictive world views, hidden theoretical assumptions, and the temptation to convert prevailing theory into prevailing dogma.

CHAPTER 11

Alien Abductions

IT WAS a seminal year for Area 51 in 1993. The Air Force filed to withdraw Freedom Ridge and White Sides, and overall the security of the secret base was heightened for the purported arrival of the new experimental stealth.

It was also the year that Bill Hamilton and his wife-to-be, Pamela, were abducted by gray aliens led by a leader who called himself "Quaylar." It was March 16, and they were parked near the Black Mailbox off Highway 375. In an *Omni* interview with Dennis Stacy, a year and a half later, Hamilton recalled the lights they both saw: "I looked at it through binoculars and it seemed to be on or near the Groom Road and casting a beam on the ground." As it drew nearer, "the light appeared to be an object the size of a bus with square light panels lifting off from the ground. The panels appeared to glow amber and blue-white."

There is a large bus that ferries workers to Area 51 early in the morning, then returns in mid-afternoon, dropping (at least some) workers at cars left parked in front of an abandoned casino at the junction of the Extraterrestrial Highway and U.S. 93.

I once had the experience of meeting that bus head on, coming around a curve not far from the border of Area 51. Even in the daylight it was a daunting experience—this was no friendly orange school bus. It was tall and broad and silver with dark windows, and it spewed a plume of choking dust after it.

However, Hamilton, the former director of investigations for MUFON Los Angeles and a MUFON field investigator since 1976, believes this wasn't a bus: "The lights rapidly resolved into two glowing orbs or discs of brilliant blue-white light, so bright they hurt my eyes." The next time Hamilton looked at his watch, approximately thirty minutes had passed. Glenn Campbell was at the Little A'Le'Inn when the couple returned. He told me, "When I saw them at Rachel, before they went out, I said to myself—I bet something happens to them. Sure enough, they came back upset, talking about the lights, but neither had any memory of an abduction at that time."

In an interview with Hamilton in May 1997, I asked him about that night—did they remember anything right after it happened? Hamilton replied, "When we went back to Rachel, I woke up at 1:17 in the morning, screaming. I scared the life out of my wife. Here I was dreaming of a dark silhouette leaning over me with a pinpoint light. As I woke, I saw the VCR light and the two merged, and I screamed."

The couple went to John Lear in Las Vegas, and Lear hypnotically regressed them both, uncovering their strange abduction. Hamilton assured me that Lear asked no leading questions, and that they simply began to do it as a way for them to relax. Hamilton says, "He was the most excellent hypnotist I have ever run across, and I couldn't believe it. I knew this guy for a while. I said, John, how did you learn this?"

Under hypnosis, the Hamiltons recovered memories of being abducted by the gray aliens and taken onboard the UFO. They had large dark eyes, and Hamilton later drew a picture of "Quaylar." On the gray alien's uniform is a little Starfleet-like insignia on his (its?) breast.

I asked Hamilton whether this wasn't a case of the mind taking elements of reality and creating a fantasy situation. But Hamilton laughed and replied that it was really the other way around. " 'Star Trek' took a lot of stuff from us. Roddenberry came to one of the meetings sometime, maybe out at Giant Rock [Spacecraft Conventions]. It gave him the ideas—the transporter idea, and the Federation idea. We could prove what we were talking about."

Hamilton served in the USAF Security Service from 1961 to 1965, and for the past twenty-seven years he's worked in data processing as a senior programmer. Hamilton has made a study of the UFO phenomenon since 1953, when he began writing and lecturing while he was still a teenager. He's written seven books, including one about his abduction experience entitled *Alien Magic*. A revision was released in 1996.

Hamilton has written UFO articles for *Search, Energy Unlimited, Borderland Sciences Journal, New Age Science Journal*, the *New Atlantean Journal*, the *Psychic Observer, UFO Magazine*, the *MUFON UFO Journal, UFO Universe*, and *Unsolved UFO Sightings*. He has also been interviewed by various network and cable television shows, including ABC News in San Diego and the Fox network television show "Sightings."

With "over one hundred personal sightings" of UFOs, Hamilton has had plenty of experience in the field. "I had telepathic contact in 1957," he explained to me, as part of an ESP experiment. Since 1958, he has participated in communication experiments using light beam transmitters, the same sort that are used to communicate across the English Channel. "We used that and we got responses," he said, adding, "In 1981, I had the classic bedroom intrusion, with the three little guys and the smell of ozone in the air. I hadn't even heard of that until Budd Hopkins. That happened in Glendale, Arizona."

Hamilton has always taken an interest in spacecraft propulsion systems and other areas of advanced technology. He spoke on the electrogravity theory of spacecraft propulsion at the Advanced Propulsion Workshop, hosted by NASA scientist Alan Holt, at the MUFON Symposium in Houston in 1980.

Since Bob Dean was also a MUFON member in Arizona, I asked Hamilton if he knew the former NATO officer. Hamilton replied that he knew Dean before he got involved in the lawsuit over his FEMA promotion. "We were the first ones to contact Bob Dean back in 1988, investigating government connections. Tal and I were putting together a video. We were going around to all those people." A few years after Hamilton's abduction by Quaylar, he became the assistant state director of MUFON Arizona. But after twenty-one years as a member of MUFON, in May 1997 he left that organization to become executive director of Skywatch International, a group founded the year before by another retired Air Force man, Colonel Steve Wilson.

Hamilton's departure coincided with the March 1997 sightings over Phoenix. These sightings were seen by so many people that Councilwoman Frances Emma Barwood asked city staff to look into reports of bright lights in the city's March skies. Barwood says she received over fifty calls, describing the same thing: something passed overhead that was huge and made no noise.

When Councilwoman Barwood's justifiable concern was ridiculed by the mayor, Skip Rimsza, Barwood stated in *The Arizona Republic* on May 20, "It's still amazing to me that no one seems to be that concerned. There definitely was something there. As to what it was, I don't have a clue. I'm kind of an open-minded skeptic."

At least half a dozen TV newscasts stated that the military had set off flares. Yet there is no military official on record admitting that flares were dropped over Phoenix that night.

Bill Hamilton, as assistant director for Arizona MUFON, was one of those trying to stamp out the "flare theory" by posting on UFO UpDates: "For the record I have stated that all analysis so far shows that NONE of the sightings on the night of March 13 over the state of Arizona have been explained and they remain unidentified, unconventional, and unknown."

When the Arizona sightings were revived in the news in June of 1997, Councilwoman Frances Barwood was interviewed by the media again, even appearing on the CBS "This Morning" show. Also featured was Richard Motzer, Arizona MUFON director, who maintained that one of the groups of lights was flares, while the major "event" couldn't be so easily explained.

When I asked Hamilton if his difference of opinion with the MUFON director had caused him to resign his position with the organization, Hamilton replied via e-mail on June 19, 1997:

> The dispute between one MUFON investigator and the rest of us is a long story. There were absolutely NO FLARES over Phoenix that night. No one saw any flares, but it seems like one of the Air Force's balloon stories. I am familiar with flares—several of the witnesses are experts on flares—evaluation: no flares were ever seen, but strange lights and objects were. Like I said, it is a long story. This guy was only a field investigator trainee, but since the State Director would not back me, I quit my position as Assistant State Director because I did not want to continue to deal with such incompetence. I am still a field investigator for the National MUFON organization and am now Executive Director of Skywatch International.

Hypnosis

Most abduction reports contain the same basic points: the victims are taken from an isolated place or from their beds in the dead of night; they are subjected to personal indignities like human testing or forced sexual encounters; then they are returned to where they came, controlled to the end mentally and physically by their captors.

The truly unexplainable abduction case takes place in daylight with multiple witnesses, with no memory loss— as in the 1975 Travis Walton abduction, witnessed by six other men. James Moseley, one of the founding fathers of ufology, heard Travis Walton and Mike Rogers speak at the fifth annual Gulf Breeze UFO Conference. As editor of the trade paper *Saucer Smear*, he wrote,

We had never met Walton before, and we never read his book, though we did see the movie. Everyone agrees that the movie scenes aboard the spacecraft are purely imaginary—deliberately made *different* from other abduction stories, just to be different! But what we hadn't realized till now was *how much* was seen of the Walton abduction by the other six men. *IF* this is true, there may be a stronger case here than in the better-known Betty & Barney Hill abduction.

One of the cornerstones of the abduction phenomenon is the use of hypnosis to uncover suppressed memories. Hypnosis is an investigative tool as old as the first recorded abduction case, described in 1966 by journalist John G. Fuller in *The Interrupted Journey*. The abduction of Barney and Betty Hill has become a classic example: the abduction took place on a lonely road, they had strange medical examinations performed on them, and then they were released after having their memories erased.

It took two months before the couple realized, while discussing their case with UFO investigators, that the 190-mile journey had taken seven hours—more than twice as long as it should have. This became known as "missing time."

Some abductees remember a lot about their experiences, some have only flashbacks or vague memories, while others exhibit signs of being traumatized sometime in their past. Like Bill and Pamela Hamilton, many abductees only remember missing time, or they experience bad dreams, until they undergo hypnotic regression.

Fred Frankel, a Harvard Medical School professor and psychiatrist in chief at Boston's Beth Israel Hospital, maintains, "Hypnosis helps you regain memories that you would not have otherwise recalled. . . . But some will be true, and some will be false. The expectation of the hypnotist and the expectation of the person who is going to be hypnotized can influence the result."

As a psychiatrist and Harvard professor, John Mack brought respectability to the abduction phenomenon. Mack is also the Pulitzer Prize–winning author of *T. E. Lawrence: A Prince of Our Disorder*, and he helped found the clinical psychiatry department at Cambridge Hospital.

In 1994 when John Mack's book *Abduction: Human Encounters with Aliens* was published, it was similar in theme to artist Budd Hopkins's books *Missing Time* (1981) and its 1992 follow-up, *Intruders*. All three books point to recurring patterns which they maintain indicate that abduction experiences are more than just random psychological delusions. Though Hopkins has no medical or psychological training, he began uncovering hundreds of abduction cases by hypnotically regressing his clients.

In an article in *Time* in April 1994, Mack's associate, Professor Frankel, stated, "Dr. Mack is ignoring the high level of suggestion and imagery that surrounds the way in which he deals with these people." The agitation of the Harvard professors was also reported in the serious scientific journal *Nature* in May 1995: "Harvard University is said to have set up a special faculty committee to investigate research by John Mack, professor of psychiatry at the Harvard Medical School, into the experiences of those who claim to have been abducted in Unidentified Flying Objects (UFOs)."

Psychologists have expressed doubts about the methodology of Mack's work, and others claim he manipulates the subjects under hypnosis. In August 1995, Mack was publicly censured, but his job at Harvard was not threatened. While Dr. Mack freely acknowledges that he is not "an expert on hypnosis," he adds, "The attacks on hypnosis didn't begin until it began to reveal information that the culture didn't want to hear."

Therapists have traditionally used hypnosis as a way to draw out a patient's fantasies, which can then be examined to understand their meaning. There have been cases where the technique was proven to create false memories. Says Ray William London, president of the American Boards of Clinical Hypnosis: "It isn't a way of validating an abduction or anything else."

At a 1997 meeting of the American Association for the Advancement of Science, several psychologists reported on their "malleable-memory" experiments. E. Loftus, professor at the University of Washington, asked a group of parents to describe events that their children had when they were young. When she went to the children, who were now adults, she "walked them through a series of real incidents and then threw in a fake one: as a young child, they had been lost in a shopping mall and were frightened and cried until an elderly person found them and reunited them with their parents." According to Loftus, nearly 25 percent of the subjects only needed a little coaxing to "remember" that they had been lost as a child. Some even supplied additional details of the nonevent.

Jennifer Freyd, a professor of psychology at the University of Oregon and author of *Betrayed Trauma: The Logic of Forgetting Childhood Abuse,* has had her own conflicts with the recovered memory phenomenon. In 1991, she herself recovered memories of abuse, only to have them publicly and vehemently denied by her family. Her parents were among the founders of "False Memory Syndrome Foundation," an organization that attempts to discredit recovered memories.

Freyd continues to analyze the subject in scholarly essays. She believes the memories that are suppressed are so traumatic that the individual must deny the existence of the event. She recounts cases of memory loss that range from vague, nonthreatening reinterpretations of the past to entire sections blanked out of a victim's life.

Freyd does admit that some false memories might be due to therapists "causing" or "implanting" them in clients. She contends that this could be entirely unconscious on the part of the therapists, who are simply searching for some reason why their clients are disturbed.

No matter which side scientists take in the debate on recovered memories, there is plenty of research to yet be done.

Physiological Research

After my interview with Bill Hamilton, I was left wondering which came first—his interest in UFOs or the UFOs' interest in him? Hamilton says he was still in grade school when he read Donald Keyhoe's book *Flying Saucers from Outer Space*. He also met early UFO contactees at the Giant Rock Spacecraft Conventions hosted by George Van Tassel.

Did this create a tendency in Hamilton to interpret his experiences as alien encounters? Or, as he claims, did his research open his mind up to comprehend what was happening to him?

The effects of a person's belief systems on what they see have been studied by Nicholas Spanos, a psychologist at Carleton University in Ottawa. In *Science News*, November 1993, Spanos claimed that UFO sightings are reported most often by people who believe in the existence of UFOs, extraterrestrials, and other paranormal phenomena, such as reincarnation. But this could simply be a correlation between those who believe and those who *report* UFO incidents—we don't have the data on other nine-tenths of the people who see UFOs and don't report them.

People who report close encounters with UFOs are typically middle-class, no-nonsense, nine-to-five citizens. According to a study in the November 1996 *Journal of Abnormal Psychology,* abductees aren't psychologically disturbed or prone to creating fantasies.

Spanos and his colleagues contend that it's people's expectations that lead some to "shape UFO episodes out of ambiguous events or unusual physical sensations that most often occur at night and in conjunction with a dream or sleep. In particular, many people may have religious beliefs that provoke unusual sensory or visual experiences that they don't normally talk about."

There is also the well-known phenomenon of sleep paralysis, a brief event that occurs just before nodding off or upon awakening. Notable is the observer's inability to move and feelings of panic, often accompanied by unusual sensations and hallucinations.

People interpret these experiences in terms they can understand. Stories of nighttime paralysis have occurred throughout human history and have been variously explained as succubi and incubi, demons, angels, ghosts, or waking nightmares.

There's also the theory of "morphic resonance," which is a kind of cumulative memory. According to one web poster discussing this esoteric subject on UFO UpDates in January 1997:

> Sheldrake and others suggest that the concepts of homing, migration, the sense of space, bonding, social organization and communication in general can be understood in terms of fields and related to known principles of physics. Through Sheldrake's suggestions, it seems reasonable to explain most phenomena in terms of morphic fields, including psi, remote viewing, precognition, false memory, reincarnation memory, and even ufo experience.

This web poster has experienced "out-of-body-experiences, RV NDE and ET contact, dreams of former life experiences, including the Civil War, as an American Indian, and over six months of dreams of a 'holocaust death.' " He believes it is "reasonable to explain all of this in terms of morphic resonance."

Some current theories turn to a natural source for abduction experiences, such as geophysical phenomena. Unusual lights were first associated with earthquakes by Charles Fort, the man known as the first ufologist. Fort wrote three books that dealt in part with the UFO phenomenon: *The Book of the Damned* (1919), *New Lands* (1923) and *Lo!* (1931).

Fort's humorous take on strange phenomena, experiences, and curiosities is carried on today by the *Fortean Times,* founded in 1973. Like Fort, the *Fortean Times* is skeptical about scientific explanations, pointing out that scientists are led by their belief systems like everyone else. Therefore scientists tend to find solutions that agree with their own theories and the "inconvenient data is ignored, suppressed, discredited or explained away."

Charles Fort once noted that the business of "finding out" is bound to offend those with closed minds or a vested interest in the status quo. So *Fortean Times* holds one of the largest collections of strange stories and odd occurrences in the world. You can find the *Fortean Times* Reporting Centre on their website, which asks, "Has something weird happened to you lately?"

Geophysical Phenomena

The geophysical source of UFOs was first scientifically studied by French researcher Ferdinand Lagarde. In a 1968 article, he presented an initial survey of the French sightings during the worldwide 1954 UFO wave. Lagarde found that 37 percent of reported UFO sightings occurred on or in the immediate vicinity of faults, and that 80 percent of the sighting localities were associated with fault lines.

Lagarde did control tests, comparing the number of communes that were near faults, and the correlation was closer to 10 percent. Lagarde concluded that "UFO sightings occur by preference on geological faults. It seems as though faults, as such, are not merely the external aspect of an irregularity in the Earth's crust, but are also the scenes of delicate phenomena—piezo-electrical, or electrical, or magnetic, and at times perhaps of gravimetric variation or discontinuity."

In 1977, Dr. Michael A. Persinger together with Gyslaine Lafreniere published "Space-Time Transients and Unusual Events," in which they described a similar study of the entire area of the United States. Results indicated that UFO sightings clustered in certain areas, with a higher correlation between UFO activity and the location of earthquake epicenters. Persinger and Lafreniere concluded that "the data consistently point towards seismic-related sources."

Persinger and Lafreniere defined this earthquake-related phenomenon as the piezoelectrical effect, originally the term used for electricity that is produced by crystals when they're subjected to pressure. The two scientists claimed that the stress caused within seismic areas could produce an "electric column" from a few feet to thousands of yards across. This electric field would ionize the air into glowing shapes that would shift as the stress in the fault shifted.

This electric field could stimulate abduction experiences, Persinger and Lafreniere contend. They base their theories on research into the stimulation of the temporal lobes of the mammalian brain. In "Space-Time Transients," they describe how an abduction event could happen:

> The electrical stimulation of the hippocampus produces lucid dreams in a waking state. Also sudden unconsciousness by electro-convulsive-like shock induced by the EM field column may produce pre-event amnesia filled with confabulation from the primary memory. If less severe the effects of the EM field column may include epileptic-like auras, vertigo, disorientation, putrid smells, voices, and feelings of a presence.

Dr. Persinger has since published more than one hundred technical articles in the areas of psychobiology, parapsychology, brain functions, and environmental health. Persinger is a professor of psychology and head of the

Neuroscience Research Group at Laurentian University, Sudbury, Ontario, but he is much better known for his theory on the piezoelectric source of UFO sightings: ". . . odd visual experiences, the profoundness, the fact that it's true reality, the intense meaningfulness, the cosmic significance of it all, the desire to proselytize, to spread the word, the sense of the personal, as if one is particularly chosen—these are all classic temporal lobe signs."

Dr. Susan Blackmore, a fairly skeptical psychologist from the University of the West of England, underwent Persinger's experiment for BBC 2's "Horizon," which aired in November 1994. Dr. Blackmore reported that the electrodes stimulating her brain cells produced an unpleasant and frightening experience, including the feeling that she was being physically manipulated by some unseen entity. Yet Blackmore was not entirely convinced by the experiment.

The piezoelectric effect has often been compared to the earth lights phenomenon. Paul Devereaux wrote a summary of the phenomenon in his 1982 book *Earth Lights,* noting a connection between tectonic events and the light phenomena in Great Britain. In 1989, Devereux's *Earth Lights Revelation* was a sequel to his first book, containing discussions of triboluminescence, or light that is produced by frictional forces, and thermoluminescence (the production of light by heating).

Most scientists agree that earth lights consist of some form of plasma or ionized gas. Devereux compared this phenomenon to a "quantum event" in that it lies within a fluctuating probability field between energy and matter. Dr. Hal Puthoff once theorized that earth lights are powered by zero-point energy (as a coincidence, at one time Persinger was also involved as a researcher in the SRI remote viewing project).

Devereaux criticized Persinger's original broad geographical study of anomalous phenomena with Lafreniere, questioning the scientific validity and conclusions drawn from "intuition" rather than the computer:

Why attempt to explain other, possibly more complex and perhaps unrelated mechanisms under the same conceptual umbrella? . . . This approach to the UFO problem cannot sensibly be conducted over the entire USA in any case the area is so vast that untenable numbers of UFO events would have to be involved. And how would one cope with the detailed geological data of such a continental area, even if it is available?

Joel Henry, Minnesota MUFON webmaster, points out that magnetic fields and electrostatic fields are not the same. When skeptics point to piezoelectric phenomena to explain abduction experiences, Henry objects that

Without electromagnetic fields (sustained over some time, yet) NO fantasies can be induced into the brain. Careful analysis of the facts and no corroboration of the so called Persinger test effect with a real abductee/experiencer to compare the two experiences leads to easy rejection of the hypothesis. All too often skeptics and debunkers generalize their facts to fit the case and ignore the ones that don't fit. Just plain bad science if you ask me.

And finally, the voice of reason, Jan Aldrich of Project 1947, asks, why isn't Persinger pursuing the National Academy of Sciences for a multimillion-dollar grant to do further studies?

If [it] exists the way the theorist claims, it could be a possible indication of earthquakes. Considering some of the current rather "far-out" correlations that are being studied (i.e. the number of lost pet advertisements in the newspaper) CSICOP and Persinger should be beating the drums to do an UFO-earthquake study. However, these little theories are *only* used to debunk a UFO sighting after the fact. This appears to be the theory and theorist's only function. There is no attempt to advance scientific knowledge.

Abductions by the Government

Evidence for military kidnappings of alleged UFO abductees has been gathered by Project-MILAB, founded by Dr. Helmut Lammer. Lammer has a Ph.D. in geophysics and experience in NASA/ESA space projects. He is the Austrian representative for the Mutual UFO Network and a member of the Society for Scientific Exploration (SSE).

Dr. Lammer has reviewed the relevant literature and contacted UFO and mind control researchers all over the world. He also compared Project-MILAB's findings with the comprehensive UFO Abduction Study by Dr. Thomas Bullard, the MUFON Transcription Project, and the MIT Abduction Proceedings.

As Lammer stated in his "Preliminary findings of Project-MILAB" published on the Alien Jigsaw website: "Not many of the popular books on the subject of UFO-abductions mentioned these experiences. Especially disconcerting are the facts that abductees recalled seeing military/intelligence personnel together with alien beings working side by side in these secret facilities."

Project-MILAB contends that abductees are used by the military for their mind control experiments, like test-targets for microwave weapons. There are also theories that abductees are being kidnapped in order for our government to learn more about their past alien contact. Lammer asserts, "It seems to me that they are interested in well investigated UFO-abduction cases. They are monitoring the houses of their victims, kidnapping and possibly implanting them with military devices sometimes shortly after an UFO-abduction experience. It appears to me that they are searching for possible alien implants too."

Katharina Wilson is the author of *The Alien Jigsaw* (1993), a self-published book that adheres with strict honesty to her journal entries—some made before she realized that her personal experiences fit the larger pattern of alien abductions. One of Wilson's conclusions is that "I had been abducted by aliens, and either some members of our government are working with them, or the aliens have manipulated me into believing our government is working with them."

Wilson's venture into self-publishing proved to be successful. She has also published *The Alien Jigsaw Researcher's Supplement,* while the first and second editions of *The Alien Jigsaw* were picked up by national bookstore chains like Barnes and Noble and B. Dalton Booksellers. In her books, Wilson admits that intense emotions are evoked by the abductions—including strong, loving feelings between herself and her abductors, in addition to painful psychological manipulation such as when the aliens test her intense love for stray cats and dogs. She has also had "Teaching Dreams" and visions of the future, including a precognition of lightning that saved her life.

Patrick Huyghe points out how important it is to have Wilson writing about her own experiences rather than "filtering" her story through abduction investigators. In Huyghe's *Omni* article "In Her Own Words: An Abductee's Story," February 1996, he writes:

Indeed, as a journalist who's investigated more than my fair share of UFO abductions, I've learned that many aspects of the so-called abduction phenomenon just don't make it into print. Instead, most investigators inevitably process the stories, molding the accounts to fit the theories they favor or the patterns they expect to find. Things that don't fit their preconceived notion of what's really happening "out there" are often deliberately left out of subsequent retellings of the tale.

Along with Puzzle Publishing, Wilson maintains the "Alien Jigsaw" website. She believes MILAB reports may be evidence that a secret military/intelligence task force has operated in North America since the early eighties, monitoring alleged UFO abductees.

Both Wilson and Dr. Lammer contend that while there are parallels, there are also "striking differences" between the experiences of abductees and mind control victims. While most UFO abduction cases begin with beings appearing suddenly in a room, instantly evoking a paralysis in their victims, the MILAB abductee reports begin with a shot from a syringe. MILAB abductees are examined in terrestrial-type rooms, very different from the spare, sterile environment of UFO abductees.

Dr. Lammer theorizes that the military uses some form of electronic jamming to "create a static which blocks out sight and sounds." The name of this phenomenon is RHIC-EDOM or Radio-Hypnotic Intracerebral Control and Electronic Dissolution of Memory (EDM), first described by Lincoln Lawrence in his 1967 book *Were We Controlled*?

The jury is still out on these issues, but as Wilson states in "Project Open Mind: Are Some Alien Abductions Government Mind Control Experiments?" (1996): "What I want to do in Project Open Mind is determine if the military and other government personnel that I report seeing during my experiences have both the motive and the means for being there."

Physical Evidence

Alien abductees often point to strange scars on their bodies—scoop marks that leave a shallow pit in the skin much like those made by "punch biopsy" medical instruments. Others have fresh cuts or bruises when they wake in the morning. Sinus cavities are commonly said to be the site where aliens leave implants, and tiny BB-like pellets have been sneezed or blown out of abductees' noses.

Physical evidence has been sought for some years, yet no alien implant has yet been proved to be extraterrestrial in origin. But researchers continue to analyze removed implants—such as the incomprehensible NIDS report, discussed earlier, from the "New Mexico Tech"—in the hopes that something "extraterrestrial" will be found.

Journalist Patrick Huyghe examined one interesting analysis of an alleged alien implant in the April 1995 *Project Open Book* article "Alien Implant Or—Human Underwear?" Huyghe describes the abduction of Richard Price that took place one evening in September 1955, near a cemetery in Troy, New York. Price remembers that a couple of humanoids took him aboard their craft and injected an implant under the skin of his penis.

Price didn't speak of the incident until nine years later, to a girlfriend who spread the story around his high school, causing Price extreme embarrassment and distress. The high school principal referred Price to a psychologist. As Huyghe describes, "He underwent a battery of psychological tests and was given various medications. But since no one had even heard of UFO abductions back then, he eventually ended up in a state hospital. He was released after three months, but only after 'admitting' to the doctors on his case that the incident had never occurred."

Then in 1981, a doctor confirmed that there was a foreign object under the skin, and he provided Price with a medical report. Since there was no discomfort, the recommendation was that nothing should be done. Then in June 1989, "Price noticed the implant protruding above the skin, and about two months later it came out. The object was roughly cylindrical, rounded at both ends, and had at least six small appendages. Tiny, measuring about 1 millimeter wide and 4 millimeters deep, it had an amber colored interior and a white shell."

Two weeks later, David Pritchard, an open-minded scientist at the Massachusetts Institute of Technology, agreed to analyze the "implant." Pritchard found that the object was composed of "the kind of material elements and chemicals—carbon, oxygen, hydrogen, and compounds—one would expect if the object were biological in origin and formed right here on planet Earth."

Thomas Flotte, a dermatopathologist at Massachusetts

General Hospital in Boston, also studied the "implant" and discovered concentric layers of fibroblasts, a type of cell found in connective tissue and extracellular material like collagen. Flotte also found cotton fibers, indicating Price's body had produced calcified tissue in response to an injury.

According to Huyghe, for decades Price has been trying to deal with his memory of that first abduction, along with two subsequent encounters. Richard Price is currently writing a book entitled *What Affects Your Life.*

Patrick Huyghe reasons that if UFO abductions are real, then there should be evidence. In "UFO Crime Lab," in the same issue of *Project Open Book,* Huyghe interviewed Victoria Alexander, a writer and UFO researcher in Santa Fe. Alexander suggests that crime-scene investigative techniques should be used to gather evidence in UFO abduction cases: "After all, crimes are supposedly being committed. The aliens are accused of unlawful entries, kidnappings, assaults, and rapes. So I think it's time we start looking at the typical bedroom abduction as a police crime-scene unit would."

Alexander is writing a manual outlining collection protocols, and designing a kit that can be used by abductees and investigators. She wants to get abductees' participation so that they "stop thinking of themselves as victims" and start trying to find a concrete answer. Alexander argues,

> Since the vast majority of abductees claim the aliens are humanoid, not robots, there should be biological and chemical traces of their presence. If these are real events, if the aliens are real, if contact is taking place, there has to be real evidence for it—latent fingerprints, fungi, particles, whatever. It's a basic tenet of criminalistics that when any two items come in contact there will be an exchange of microscopic particles.

One of the things Alexander recommends is for "conscious repeaters," those people who feel they are abducted over and over again, to take a urine sample the morning after and have it analyzed. "Lab tests of urine should show if the body has undergone any stress. And if the abductee wakes up with a bloody nose, they should keep a sample of that, too, for later analysis."

Alexander knows that with abductees collecting this evidence themselves, there will be smudged fingerprints and contaminated samples. But there's little choice when no one else is willing to do it. She hopes that with some evidence gathered, professionals will begin to take an interest.

Huyghe quotes Thomas Van Valkenburgh, bureau chief of the Department of Public Safety's crime lab at the New Mexico State Police headquarters in Santa Fe, who finds Alexander's suggestion feasible. He also admits that police bureaus may turn down requests from abductees who want their homes examined, so people "are probably going to have to do it themselves, at least at first." The next step is getting the UFO organizations involved so that researchers can help administer the tests in order to control the procedure.

Most abductees would agree to do anything to discover the truth. Almost all claim that their experiences have dramatically affected their lives. That's why John Velez posted an article on UFO UpDates that was written by his wife's cousin, Paul Vitello, in response to the Heaven's Gate suicide.

Paul Vitello is a Pulitzer Prize–winning news journalist, and his article "It's a Struggle, Staying Grounded," was published in *Newsday* on Sunday, March 30. Vitello described his long friendship with Velez and remembers the first time Velez confided that he had been abducted by aliens. Vitello said his skin turned cold:

> It was not just because the story he told was chilling, or because I could see the fear in his face as he described new scars on his body and on those of others like him who have been abducted, or as he bravely told of his decision to help "researchers" collect military radar and videotape evidence of the many recent visitations on

earth by extraterrestrials. I felt clammy, mostly, at seeing a person I thought I knew transformed before my very eyes into someone I couldn't really ever know.

Velez posted Vitello's article as a rebuttal to those who claim abductees are simply trying to get attention: "The price that I (we) have paid, (and continue to pay) for giving up to the higher dictates of my (our) conscience is not something easily assessed. It has cost me, and my loved ones dearly. All for the sake of telling the truth."

CHAPTER 12

UFOs in Popular Culture

A GALLUP poll taken in March 1987 found that nearly 50 percent of the respondents believed that UFOs are actually extraterrestrial craft piloted by aliens. In the past ten years, the popular belief in the ET hypothesis for UFOs has risen, and now, according to a recent CNN/*Time* poll, 64 percent of the respondents said that aliens have contacted humans, and 37 percent said aliens have contacted the U.S. government.

Are incidences of UFO contact increasing or are people more disposed to see UFOs? Even back in 1952, the Project Blue Book director, Edward J. Ruppelt, thought they were getting only about 10 percent of the reports. Francis Ridge, project coordinator for the Lunascan Project, points out that currently there are over 130,000 reports on UFOCAT, with primary entries around 100,000. The UFO Filter Center has over 4,000 listed on Ridge's Regional Sighting Information Database for Missouri, Illinois, Indiana, Ohio, Kentucky, and Tennessee.

And it's not just sightings—the CNN/*Time* poll says that half the people polled believe that humans have been abducted by aliens. This belief is so widespread that London insurance brokerage Goodfellow, Rebecca, Ingrams, Pearson announced in August 1996 that it would offer insurance policies to cover people who have been abducted. For a premium of $150 a year, you will receive about $160,000 if you can prove the abductor was not from Earth. If the insured is impregnated during the abduction, the payoff is double—and this "impregnation" clause is offered to both men and women!

UFOs in the Media

The mass media has done its fair share of raising awareness of the UFO phenomenon, especially through television shows like "Sightings" and "Unsolved Mysteries." In the nineties, The Learning Channel and Discovery began to broadcast and produce numerous UFO documentaries, even sponsoring "UFO weeks" in their programming.

Heading the list of fictional portrayals of UFOs—and leaning heavily on the government conspiracy angle—is "X-Files." Every week two FBI agents, Fox Mulder and Dana Scully, handle the more "far out" cases of UFO sightings, alien abductions, and other paranormal encounters that the Bureau officially wants nothing to do with. Just one example of life melding with fiction in "X-Files" is the fact that one of Mark Farmer's photographs of Area 51 graces the wall of Mulder's office on the show.

For decades, shows like "Star Trek," and more recently, "Babylon 5," have suggested futuristic universes filled with viable human/alien interaction. The science fiction genre has been gathering impetus in Hollywood, with numerous big-budget movies that mix *Die Hard* action and adventure with science, such as *Total Recall* and *Twelve Monkeys*.

Extraterrestrials have always been worth big money. Carl Sagan, perhaps the supreme skeptic of the ET hypothesis, got a record-breaking advance for his book *Contact*. Even though the book wasn't written yet, Sagan received payment of two million dollars in 1984. Sagan collaborated on the screenplay with his wife, Anne Druyan, but it languished for years before finally being developed. Jodie Foster plays the lead, a radio astronomer who first discovers the alien signals through the SETI project.

The use of radio telescopes to establish contact with aliens first appeared in John Elliot's *A for Andromeda* (1962), which was more skeptical of the benefits to mankind. Sagan's scientist-protagonists are portrayed as eager to meet and establish significant contact with aliens, focusing on the need for humans to rise to the intellectual challenge offered by the alien civilization.

Close Encounters of the Third Kind (1977) offered a similar kinder-gentler view of alien contact, in the same vein as Steven Spielberg's sweet and cuddly *ET,* who is hounded by nasty government agents. Almost all the aliens in the 1970s, like those in *Cocoon,* were the good guys. Then Ridley Scott's *Alien* (1979) reverted to the 1950s paranoia of terrifying monsters who want to invade and destroy us, reminiscent of *Invasion of the Body Snatchers* (1956).

In the October 1996 issue of *Alien Encounters,* Dr. J. D. Jaye, a psychologist and sociologist, summed up the fear of aliens that seems to be reflected in current popular culture:

> The fact that the concept of the "evil alien" is so prevalent at the moment is purely a reflection on the state of the times. If you look back a decade, when the United States was experiencing a boom under Reaganism, people felt considerably more secure than they do now. The "enemies" of the '80s were still the old Cold War foes of the Soviet Union, as they represented the greatest threat to our way of life.

The last time Americans felt so uneasy was in the 1950s, when the possibility of nuclear annihilation was always in the back of everyone's mind. Dr. Jaye believes that the image of the alien we see in *Independence Day* and *Mars*

Attack! is "simply a personification of our own fears and insecurities."

Conspiracy theories often claim that the government has been preparing the public for alien contact though the development of the 1980s ET films. But then the rumors go on to say that in the late eighties there was a "falling out" between the aliens and their government handlers.

Media propaganda has certainly been used by the government since the modern UFO phenomenon began, but it's quite a leap from there to conspiracies of alien-human co-operation. Yet some claim that *Independence Day* was created as part of an elaborate disinformation plot.

Den Devlin, screenwriter and producer of *Independence Day*, explains that the government wasn't involved in the production. In fact, the producers tried to get the military's support for the movie, figuring, why not? After all, the president and the Department of Defense are the good guys.

And the military's response? According to Devlin, in an interview in *Alien Encounters* in September 1996, they said, "Great, we love it. We're all set to join you, but there is one little thing. Can you remove any reference to Area 51?"

Using cinematic license, the movie proposes that Area 51 is where the alien bodies and saucer debris from the 1947 Roswell crash were taken. You have to forget the fact that Area 51 didn't even exist at the time, and that most Roswell experts agree that the debris was transported to Wright-Patterson Air Force Base in Ohio. Yet Devlin decided that he would rather have the action take place at Area 51, so the producers made do without using the Air Force's bases or planes.

The Air Force needn't have worried—they wouldn't have recognized Devlin's Area 51. The movie base sits in plain sight, in the middle of vast salt flats. Scores of RVs drive right up to a gate in a barbed wire fence, protecting a pristine complex, and they are simply waved through by accommodating security guards! The real Area 51, as noted earlier, is a vast collection of hangars and metal-sided buildings tucked into a desert valley that is concealed on all sides by mountains. No one can get within miles because of the sensors that have been planted around it.

Of course, *Independence Day* broke box office records when it was released on July 4, 1996. After only two months, it had made over $200 million in America alone. Most compared it to big-budget films like *Towering Inferno* and *The Poseidon Adventure,* even though the invading alien saucers were an obvious takeoff on Orson Welles's adaptation of the British writer H. G. Wells's "War of the Worlds" (1898). For a hundred-year-old concept, it held up rather well. Yet as numerous critics pointed out, the script is painfully bad, even for science fiction.

The special effects in *Independence Day* make up for the corny "the president to the rescue" bit and the limp-tentacled alien in a bag. Most of the major metropolitan regions in the world are blown up quite effectively. Watching the White House explode is surely a seminal moment in anyone's moviegoing experience—although the review in *The Wall Street Journal* noted, "As I watched the alien invaders in *Independence Day* zap the White House and pretty much everything else on the face of the earth, I tried my best to suspend disbelief, and succeeded in the wrong way. In a summer of aggressively dumb big movies, I do believe this one is the dumbest. . . ."

Yet the movie had a very real impact on at least one aspect of ufology in Great Britain. When it was released, the *Evening Standard* asked the Ministry of Defense whether there was a contingency plan to deal with an alien invasion. The MoD said that would be an instance of "civil defense" and would be dealt with by the Home Office. But when the *Evening Standard* asked the Home Office about its plans, it said that if aliens did invade, then the Ministry of Defense would rally and take care of the problem.

Independence Day wasn't the first movie to depict aliens at Area 51, but it's had the most impact so far. After its release, IRS Media stopped work on its own Area 51 movie, which also depicted the Groom Lake facility as the

place where alien research is done. The film looked like it
was ready to roll in June 1996 when Robert Carradine came
on as director. But now it may be delayed permanently.
The project's projected budget was five to eight million
dollars, "depending on the special effects."

The first Area 51 movie was *Aurora: Operation Intercept,* an HBO made-for-cable broadcast in early 1995.
Glenn Campbell noted that the movie used his Area 51
patch on the uniforms of the flight suits, and according to
his review in the *Desert Rat:*

> We watched it recently in fast forward, which is prob-
> ably the best way. It is a male action-adventure melo-
> drama most closely resembling a low-budget James
> Bond flick. A beautiful chick with a Russian accent fills
> the Blofeld role of seeking world domination through
> science. Only our hero and his fast Aurora can save the
> day. No stars in this one, only forgettables. Contains lots
> of good computer graphics of a romanticized version of
> the alleged plane, and there are a couple of nighttime
> scenes at "Groom Lake Air Force Base, Nevada" (aka
> some airport in the L.A. area).

Glenn Campbell's Area 51 site on Ufomind also has
some of the more recent popular uses of the name "Area
51." Not only is there a clothing and New Age music store
called "Area 51" in Miami Beach, but two recent novels
incorporated the theme of aliens and government cover-up
at Area 51: *Dreamland* (1995), by Hilary Hemingway and
Jeffry P. Lindsay (the granddaughter of Ernest Hemingway
and her husband), and *War Heaven* (1997), which opens
with the Roswell crash and is filled with maddening errors
if you're serious about trying to understand experimental
R&D aircraft. The best is *Area 51,* 1997, by Robert Doherty
featuring realistic military jargon and current UFO events.

Alien-inspired art can command high prices, such as David Huggins's paintings, which cost around two thousand
dollars each. *The New York Times* mentioned Huggins in a

September 1996 review: ". . . David Huggins, another self-described abductee, paints graphic and disturbing images from a lifetime of supposed encounters, including babies he fathered with alien mothers. The women have the bodies of *Playboy* centerfolds and the familiar gray alien heads with sloe eyes. . . ."

The UFO phenomenon has crept into music as well. Ozric Tentacles' techno-offshoot band, Eat Static, features on the cover of their album *Abduction* a flying saucer beaming a ray onto a stone circle, a very topical combination of New Age and the UFO phenomenon. And in August 1996, an "Abduction" Rave party took place near Area 51. The press release from Zzyzx Productions anticipated thousands of participants:

> The government has been withholding information pertaining to the secret base located at Area 51 on Groom Lake (it's a dry lake) from the people of the world. We want to know what is really going on there, and this is your chance to help find out . . . while busting some phat trancey grooves on top of the speaker stacks. Abduction will have petitions ready for you to sign indicating that you want the government to tell us what is really going on. In essence, this is a political rally . . . and an alien invocation at the same time. :)

As it turned out, there was no live music at the event, just lyric-free techno music, and "more sheriff deputies than participants" as one Rachel resident said. Glenn Campbell followed the loose production of the event in his *Desert Rat,* finally summing up, "I haven't the faintest clue what motivates those phat trancy groovesters."

ET Highway

Nevada has always been a one-industry economy. It used to be mining, but now casinos and tourism are the local cash cow. When mining communities were the norm, there was a rugged individualism in the state. This attitude of minding your own business must have served the needs of the military quite well when Area 51 was being developed.

More recently, the federal government could take some media training from Nevada politicians, who inaugurated the Extraterrestrial Alien Highway with the publicity team from Twentieth Century–Fox that was promoting *Independence Day*.

State Route 375 was renamed the Extraterrestrial Highway by the Nevada Transportation Board in February 1996. Practically the only thing noteworthy on the lonely ET Highway is the tiny "town" of Rachel, a collection of trailers crouched next to the road, almost lost in the midst of an enormous desert valley. Further south is the Mailbox Road and the Groom Lake Road, well-maintained dirt "highways" leading to the border of Area 51, as well as points such as the Medlin ranch and various cattle guards along the border of the Nellis Range.

Governor Bob Miller and other state officials formally dedicated the highway on April 18, 1996. Twentieth Century–Fox sent a whole convoy of movie stars, reporters, and production staff to the opening ceremony in Rachel. This served the dual purpose of promoting *Independence Day* and the new highway designation.

The convoy to Rachel sounds like a silly "Best of Home Video" clip. I knew something was up as soon as I heard that Mark Farmer (aka Agent X) somehow got in the lead of the convoy in his rented red convertible. Farmer followed the yellow arrow (which some unknown jokester had posted) and turned off on Groom Lake Road, leading the entire convoy straight toward Area 51. The Cammo Dudes must have been having heart attacks when they saw all those buses coming. Then Farmer turned again, onto the Mailbox Road, leading the convoy of media back to Route 375 where they belonged.

Glenn Campbell wasn't amused by the media hoopla surrounding the establishment of the ET Highway. Campbell was one of the few who pointed out the questionable logic of the State of Nevada endorsing a movie that was not even filmed locally.

The governor never consulted his constituents before signing an agreement with the Fox studio for a joint promotion. From the moment the ET Highway was proposed by State Assemblyman Roy Neighbors as a 1995 bill, Campbell claims that civil rights and fundamental procedural policies were ignored. A hearing was held, but local residents received no official notice. Though the state assembly unanimously passed the measure to designate State Route 375 "The Extraterrestrial Alien Highway," the state senate considered the bill "frivolous" and killed it.

Governor Bob Miller must have seen a gold mine in the potential tourist returns, because the following month he passed the measure in a meeting of the State Transportation Board (which he chairs). Almost immediately thereafter, he flew to Hollywood to negotiate the publicity deal with Twentieth Century–Fox.

This remote highway runs through seriously inhospitable desert. On the first page of his *"Area 51" Viewer's Guide*, Campbell warns of the dangers:

This area, at an elevation of 5,000 feet, can be bitterly cold in the winter and at night, and high winds are common. Many people come here thinking deserts are always hot and have been ill-prepared for the elements. If you choose to leave the maintained roads, remember that this is a remote area with little hope of rescue should you get into trouble away from the paved highway. In the summer, sunburn is a danger, and running out of water on a hike can be deadly.

But if you do drive to the border of Area 51 and see the security measures that have been taken, and you cruise the Internet to hear the stories of employees at the base who have been sworn to absolute secrecy for decades, where fantastic alien technology is being developed, then you begin to understand how this black-project base is beyond our reach. Area 51 is a little nation within a nation existing outside the bounds of American law, while paradoxically, it is also one of the crown jewels of the Department of Defense.

UFOs on the Internet

If you want to see Area 51, you can climb Tikaboo Peak. But Campbell warns,

> If you are not in good physical shape, you will die on this hike. If you try to hike at night, you will also die. In the winter, your car will get stuck in snow or mud before you reach the trailhead and you will die right there, miles from help. You could die if you miss the trail markers and get lost, and you could die from a lightning strike at the exposed summit. At 8000 feet, you could die from cold, wind and exposure most of the year.

Or thanks to the Internet, you can sit safely in your own living room and roam the world, exploring Area 51 and the global UFO phenomenon. You can see video clips of UFOs flying over Phoenix in 1997, or compare the Nellis footage and the Brazil UFOs. You can even hear the sound of a crop circle being made.

The *Area 51 Security Manual* is available on the Internet, the same one the Department of Defense tried to smother with retroactive classification, sealing Jonathan Turley's offices to this day. The Air Force Academy textbook is also posted on various sites, and you can see for yourself what the cadets in the physics department were being taught about UFOs as late as 1970.

You can find quotes from books that aren't available in the United States. I found interesting passages posted from Nick Pope's *Open Skies, Closed Minds*, which at that time was available only through Simon & Schuster, England. In discussing what sort of people submitted UFO reports to the Ministry of Defense during his three-year tenure at the UFO desk, Pope stated:

> They come from all walks of life, both sexes, all ages. Most of them—and this is what made their stories so convincing for me—came forward tentatively, embarrassed, and sorry for taking up my time. The vast majority did not believe in alien civilizations and wanted to avoid publicity at all costs, and to keep away from civilian UFO groups. Without the lure of money or limelight, it is difficult to see why they would have reported their experiences unless their accounts are genuine.

The Internet offers access to thousands of books and videos that are for sale—everyone's version of the "truth," all for only $14.95 plus tax and shipping. But you'll have to wade through the marketing to get to the meat of the UFO phenomenon. Everyone's in on the act—Art Bell sells his "Levitron," a floating magnet, while Jarod-2 sells a nice deck of "alien" playing cards that has tiny flying saucers on the face of each card.

You can buy aliens on everything from cups to computer mouse pads to T-shirts and baseball caps. While writing this book, my sister Becky sent me a "genuine" Area 51 "Special Agent Security Pass." That and an auxiliary membership in the Groom Lake Interceptors should get me a bored stare from the Cammo Dudes the next time I go back to Area 51.

I like to keep up on my Area 51 rumors as well as the facts on the Area 51 E-mail List Archives or UFO UpDates, such as this post from an anonymous source on January 8, 1997:

> My mother just recently told me that the passenger airliner that she road in made an emergency landing at Area 51 while she was on the way to Las Vegas from San Francisco. . . . She told me that while the plane was on the ground, her jetliner was surrounded by at least

10–15 military vehicles. All of them had their machine guns trained on the airplane. While the passengers were waiting, the air force refueled the plane and let the plane take off with a full fighter escort out of the restricted airspace.

These postings are immediately debunked by the more savvy armchair ufologists, "1. More than likely all windows would have been ordered closed by order of the Air Force. I doubt if a free-for-all of picture taking would be allowed."

The World Wide Web is the ultimate case of "buyer beware." Enjoy the freedom of the Internet for its entertainment value, but don't take any hearsay as fact. Rumors are usually just that, and are often embellished into outright hoaxes, like those who went wild over the sightings of a Hale-Bopp "companion." Some people added luminous objects to photographs of the comet and posted them for ufologists who were looking to have their theories confirmed.

You can also find serious Internet networks such as CU-FON, the Computer UFO Network, a free international telecommunications system for factual information on unidentified flying objects. CUFON also posts "Interviews" with senior ufologists, such as Richard Hall, current chairman of the Fund for UFO Research (FUFOR) and author of *Uninvited Guests: A Documented History of UFO Sightings, Alien Encounters and Coverups* in 1988. Hall has some good advice for increasing professionalism and promoting serious interest among scientists: "Don't believe half of what you read about UFOs, and subject the other half to rigorous analysis before taking it seriously. Work toward establishing the hard-core database on what constitutes the UFO mystery and don't confuse it with speculation and wild imagination."

Take a look at the declassified documents and judge for yourself. Many of the pertinent UFO documents, particularly those that are being investigated, are posted on the CUFON website as well as other private websites, such as the Black Vault. Or you can directly access declassified government documents yourself from the National Archives and the CIC, the database for the Department of Energy.

A citizen's guide to using the Freedom of Information Act and the Privacy Act of 1974 is available to help you request government records. This guide is produced by the House Committee on Government Operations, and provides detailed information on locating records, fees, requirements for agency responses, reasons for denial, and appeals.

The Internet allows ufologists to exchange information rapidly and it helps cut down on wasteful duplication of effort. Our government's predisposition to classify information has helped conspiracy theories flourish, but now, with the Cold War's end and the rise of the Internet, informational access will certainly help force the federal bureaucracy into a new era of openness.

UFO Organizations

In the past few years, the Internet has allowed authors and organizations to reach millions of people, instead of a mere two hundred attendees at a UFO convention. Yet the backbone of ufology is the civilian UFO organizations, which have contributed important research and grassroots involvement since long before the government stopped officially investigating UFOs.

In October 1969, two months before the end of Project Blue Book, the National Investigations Committee on Aerial Phenomena (NICAP) acquired a copy of the textbook from the Air Force Academy's department of physics, Space Science course #370. NICAP widely distributed the UFO chapter of the Academy textbook, causing the Air Force some embarrassment due to the contradiction between their official policy and what they were teaching their cadets. Without NICAP, no one would have known about the textbook.

NICAP was formed in October 1956 by a group of people under the direction of T. Townsend Brown, a former

Navy physicist and space-propulsion researcher. But within months Major Donald Keyhoe was in charge—Keyhoe was the author of a number of seminal books on the UFO phenomenon, such as *The Flying Saucers Are Real* (1950) and *Flying Saucers from Outer Space* (1953). NICAP published the *UFO Investigator* to report on its findings, and at its height had twelve thousand members and received forty thousand letters a year.

NICAP was basically a national center for the collection and evaluation of UFO reports. Though NICAP was a civilian UFO organization, it also had its share of CIA involvement. The most infamous CIA employee to be on the board of NICAP was Vice Admiral Roscoe Hillenkoeter, the first director of the CIA when it was formed in 1947. Hillenkoeter even signed a statement to Congress on August 22, 1960: "Behind the scenes high-ranking Air Force officers are soberly concerned about the UFOs. But through official secrecy and ridicule, many citizens are led to believe the unknown flying objects are nonsense. . . . I urge immediate Congressional action to reduce the dangers from secrecy about unidentified flying objects."

Keyhoe and Hillenkoeter were Naval Academy classmates, and both were known to believe in the ET hypothesis of UFOs. Yet Hillenkoeter's participation only lasted a few years, until he resigned from NICAP, saying that the Air Force shouldn't be criticized for its handling of UFOs.

Francis Ridge was also involved in NICAP during the early sixties. During one regional flap in southern Illinois in the summer of 1963, Ridge met a team of physicists from Project Blue Book. One of the men was Hector Quintanella, who would go on to become the next Blue Book director. As Ridge recalls:

The case involved a close encounter witnessed by at least a half a dozen people, a car chased by a UFO, vehicle interference, possible radiation, dead phone lines when the UFO was nearby, etc. The explanation by Blue Book was "the Planet Jupiter", then later "a refueling operation". Neither of these things cause a boy to become terrified and go into shock. He was afraid to go outside for weeks and lost 18 lbs. His father grabbed a shotgun, saw the object, then put it down. This statistic was NOT logged under Unknown as it should have been. This was an explained case, that is, according to Blue Book.

The CIA's involvement with NICAP and other civilian UFO organizations was quite likely due to the covert recommendations of the Robertson panel. The NICAP/CIA interaction is not specifically documented, yet a general belief has risen in the UFO community that NICAP was "destroyed" by the CIA when it instigated the removal of Keyhoe exactly two weeks before the closure of Project Blue Book in 1969. This rumor has been repeated by reputable UFO researchers, but Jerome Clark in the *UFO Encyclopedia*, Barry Greenwood, and Loren Gross maintain that NICAP fell apart for financial reasons. Jan Aldrich of Project 1947 insists, "If the CIA wanted to destroy NICAP why didn't they destroy the files as well? Why did the CIA allow CUFOS to purchase the files with the help of several 'angels'?"

In the past few years a remarkable triumvirate coalition has formed between the three main UFO investigative groups in America—CUFOS, FUFOR, and MUFON. The CFM UFO Research Coalition is a collaborative effort to share personnel and other research resources, and to fund and promote the scientific study of the UFO phenomenon.

MUFON, the Mutual UFO Network, is the oldest and largest of the three groups. Established in 1969, it now has more than five thousand members, field investigators, and research consultants worldwide. They sponsor worldwide conferences, seminars, and symposiums, including the annual International UFO Symposium. MUFON publishes the monthly *MUFON UFO Journal*, with Dennis Stacy formerly as editor, as well as an annual collection of symposium proceedings.

MUFON trains UFO field investigators and directs amateur radio networks to receive and disseminate UFO sighting reports. It also publishes a comprehensive guide available to anyone interested in conducting UFO investigations. MUFONET is MUFON's computer BBS system on the Internet.

Local chapters, such as Las Vegas MUFON, can be great sources of UFO reports and regional information. These groups often distribute newsletters and feature lectures by ufologists. I attended a MUFON meeting in Las Vegas—a discussion by Glenn Campbell of the common electromagnetic effects people report while in the vicinity of a UFO. At the next meeting, George Knapp showed an early interview with Lieutenant Colonel Philip Corso discussing information not found in his recent government insider's book, *The Day After Roswell*.

CUFOS, the J. Allen Hynek Center for UFO Studies, was founded by J. Allen Hynek. It has always been an international group of scientists, academics, investigators, and volunteers who are dedicated to the examination and analysis of the UFO phenomenon. CUFOS maintains one of the world's largest collections of original data about the UFO phenomenon, including sightings and contacts, along with a large library of related books and magazines.

CUFOS maintains a national network of field investigators who interview witnesses and examine physical evidence. CUFOS publishes the quarterly *International UFO Reporter*, with Jerome Clark as editor, and the annual, refereed *Journal of UFO Studies*. CUFOS is dedicated to promoting public understanding of the UFO phenomenon through their publications and public engagements.

FUFOR, the Fund for UFO Research, is the first—and only—organization exclusively dedicated to providing financial support for scientific research into all aspects of the UFO phenomenon. It makes available publications and reports that contain sound empirical study worthy of serious interest by government leaders, scientists, and public media. FUFOR is not a membership organization, yet many reports that have been cited in this book were funded by FUFOR, such as Project 1947, and research by Dr. Jack Kasher, Dr. Richard Haines, Kevin Randle, Stanton Friedman, and others. More than thirty grants have been given to aid research into case investigations, historical documentation and photographic analyses.

The FUFOR website specifically states it is "conservative," not for people seeking entertainment. The Fund raises money to support significant scientific research and educational projects, yet it miraculously operates without an office or a paid staff, devoting all of its revenues to its mission.

The Fund sponsors two annual awards: the Isabel L. Davis Award for excellence in UFO research, and the Donald E. Keyhoe Award for investigative journalism. As the current chairman, Richard Hall, stated in his Message dated June 5th, 1997:

> . . . Focus should be on craft-like objects (i.e., structured, metallic-appearing, ports or body lights) and objects that accelerate rapidly from a standstill, make sharp turns, give off brilliant luminosity, and otherwise do not resemble human technology at all. We are open-minded about the possibilities of what UFOs may represent, but only careful and critical-minded study will provide reliable information.

Thanks to the Supreme Court, the informational flow of the Internet is not likely to be stifled soon. Our world is facing an information explosion the likes of which hasn't been seen since the invention of the printing press—which ushered in the Renaissance of science and art.

After all my research on the UFO phenomenon, I have to agree with Richard Haines, Paul Hill, James McDonald, Bernard Haisch, and so many other reputable scientists— *something* is happening in our skies. To discover the cause, we can only continue to use our eyes to see the world around us, record it faithfully, and work toward the next step in understanding humanity's place in the universe.

SELECTED
BIBLIOGRAPHY

(sources will be cited only in the first chapter they appear)

Chapter 1

Area 51 Research Center
Glenn Campbell
Ufomind
Mailbox: Campbell@ufomind.com
http://www.ufomind.com

Glenn Campbell, with contributions by Tom Mahood. *"Area 51" Viewer's Guide,* Area 51 Research Center, 1995.

Bluefire
Tom Mahood
Mailbox: mahood@mail.serve.com
http://www.serve.com/mahood/bluefire.htm

McGinnis Military Secrecy
Paul McGinnis
Mailbox: PaulMcG@aol.com
http://www.frogi.org/secrecy.html

Coordination and Information Center (CIC)
P.O. Box 98521
Las Vegas, NV 89193-8521
Phone: 702-295-0731
http://www.doe.gov

Ben Rich. *Skunk Works: A Personal Memoir of My Years at Lockheed,* Leo Janos, 1994.

Tim Weiner. *Blank Check: The Pentagon's Black Budget,* Warner Books, 1990.

Police Call from Radio Shack, Hollins Radio Data, copyright 1996.

Charles W. Bahme and William M. Kramer. *The Fire Officers' Guide to Disaster Control,* Delaware State Fire School, 1993. Available through the Fire Engineering Book Service at 800-752-9768.

Chapter 2

Major Donald G. Carpenter and Lieutenant Colonel Edward R. Therkelson, U.S. Air Force Academy. *Introductory Space Science,* Volume II, Department of Physics, class 370 textbook, Chapter 33, Unidentified Flying Objects, 1968.

Ted Hubbard. "Air Academy Text Book Urges More Study of UFO Sightings," *Lemoore Advance* (October 8, 1970).

CUFON (Computer UFO Network)
UFO Reporting and Information Service
Jim Klotz, SYSOP

P.O. Box 832
Mercer Island, WA 98040
Phone: 206-721-5035
http://www.cufon.com

UFO Magazine
Vicki Cooper, editor and publisher
Don Ecker, Research Directory
P.O. Box 1053
Sunland, CA 91041

Seton Lloyd. *The Archaeology of Mesopotamia: From the Old Stone Age to the Persian Conquest,* Thames & Hudson, 1984.

Jacques Vallée. *Dimensions: A Casebook of Alien Contact,* Ballantine Books, a division of Random House, Inc., 1989.

Erich von Daniken. *Chariots of the Gods?,* a Berkley Book published by arrangement with G. P. Putnam's Sons, 1968.

Peter James and Nick Thorpe. *Ancient Inventions,* Ballantine Books, 1994.

George Frederick Kunz. *The Curious Lore of Precious Stones,* J. B. Lippincott Company, 1913 [published by Dover Publications Inc., 1971].

John Clute. *Science Fiction: The Illustrated Encyclopedia,* Dorling Kindersley Publishing Inc., 1995.

John Clute and Peter Nicholls. *Grolier Multimedia Encyclopedia of Science Fiction,* Grolier Electronic Publishing, Inc., 1993.

UFO Roundup
Masinaigan Productions
Joseph Trainor, editor

Mailbox: Masinaigan@aol.com
http://www.ftech.net/~ufoinfo/roundup.hts

Paris Flammonde. *UFO Exist!*, Ballantine, a division of Random House, Inc., 1976.

Mark Milchiker. "Konstantin Eduardovich Tsiolkovsky: Time to Study the Facts," *SPUTNIK*, October 1989.

Nicholas Roerich Museum
319 West 107th Street
New York, NY 10025 USA
Phone: 212-864-7752
Fax: 212-864-7704
Mailbox: info@roerich.org
http://www.roerich.org

Project 1947
Jan L. Aldrich
P.O. Box 391
Canterbury, CT 06331
Phone: (860) 546-9135
Message: 1-800-864-1000
Mailbox: jan@cyberzone.net
Internet UFO Group Project
http://www.iufog.org/

Fund for UFO Research (FUFOR)
P.O. Box 277
Mount Rainier, MD 20712
Phone/Fax: 703-684-6032
http://www.fufor.org

International UFO Reporter
Published by CUFOS (J. Allen Hynek Center for UFO Studies)
Jerome Clark, editor

2457 West Peterson Avenue
Chicago, IL 60659

Chapter 3

Dr. J. Allen Hynek. *The UFO Experience: A Scientific Inquiry,* H. Regnery Co., 1972.

Dr. J. Allen Hynek. *The Hynek UFO Report,* Sphere Books, 1978.

CUFOS (J. Allen Hynek Center for UFO Studies)
2457 W. Peterson Avenue
Chicago, IL 60659
Phone: 312-271-3611
Fax: 312-465-1898
http://www.cufos.org/index.html

Lunascan Project
Francis Ridge
Mailbox: slk@WORLD.EVANSVILLE.NET
UFO Filter Center
http://www.title14.com/ufofc/

E. J. Ruppelt. *The Report on Unidentified Flying Objects,* Doubleday & Co./paperback edition, Ace Books, 1956.

D. E. Keyhoe. *Flying Saucers Are Real,* Fawcett Publications, 1950.

David Michael Jacobs. *The UFO Controversy in America,* Indiana University Press, 1975.

Lawrence Fawcett and Barry J. Greenwood. *The UFO Cover-Up [Clear Intent],* Simon & Schuster, 1984.

E. Condon, and Associates. *Scientific Study of U.F.O.'s,* Bantam, 1969.

David Saunders. *UFOs? Yes! Where the Condon Committee Went Wrong,* Signet, 1968.

Hector Quintanella, Jr. "The Investigation of UFOs," *Studies in Intelligence,* Volume 10, #4, Fall 1966.

P. A. Sturrock. "An Analysis of the Condon Report on the Colorado UFO Project," *Journal of Scientific Exploration,* Volume 1: Number 1: Article 5, 1996.

Carl Sagan and Thornton Page, editors. *UFOs: A Scientific Debate,* Cornell University Press, 1972.

The Journal of Scientific Exploration
P.O. Box 5848
Stanford, CA 94309-5848
Phone: 415-593-8581
Fax: 415-595-4466
Mailbox: sims@jse.com
http://www.jse.com

Chapter 4

CAUS (Citizens Against UFO Secrecy)
Barry Greenwood
P.O. Box 176
Stoneham, MA 02180
Phone: 617-438-5187

James Bamford, *The Puzzle Palace: A Report on America's Most Secret Agency,* Houghton Mifflin, 1982.

Terry Hansen, "The Psychology of Dreamland: How Secrecy Is Destroying Public Faith in Government and Science," 1995.

Nick Pope, *Open Skies, Closed Minds,* Pocket Books, Simon & Schuster, Ltd., UK, 1996.

Project FT (Project Flying Triangle)
Victor J. Kean, Omar Fowler, and Ron West
Mailbox: 100545.1507@COMPUSERVE.COM

CNN
http://www.cnn.com/US/9706/19/ufo.lights/index.html

Skywatch International
Tom King, AZ Dir
Jason DeGraf
Mailbox: gilgamesh@cyberconnect.com
Mailbox: xalium@netwrx.net
OVNI CHAPTERHOUSE http://personal.netwrx.net/xal-
ium/ufovideo.htm

UFO UpDates
Distributed by the Alberta UFO Research Association
Errol Bruce-Knapp
Toronto, Ontario, Canada
Phone: 416-696-0145
Mailbox: updates@globalserve.net
http://www.ufomind.com/ufo/updates

Federation of American Scientists
307 Massachusetts Ave. NE
Washington, DC 20002
Phone: (202) 546-3300
Mailbox: fas@fas.org
http://www.fas.org/

The Groom Lake Desert Rat
"The Naked Truth from Open Sources"
Issue #25, April 15, 1995
Issue #12, July 20, 1994
Glenn Campbell
http://www.cris.com/~psyspy/area51/desert__rat

Donovan Webster. "Area 51," *The New York Times Sunday Magazine,* June 24, 1994.

Information Security Oversight Office
National Archives and Records Administration
700 Pennsylvania Avenue, NW
Washington, DC 30408

John J. Fialka. *War by Other Means,* W. W. Norton & Co., 1997.

Chapter 5

Steve Douglass and Bill Sweetman. "Hiding in Plane Sight," *Popular Science,* May 1997.

Anthony Cave Brown. *Bodyguard of Lies,* Harper & Row, 1975.

ORTK Bulletin, August 1995
OPERATION RIGHT TO KNOW (ORTK)
P.O. Box 2911
Hyattsville, MD 20784
Mailbox: hines/ortk.html
http://galaxy.tradewave.com/editors/mark-

Stanton Friedman and Don Berliner. *Crash at Corona,* Paragon House, 1992.

Stanton Friedman. *Top Secret/Majic,* Marlowe & Company, 1996.

Dennis Stacy. "Cosmic Conspiracy: Six Decades of Government UFO Cover-Ups, Part One" (in a six-part series), *Omni Magazine,* Volume 16, No. 7, April 1994.

Frank Scully. *Behind the Flying Saucers,* Henry Holt and Co., 1950.

Flying Saucer Review Magazine
FSR Publications Ltd
P.O. Box 162
High Wycombe, Bucks. HP13 5DZ England
http://www.cee.hw.ac.uk:80/~ceewb/fsr/fsrhome.htm

Norio Hayakawa
GroomWatch
P.O. Box 599
Gardena, CA 90248
Phone: 310-784-7705
Mailbox:norioa51s4@aol.com

Saucer Smear
James W. Moseley, Editor and Supreme Commander
P.O. Box 1709
Key West, FL 33041
http://www.mcs.com/~kvg/smear.htm

The Spot Report (also the *Cowflop Quarterly*)
Robert Todd
2528 Belmont Avenue
Ardmore, PA 19003-2617

Just Cause
(now known as UFO Historical Review)
Barry Greenwood
P.O. Box 176
Stoneham, MA 02180

Heaven's Gate
http://www.harborside.com/home/a/angel

Jacques Vallée. *Messengers of Deception,* And/or Press,
1979.

Lee Shargel. *Voice in the Mirror,* Oughten House
Publications, 1997.

Chapter 6

"Recollections of Roswell, Part II"
Fund for UFO Research
P.O. Box 277
Mt. Rainier, MD 20712
Phone/Fax: 703-684-6032
http://www.fufor.org

International Roswell Initiative
3105 Gables Drive
Atlanta, GA 30319 USA
Phone: 404-240-0655
Mailbox: roswelldec@aol.com
http://www.roswell.org
IRI Bulletin #3 (August 9, 1995)

Benson Saler, Charles A. Ziegler, Charles B. Moore. *Ufo Crash at Roswell: The Genesis of a Modern Myth*, Smithsonian Institute Press, July 1997.

MSNBC
http://www.msnbc.com/news/

CNI News
(Global News on Contact with Non-human Intelligence)
Michael Lindemann, editor
distributed by the 2020 Group
Mailbox: CNINewsl@aol.com.
http://www.cninews.com
http://www.iscni.com/

Donald R. Schmitt and Kevin D. Randle. *UFO Crash at Roswell*, Avon Books, 1991.

Colonel Philip J. Corso (Ret.), with William J. Birnes. *The*

Day After Roswell, Pocket Books, Simon and Schuster, 1997.

"Strange Universe"
syndicated half-hour daily newsmagazine
Produced by Chris-Craft/United Television
Distributed by RYSHER Entertainment
http://www.rysher.com/strangeuniverse

Trey Stokes
"How to Build an Alien"
http://www.trudang.com

Kent Jeffrey. "Santilli's Controversial Autopsy Movie (SCAM)," *International Roswell Initiative (IRI) Bulletin,* #5.

Randy Koppang, "Resolving History and the Rights of Man: A Dialogue with Robert O. Dean," April 1, 1995.
Stargate International Website
http://www.rtd.com/%7Estargate/Stargate.html

Stargate International Inc.
2732 S. Gwain Pl.
Tucson, AZ 85713
Phone: 520-882-9544
Fax: 520-882-4907
Mailbox: stargate@rtd.com
http://www.rtd.com/%7Estargate/stargate.html

Fortean Times
Bob Rickard and Paul Sieveking, editors
U.S. subscriptions:
P.O. Box 754
Manhasset, NY 11030-0754
London:
John Brown Publishing Ltd.
The Boathouse, Crabtree Lane

Fulham, London SW6 6LU, UK
Phone: 0171 470 2400
FAX: 0171 381 3930
E-mail: bobr@forteana.win-uk.net
http://www.forteantimes.com/

Chapter 7

Intruders Foundation Online
John Velez
Mailbox: jvif@spacelab.net
http:www.spacelab.net/~jvif/bhhp.html

Barry Greenwood. "Projects Sign and Grudge Records Released," *Just Cause* (Citizens Against UFO Secrecy), #49, December 1996.

James C. Goodall. *America's Stealth Fighters and Bombers,* Motorbooks International Publishers, 1992.

Michael Skinner and George Hall. *Red Flag: Air Combat for the 1990s,* Motorbooks International Publishers, 1993.

Project Black: The Intercept Files
Steve Douglass
Mailbox: Steve1957@aol.com or webbfeat@arn.net
http://www.perseids.com/projectblack

Intercepts Newsletter
Published by Steve and Teresa Douglass
P.O. Box 7176
Amarillo, TX 79114-7176
Mailbox: Steve1957@aol.com or webbfeat@arn.net

Area 51 Mailing List
Mailbox: area51@lists.best.com
http://www.ufomind.com

Mutual UFO Network (MUFON)
103 Oldtowne Road
Seguin, TX 78155-4099

Michael Curta, sightings reports
P.O. Box 470776
Aurora, CO 80047-0776
Phone: 210-379-9216
Mailbox: 71542.1030@compuserve.com

Encounters
Paragon Publishing Ltd, Paragon House
Richard Forsyth, editor
St. Peter's Road
Bournemouth, Dorset, England BH1 2JS
Mailbox: aardvark@paragon.co.uk

Chapter 8

Dr. Richard F. Haines. *Melbourne Episode: Case Study of a Missing Pilot,* LDA Press, 1987.

Dr. Richard F. Haines. *Observing UFOs,* Nelson-Hall Publishers, 1980.

Dr. Richard F. Haines. *UFO Phenomena and the Behavioral Scientist,* The Scarecrow Press, 1979.

Dr. Richard Haines. *Project Delta: A Study of Multiple UFOs,* LDA Press, 1994.

KUFOR (Karel's UFO Research)
Karel Bagchus
Postbus 5222
1410 AE Naarden, The Netherlands
Phone: (+31) 035-699 87 00
Fax: (+31) 035-695 11 99
Mailbox: Karel@worldonline.nl
http://www.worldonline.nl/~karel/ufo/

Jack Kasher, Ph.D. *A Scientific Analysis of the Videotape Taken by Space Shuttle Discovery on Shuttle Flight STS-48 Showing Sharply Accelerating Objects,* FUFOR: Perfectbound.

AUFORA
News & Information from the world of UFOlogy
AUFORA Web: http://www.aufora.org/
AUFORA News: http://www.aufora.org/news/
AUFORA Discussion: http://www.aufora.org/discuss/

John Locker, G7-MIZ
http://www.cybase.co.uk/satcom/

UFO Universe, Volume 1, No. 3, Condor Books (351 West 54th St., New York, N.Y. 10019).

Timothy Good. *Above Top Secret: The Worldwide UFO Cover-up,* William Morrow and Company, Inc., 1988.

Frank Edwards. *Flying Saucers: Here and Now!,* Lyle Stuart, 1967.

MUFON Ontario's Home Page:
http://auraland.com/mufon/index.htm

CSETI (Center for the Study of Extraterrestrial Intelligence)
P.O. Box 15401
Asheville, NC 28813
Phone: 704-274-5671
Fax: 704-274-6766

Chapter 9

"Dreamland" and "Coast to Coast"
Art Bell

P.O. Box 4755
Pahrump, NV 89041-4755
Chancelor Broadcasting Company
Phone: 541-664-8829
Fax Number: 702-727-8499
Mailbox: artbell@aol.com
http://www.artbell.com

George Knapp, "UFOs: The Best Evidence," UFO Audio-Video Clearinghouse (P.O. Box 342, Yucaipa, CA 92399).

John Kirby. "An Interview with Robert Lazar," *MUFON UFO Journal,* October 1993.

Area 51/Area 54 UFOs & Boblazar, Tridot Productions, Ltd.
http://www.banzai-net.com/tridot/1S4.htm

Donald Keyhoe. *The Flying Saucer Conspiracy,* Henry Holt, 1955.

Chapter 10

Paul Hill. *Unconventional Flying Objects: A Scientific Analysis,* Hampton Roads Publishing Company, 1995.

The Society for Scientific Exploration
P.O. Box 5848
Stanford, CA 94309-5848
Phone: 415-593-8581
Fax: 415-595-4466
Mailbox: sims@jse.com
http://www.jse.com/index.html

The SETI League, Inc.
P.O. Box 555
Little Ferry, NJ 07643
Phone: 201-641-1770

Fax: 201-641-1771
Mailbox: join@setileague.org

The Planetary Society
65 North Catalina Avenue
Pasadena, CA 91106-2301
Fax: 818-793-5528
Mailbox: tps@mars.planetary.org
http://planetary.org/default.html

Veritay Technology Inc.
4845 Millersport Highway
P.O. Box 305
East Amherst, NY 14051

Science, Logic and the UFO Debate
Brian Zeiler and Jean van Gemert
Mailbox: bdzeiler@ANet-chi.com
Mailbox: jeanva@oos.nl
http://www.primenet.com/~bd Zeiler/index2.htm

Jacques Vallée. *Forbidden Science: Journals, 1957–1969,*
North Atlantic Books, 1992.

Jacques Vallée. *Dimensions: A Casebook of Alien Contact,*
Contemporary, 1988.

William R. Corliss. *Handbook of Unusual Natural Phenomena,* Crown Publishers Inc., 1986.

H. E. Puthoff, Ph.D.
Institute for Advanced Studies at Austin
4030 W. Braker Lane, Ste. 300
Austin, TX 78759
Mailbox: Puthoff@aol.com

National Institute for Discovery Science
1515 E. Tropicana Suite 400

Las Vegas, NV 89119
Phone: 702-798-1700
Fax: 702-798-1970
Mailbox: discsci@anv.net
http://www.accessnv.com/nids

John Alexander, Richard Groller, and Janet Morris. *The Warrior's Edge,* William Morrow and Company, 1990.

Chapter 11

Bill Hamilton. *Alien Magic,* Greenleaf Publications, 1996.
Phone: (800) 905-UFOS (8367)

John G. Fuller. *Incident at Exeter/Interrupted Journey,* Fine Communications, 1996/1966.

John Mack. *Abduction: Human Encounters with Aliens,* Scribner, 1994.

Jennifer Freyd. *Betrayed Trauma: The Logic of Forgetting Childhood Abuse,* Harvard University Press, 1996.

Nicholas Spanos, *Science News,* Volume 144, November 13, 1993.

Paul Devereaux. *Places of Power: Secret Energies at Ancient Sites: A Guide to Observed or Measured Phenomena,* Blandford Press, 1990.

Minnesota MUFON
Joel Henry, Webmaster
http://www.wavefront.com/~jhenry/index.html

"Preliminary findings of Project-MILAB: Evidence for military kidnappings of alleged UFO-abductees"
Dr. Helmut Lammer, Ph.D.

Postfach 76
A-8600 Bruck/Mur Austria
Mailbox: lammerh@bkfug.kfunigraz.ac.at>

Patrick Huyghe. "In Her Own Words: An Abductee's Story," *Omni Magazine,* Volume 17, No. 9, January-February 1996.

"The Alien Jigsaw: True Experiences of Alien Abduction"
Katharina Wilson
Puzzle Publishing
P.O. Box 230023
Portland, OR 97281-0023
Mailbox: kwilson@alienjigsaw.com
http://www.alienjigsaw.com

Katharina Wilson. *The Alien Jigsaw,* Puzzle Publishing, 1993.

Katharina Wilson. *The Alien Jigsaw Researcher's Supplement,* Puzzle Publishing, 1994.

Patrick Huyghe. "Alien Implant Or—Human Underwear?" *Project Open Book,* Volume 17, No. 7, April 1995.

"UFO Crime Lab," *Project Open Book,* Volume 17, No. 7, April 1995.

Chapter 12

Rutgers UFO WWW page
http://www.rutgers.edu/ufo.html
FTP directory /pub/ufo at ftp.rutgers.edu
ftp://ftp.rutgers.edu/pub/ufo

The Black Vault
http://www.blackvault.com/

PARANET
Newsgroups:
alt.paranet.ufo
alt.alien.research
alt.alien.visitors

Richard Hall. *Uninvited Guests: A Documented History of UFO Sightings, Alien Encounters and Coverups,* Aurora Press, 1988.

Richard H. Hall, editor. *The UFO Evidence,* Barnes and Noble, 1997.

UFO
ORGANIZATIONS
AND RESOURCES

Abductees Anonymous
266 W. El Paso Avenue
Clovis, CA 93611-7119
http://www.CyberGate.com/~ufonline/

Aerial Phenomenon Research: The Indiana Group
18 Davis Drive
Mt. Vernon, IN 47620
Phone: 812-838-3120
Fax: 812-838-9843

Alberta UFO Research Association
Mailbox: watanabe@acs.ucalgary.ca
http://www.aufora.org
http://ume.med.ucalgary.ca/aufora/

Anathem Research
A division of AnathemÆnterprises
Doc Hambone, Research Director
2002-A Guadalupe St. #227

Austin, TX 78705
Mailbox: hambone@io.com
http://www.io.com/~hambone/index.html

Archives for UFO Research (AFU)
P.O. Box 11027
S-600 11 Norrkoping Sweden
Mailbox: afu@ufo.se
http://www.anders.liljegren@norrkoping.mail.telia.com

Area 51 Research Center
P.O. Box 448
Rachel, NV 89001
Mailbox: Campbell@Ufomind.com
http://www.Ufomind.com

BUFORA (The British UFO Research Association)
Suite 1
2C Leyton Road
Harpenden, Herts, AL5 2TL,
England
Phone: 01924 444049
Mailbox: bufora@dial.pipex.com
Mailbox: bufora@stairway.co.uk
http://www.bufora.org.uk

CISU—Centro Italiano Studi Ufologici
Mailbox: cisu@ufo.it
http://www.alpcom.it/~ufo

Cleveland Ufology Project (CUP)
7653 Normandie Boulevard C-33
Cleveland, OH 44130
Phone: 216-243-0782

CNI News
(Global News on Contact with Non-human Intelligence)
Michael Lindemann, editor

distributed by the 2020 Group
Mailbox: CNINewsl@aol.com.
http://www.cninews.com

Committee for the Scientific Claims of the Paranormal
(CSICOP)
P.O. Box 229
Central Park Station
Buffalo, NY 14215
Phone: 716-834-3222
http://www.csicop.org/

Crop Circle Connector
Mailbox: mjfussell@marque.demon.co.uk
Mailbox: anasazi@uk.pipeline.com
http://www.hub.co.uk/intercafe/cropcircle/connector.html

CSETI (Center for the Study of Extraterrestrial Intelligence)
P.O. Box 15401
Asheville, NC 28813
Phone: 704-274-5671
Fax: 704-274-6766

CUFON (Computer UFO Network)
UFO Reporting and Information Service
Jim Klotz, SYSOP
P.O. Box 832
Mercer Island, WA 98040
Phone: 206-721-5035
http://www.cufon.com

CUFOS (J. Allen Hynek Center For UFO Studies)
2457 W. Peterson Avenue
Chicago, IL 60659
Phone: 312-271-3611
Fax: 312-465-1898

Mailbox: hynek@cufos.org
http://www.cufos.org/index.html

Erickson Paranormal Research Foundation
E.P.R.F.
12426 S.E. Tibbetts Street
Portland, OR 97236
Phone: 503-760-4543
Fax: 503-760-6327
http://www.teleport.com/~captkirk/

Fund for UFO Research (FUFOR)
P.O. Box 277
Mount Rainier, MD 20712
Phone/Fax: 703-684-6032
http://www.fufor.org

ICAAR (The International Center for Aerial and Abduction
Research)
P.O. Box 154
Goffstown, NH 03054

The International Society for UFO Research (ISUR)
Mailbox: isur@america.net
http://www.isur.com

The International UFO Museum and Research Center
114 North Main
Roswell, NM 88201
Phone: 505-625-9495
Fax: 505-625-1907

Internet UFO Skeptics
Mailbox: iufos@pobox.com
http://www.geocities.com/Area51/Corridor/8148/iufos.html

Internet UFO Group Project
PROJECT 1947

Mail List: John Stepkowski and Zac Elston
http://www.iufog.org/

Intruders Foundation
P.O. Box 30233
New York, NY 10011
Phone: 212-645-5278
Mailbox: jvif@spacelab.net
http://www.spacelab.net/~jvif/bhhp.html

ISCNI (The Institute for the Study of Contact with Non-human Intelligence)
3463 State Street #440
Santa Barbara, CA 93105
Phone: 800-41-ISCNI or 805-563-8500
Fax: 805-563-8503
http://www.iscni.com/

International Committee for UFO Research (ICUR)
P.O. Box 314
Penn, High Wycombe
Buckinghamshire, HP10 8PB, England
http://dspace.dial.pipex.com/town/square/el82/icur.htm

International Society for UFO Research
P.O. Box 52491
Atlanta, GA 30355
Phone: 770-424-1623
Mailbox: isur@america.net
http://www.isur.com/

KUFOR—Karel's UFO Research
Postbus 5222
1410 AE Naarden The Netherlands
Phone: (+31) 035-699 87 00
Fax: (+31) 035-695 11 99
Mailbox: Karel@worldonline.nl
http://www.worldonline.nl/~karel/ufo/

London UFO Studies
10a Tudor Road
Barking, Essex IG11 9RX, London
Phone: 0181 270 9919

Malta UFO Research
Mailbox: mufor@maltanet.net
http://www.mufor.org/

Minnesota MUFON
4620 Garrett Ave. #104
Apple Valley, MN 55124
Phone: 612-431-2426
Mailbox: lynnbl@ix.netcom.com.
http://www.wavefront.com/~jhenry/index.html

MUFON (Mutual UFO Network, Inc.)
103 Oldtowne Road
Seguin, TX 78155-4099
Phone: 830-379-9216
Fax: 830-372-9439
Mailbox: mufonhq@aol.com
http://www.mufon.com
UFO Hotline: 1-800-UFO-2166

MUFON—Arizona Chapter
1433 W. Huntington
Tempe, AZ 85282
UFO Hotline: 602-967-6265

MUFON—Las Vegas, Nevada
6057 Sunkiss Drive
Las Vegas, Nevada 89110
Phone: 702-242-2294

Multi-National Investigations Cooperative on Aerial Phenomena (MICAP)

P.O. Box 172
Wheat Ridge, CO 80034-0928

National UFO Reporting Center
P.O. Box 45623
University Station
Seattle, WA 98145
UFO hotline 206-722-3000
Mailbox: ufocntr@nwlink.com
http://www.nwlink.com/~ufocntr

NESUFOIG (New England Studies of Unidentified Flying
Objects Investigative Group)
18 N. Blandford Rd.
Blandford, MA 01008
Mailbox>starchas@sprynet.com
http://home.sprynet.com/sprynet/starchas/

New York Fortean Society
John A. Keel
Box 20024
New York, NY 10025

NICAP (National Investigations Committee on Aerial Phenomena, Inc.)
10 Linden Street
Congers, NY 10920
Mailbox: plawrence@nicap.com
http://www.nicap.com/

Operation Right to Know (ORTK)
20 Newton Gardens
Ripon, North Yorks HG4 1QF, London
Phone: 01765 602898
P.O. Box 2911
Hyattsville, MD 20784
http://galaxy.tradewave.com/editors/mark-hines/ortk.html

OPUS (Organization for Paranormal Understanding and Support)
P.O. Box 273273
Concord, CA 94527
Phone/Fax: 510-689-2666 or toll free 888-999-OPUS
Mailbox: cd001400@interramp.com
http://www.avante-garde.com/opus/

Panasia/Pacific/Americas UFO Network (PAPAUFON)
756 Clara Drive
Palo Alto, CA 94303-3905
Phone: 415-858-2235
Mailbox: ttor@a.crl.com

PARANET
Newsgroups:
alt.paranet.ufo
alt.alien.research
alt.alien.visitors

Project 1947
Jan Aldrich
P.O. Box 391
Canterbury, CT 06331
Phone: 860-546-9135
Mailbox: jan@cyberzone.net
http://www.iufog.org/

Quest International
18 Hardy Meadows
Grassington, Skipton
North Yorks, BD23 5LR, London
Phone: 01756 752216

The Raven Team (UFO investigations in S. Oregon and N. California)
4455 Jump off Joe Creek Road
Grants Pass, OR 97526

Phone: 1-541-479-2288
Pager: 1-800-223-3737 PIN 1303
Mailbox: dreamer@mail.chatlink.com

Russian Ufology Research Center
5700 Etiwanda Avenue
Suite 215
Tarzana, CA 91356
Mailbox: pshill@mail.idt.net

Rutgers UFO WWW page
http://www.rutgers.edu/ufo.html

Skywatch International
Tom King, AZ Dir
Mailbox: skywatch@phoenix.net
http://www.wic.net/colonel/ufopage.htm

Society for Scientific Exploration
ERL 306, Stanford University
Stanford, CA 94305
Phone: 415-693-8581
Fax: 415-595-4486

SOBEPS—Société Belge d'Étude des Phénomènes Spatiaux
(Belgian Society for the Study of Space Phenomena)
74 Avenue Paul Janson, B-1070
Brussels, Belgium

SOSOVNI Quebec
Jacques Poulet, Director
Case Postale 143
St.-Jean-sur-Richelieu, QC
Canada J3B621
http://www.cam.org/~martine/index.html

Scientific UFO Investigative Team (S.U.F.O.I.T.)
/ Paranormal Activity Research Association (PARA-4)

Commerce City, Colorado
Mailbox: sufoit@juno.com
http://www.geocities.com/Area51/1722

Tasmanian UFO Information Center
Mailbox: tufoic@netspace.net.au
http://server.netspace.net.au/~tufoic/

Temporal Doorway
Mark Cashman
Mcashman@ix.netcom.com
http://www.geocities.com/SoHo/Lofts/5623/

UFO Contact Center International (UFOCCI)
19519 SE 270th Pl., Suite 73
Kent, WA 98042
Phone: 206–630-3399
Fax: 206–630-3033
Mailbox: AGarou7410@aol.com

UFO Filter Center
Francis Ridge
Mailbox: slk@world.evansville.net
http://www.titlel4.com/ufofc/

UFO Folklore
DanTronix Productions
Mailbox: geibdan@qtm.net
http://www.qtm.net/~geibdan/framemst.html

UFOIA INTERNATIONAL
P.O. BOX 261486
San Diego, CA 92196-1486
Phone: 619-546-9639
Mailbox: UFOIA@aol.com, UFOIA2@aol.com,
mich@glo.be
http://members.aol.com/ufoia

UFOINFO
Mailbox: john@ufoinfo.ftech.co.uk
http://www.ftech.net/~ufoinfo/

Ufology Research of Manitoba
UFO UpDates
P.O. Box 1918
Winnipeg, Manitoba
Canada R3C 3R2
Mailbox: rutkows@cc.umanitoba.ca
http://www.freenet.mb.ca/iphome/u/ufo/index.html
UFORA/UFONLINE UFO RECORDS ADMINISTRA-
TION
Mailbox: ufologik@usa.net
http://www.geocities.com/Area51/Vault/1183/

UFO Update AZ
12629 N. Tatum Blvd., Suite 109
Phoenix, AZ 85032
Phone: 602-494-9279
Mailbox: EZDD95B@prodigy.com

Victorian UFO Research Society (VUFORS)
P.O. Box 43
Moorabbin, Victoria 3189, Australia
Mailbox: vufors@ozemail.com.au
http://www.ozemail.com.au/~vufors

Like other residents of the strange communities of Crestone and the Baca, Christopher O'Brien was drawn to the sacred valley of Native American myth. He was soon compelled to document, in disturbing detail, the inexplicable events unfolding around him and the questions they raised:

- **What is the truth behind the nightly light show of UFOs pulsing and glowing across the sky?**
- **What are the strange rumbling noises coming from underground?**
- **What is the origin of a mysterious crystal skull found in the Baca?**
- **And most frightening of all, who is responsible for the scores of cattle left bloodless and mutilated in inhuman fashion?**

Including fascinating and sometimes frightening firsthand accounts by residents of the area, *The Mysterious Valley* reveals the story of one of the most bizarre regions on the face of the earth and its chilling implications for the rest of humanity.

THE
MYSTERIOUS VALLEY
CHRISTOPHER O'BRIEN